EDUCATION and the
AMERICAN INDIAN

Second Edition

EDUCATION and the AMERICAN INDIAN

The Road to Self-Determination Since 1928

Margaret Connell Szasz

UNIVERSITY OF NEW MEXICO PRESS

Albuquerque

In memory of Stanley Smartlowit,
whose commitment to better schooling
for the Yakima Nation demonstrated
the unique possibilities for self-
determination in Indian education

PREFACE

In his pioneering study, *The Education of American Indians: A Survey of the Literature* (1969), Brewton Berry stressed the need for a comprehensive analysis of American Indian education. As Berry pointed out, one of the greatest problems in writing on this topic was the sheer amount of information available. While the records of Congress contain a great deal of material, they pale in comparison with that stored in the National Archives. At the Washington National Record Center in Suitland, Maryland, for example, the documents are housed in cardboard cartons that seem to go on forever.

Printed material, however, provided only one source for this study. Interviews with those involved in Indian education were equally important. No account of Indian education would be complete without contributions from both Indian students and Indian Bureau administrators. Oral history, therefore, offered another dimension to the written record. The variety and extent of these sources—congressional records, archival documents, and interviews—posed the major challenge for the writer. Synthesis was necessary for survival.

The present study appeared to have natural boundaries. It begins in 1928 with the Meriam Report and continues through the 1969 Kennedy Report and its immediate aftermath. The topic itself, however, was less easily defined. There are many kinds of Indian education and all of them could not be given equal weight. I chose, therefore, to concentrate on education directed by the Indian Bureau and, in the final chapters, on schools controlled by the Indian people themselves. I also included a brief history of the role of the federal government in public schooling for Indian children. Limitations of space, however, meant that others would be excluded, the most important being Indian children in eastern states (who historically have not been under the jurisdiction of the Indian Bureau) and Indian children in major urban areas. Alaskan Native children are mentioned only briefly; their school conditions are unique and should be the subject of a separate study.

Those who helped me in the early drafts were Richard N. Ellis, Gerald D. Nash, and William Dabney, all professors in the History Department at the University of New Mexico. More recent drafts have benefited from the sharp eye of Wanda Conger of the University of New Mexico Press.

Many of the interviews were conducted when I served as a research assistant for the American Indian History Research Project at the University of New Mexico. In this connection, special thanks are due to Sandy Gurulé, Sharon Suazo, and Connie Talley.

During my research trips to Washington, D.C., the staff at the National Archives was very helpful. I would especially like to thank Robert Kvasnicka, Richard S. Maxwell, and Sarah Jackson. At the University of New Mexico library, Dorothy Wonsmos completed interlibrary loans with efficiency and skill.

Former Indian Bureau administrators who provided invaluable insights gleaned from decades of personal experience include Hildegard Thompson and Madison Coombs, both of whom were faithful correspondents, as well as George Boyce and Robert Young, who also gave generously of their time.

During my visits to Rough Rock Demonstration School and Navajo Community College, a number of people gave me interviews despite their heavy schedules. These included Dillon Platero, Robert Roessel, Anita Pfeiffer, and Ned Hatathli.

In Albuquerque I have relied on the expertise of Myron Jones, who probably knows more about federal programs for Indian children in public school than anyone else in the country. I would also like to thank Henry M. Owl for his concern and assistance. In addition, Jerry Ingram deserves special appreciation for his original painting, which appears on the jacket of the book.

Each work that I complete in American Indian history owes a debt to Robert Jim, who gave his life in service to his people—the Confederated Bands and Tribes of the Yakima Indian Nation.

To those who have given me long-term assistance with the multiple responsibilities of research, writing, and family—Helen and Carl Connell, Helen and John Garretson, Mary and Frank Szasz, and Mary and Charles Gibbs—I can only express my gratitude for their patience and endurance. Finally, I would like to thank my husband, whose encouragement was the catalyst that transformed more than four years of work into the present study.

CONTENTS

List of Illustrations

Following page 140

1. Will Carson Ryan
2. Willard Walcott Beatty
3. John Collier
4. "Best girls squad for the year," Chilocco
5. "Best boys company," Chilocco
6. "Dairying at the Albuquerque Indian School"
7. Instruction in auto mechanics, Haskell Institute
8. "Domestic science at the Albuquerque Indian School"
9. "Kewonga Public School, Potawatomi Indian Reservation"
10. "Bridger 4H Potato Club meeting," Cheyenne River Agency
11. "Navajo rug weavers at the Albuquerque Indian School"
12. "Football team in action," Chilocco
13. Orchestra, Haskell Institute
14. Parade, Haskell Institute
15. "Afternoon tea given during Christmas holiday," Navajo Special Program
16. "Girls leaving for jobs," Navajo Special Program
17. Hildegard Thompson
18. Student government, Haskell Indian Junior College
19. Physical Education building, Southwestern Indian Polytechnic Institute
20. High school graduating class, Institute of American Indian Art
21. Graphics class, Institute of American Indian Art
22. Administration building, Institute of American Indian Art
23. Camp Chaparral summer school, Yakima Reservation
24. Children at Rough Rock Demonstration School
25. "Making Navajo fried bread," Rough Rock Demonstration School
26. High school students, Rough Rock Demonstration School
27. Cafeteria, Navajo Community College
28. Dormitories, Navajo Community College

Maps

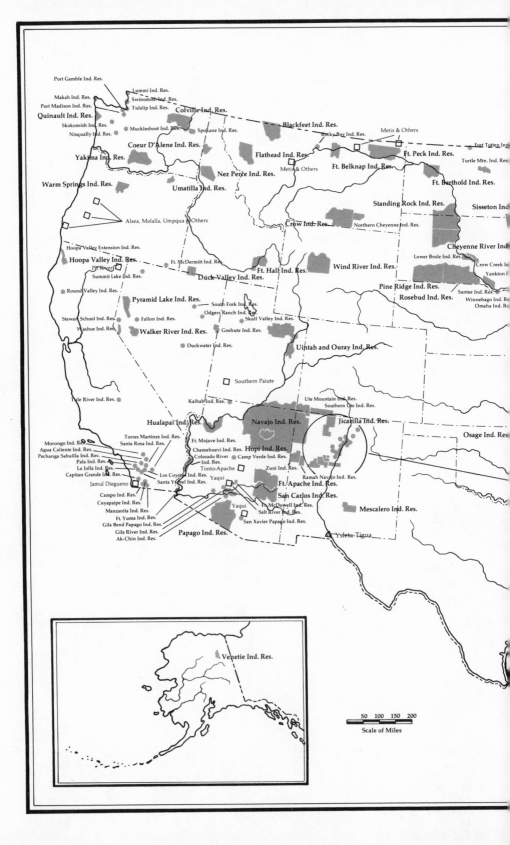

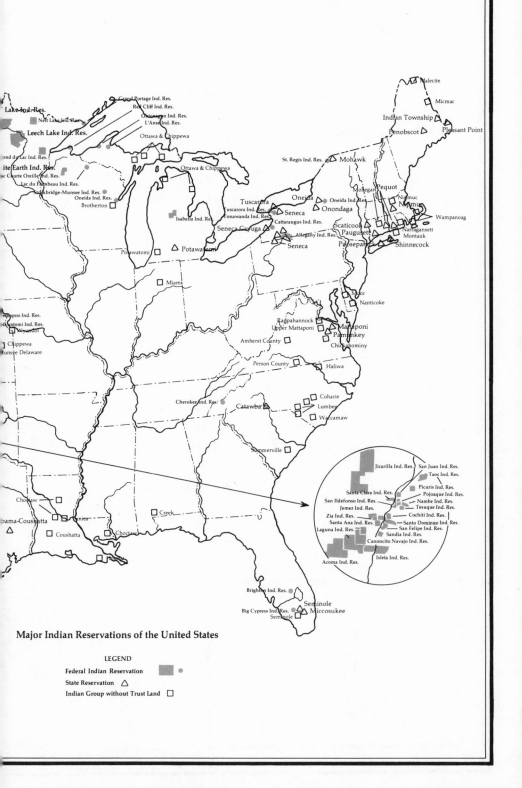

Major Indian Reservations of the United States

LEGEND

Federal Indian Reservation

State Reservation △

Indian Group without Trust Land ☐

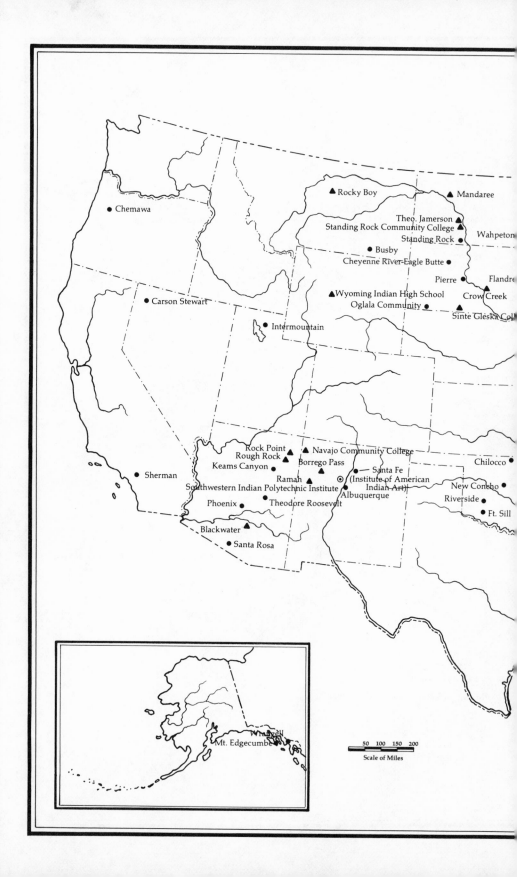

skell (Indian Jr. College)

Seneca
Sequoyah

Bogue Chitto and Choctaw Central
Conehatta

Miccosukee

Indian Schools in the United States

●   Bureau of Indian Affairs Boarding School (1970)

▲   School Contracted to Indian Group for Operation (1973) or
    Indian Community College

⊙   Southwestern Indian Polytechnic Institute

See tables on page xvi.

Boarding Schools Operated by the Bureau of Indian Affairs
(Fiscal Year 1970)

Bureau of Indian Affairs Area	State	School and Post Office Address
ABERDEEN	North Dakota	Standing Rock, Fort Yates, N. Dak. Wahpeton, Wahpeton, N. Dak.
	South Dakota	Cheyenne-Eagle Butte, Eagle Butte, S. Dak. Flandreau, Flandreau, S. Dak. Oglala Community, Pine Ridge, S. Dak. Pierre, Pierre, S. Dak.
ALBUQUERQUE	New Mexico	Albuquerque Indian, Albuquerque, N. Mex. Institute of American Indian Arts, Santa Fe, N. Mex.
ANADARKO	Kansas	Haskell Indian Jr. College, Lawrence, Kans.
	Oklahoma	New Concho, Concho, Okla. Chilocco, Chilocco, Okla. Fort Sill, Lawton, Okla. Riverside, Anadarko, Okla.
BILLINGS	Montana	Busby, Busby, Mont.
JUNEAU	Alaska	Mt. Edgecumbe, Mt. Edgecumbe, Alaska Wrangell Institute, Wrangell, Alaska
MUSKOGEE	Mississippi	Bogue Chitto, Rt. 2, Philadelphia, Miss. Conehatta, Conehatta, Miss. Choctaw Central, Philadelphia, Miss.
	Oklahoma	Seneca, Wyandotte, Okla. Sequoyah, Talequah, Okla.
NAVAJO	Arizona	Chinle, Chinle, Ariz. Crystal, Fort Defiance, Ariz. Denehotso, Kayenta, Ariz. Dilcon, Winslow, Ariz. Greasewood, Ganado, Ariz. Hunters Point, St. Michaels, Ariz.

Bureau of Indian Affairs Area	State	School and Post Office Address
	Arizona	Kaibeto, Lower, Tonalea, Ariz.
		Kaibeto, Upper, Tonalea, Ariz.
		Kayenta, Kayenta, Ariz.
		Kinlichee, Ganado, Ariz.
		Leupp, Leupp, Ariz.
		Low Mountain, Chinle, Ariz.
		Lukachukai, Lukachukai, Ariz.
		Many Farms Elem., Chinle, Ariz.
		Many Farms High, Chinle, Ariz.
		Navajo Mountain, Tuba City, Ariz.[a]
		Nazlini, Ganado, Ariz.
		Pine Springs, Houck, Ariz.
		Piñon, Piñon, Ariz.
		Rock Point, Chinle, Ariz.
		Rocky Ridge, Tuba City, Ariz.
		Seba Delkai, Winslow, Ariz.
		Shonto, Tonalea, Ariz.
		Teecnospos, Teecnospos, Ariz.
		Toyei, Ganado, Ariz.
		Tuba City, Tuba City, Ariz.
		Wide Ruins, Chambers, Ariz.
NAVAJO (cont'd.)	New Mexico	Baca, Prewitt, N. Mex.
		Cañoncito, Laguna, N. Mex.
		Cheechilgeetho, Gallup, N. Mex.
		Chuska, Tohatchi, N. Mex.
		Crownpoint, Crownpoint, N. Mex.
		Dlo'ay Azhi, Thoreau, N. Mex.
		Dzilth-Na-O-Dith-hle, Bloomfield, N. Mex.
		Lake Valley, Crownpoint, N. Mex.
		Mariano Lake, Gallup, N. Mex.
		Nenahnezad, Fruitland, N. Mex.
		Pueblo Pintado, Crownpoint, N. Mex.
		Sanostee, Little Water, N. Mex.
		Shiprock, Shiprock, N. Mex.
		Standing Rock, Crownpoint, N. Mex.
		Toadlena, Toadlena, N. Mex.
		Tohatchi, Tohatchi, N. Mex.
		Torreon, Cuba, N. Mex.
		White Horse, Crownpoint, N. Mex.
		Wingate Elem., Fort Wingate, N. Mex.
		Wingate High, Fort Wingate, N. Mex.
	Utah	Aneth, Aneth, Utah
		Intermountain, Brigham City, Utah
		Navajo Mountain, Tuba City, Ariz.[b]

Bureau of Indian Affairs Area	State	School and Post Office Address
PHOENIX	Arizona	Keams Canyon, Keams Canyon, Ariz. Phoenix Indian, Phoenix, Ariz. Santa Rosa, Sells, Ariz. Theodore Roosevelt, Fort Apache, Ariz.
	Nevada	Stewart, Stewart, Nev.
	California	Sherman Indian High, Riverside, Calif.
PORTLAND	Oregon	Chemawa, Chemawa, Oregon

^aSee NAVAJO, Utah.
^bSee NAVAJO, Arizona.

SOURCE: *Statistics Concerning Indian Education* (Lawrence, Kansas: Haskell Press, 1970), pp. 12–16.

Schools Contracted to Indian Groups for Operation (Fiscal Year 1973)

School	Post Office Address
Blackwater Day School	Sacaton, Ariz.
Borrego Pass Day School	Crownpoint, N. Mex.
Busby Boarding School	Busby, Mont.
Crow Creek High School	Fort Thompson, S. Dak.
Mandaree Day School	New Town, N. Dak.
Miccosukee Day School	Homestead, Fla. (Box 1369)
Ramah Navajo Day School	Ramah, N. Mex.
Rock Point Boarding School	Chinle, Ariz.
Rough Rock Boarding School	Chinle, Ariz.
St. Michael Day School	St. Michael, N. Dak.
Theo. Jamerson Day School	Bismarck, N. Dak.
Wyoming Indian High School	Ethete, Wyo.

SOURCE: *Statistics Concerning Indian Education* (Lawrence, Kansas: Haskell Press, 1973), p. 40.

Commissioners of Indian Affairs

Charles J. Rhoads	1929–1933
John Collier	1933–1945
William A. Brophy	1945–1949
John R. Nichols	1949–1950
Dillon S. Myer	1950–1953
Glenn L. Emmons	1953–1961
Philleo Nash	1961–1966
Robert L. Bennett	1966–1969
Louis R. Bruce	1969–1972
Morris Thompson	1973–1976

Directors of Indian Education
for
The Bureau of Indian Affairs

Will Carson Ryan, Jr.	1930–1935
Willard Walcott Beatty	1936–1952
Hildegard Thompson	1952–1965
Carl Marburger	1966–1967
Charles N. Zellers	1967–1970
James E. Hawkins	1971–1973
Clennon E. Sockeye	1974–1975
William G. Demmert, Jr.	1976–

1

INTRODUCTION

The Bureau of Indian Affairs became involved in Indian education in the late nineteenth century when the United States government first accepted its responsibilities for educating the Native American. By 1928, the Indian Bureau's Education Division had been directing Indian schooling for almost fifty years. Bureau educators in this decade were optimistic about the new directions being taken by Indian Service education. Their optimism was not unfounded, for a number of conditions were in their favor. They had the support of John Collier, Commissioner of Indian Affairs from 1933 to 1945; they had the support of Congress; and they had adequate funds for experimentation. In short, they saw a bright future ahead.

Forty years later, in 1970, critics of the Indian Bureau charged that Indian education had not improved measurably during these four decades. There were more children in school, but the quality of their education was as inferior as it had been in 1928. This type of anti-Bureau criticism was crystallized in the report of the Senate Special Subcommittee on Indian Education (*Indian Education: A National Tragedy—A National Challenge,* 1969, more commonly known as the Kennedy Report). This report, which has received extensive publicity in recent years, approached the issues of Indian education almost exclusively through an analysis of contemporary problems. Consequently, it suffered from the limitations imposed by a one-dimensional perspective. Instead of treating the historical causes for the failures of Indian education, it concentrated on the results.

To date there has been no historical account of this critical period

1

in American Indian education from 1928 to 1973. The two types of studies that have become popular—historical monographs on regional or tribal education and general accounts of contemporary Indian schooling—are restricted by their narrow scope. A broad historical coverage is needed to trace the conditions that have molded Indian education since 1928 and to suggest that the problems of the 1960s were the direct result of these conditions.

In 1930, statistics suggested that Indian education was one of the most successful programs of the Indian Bureau. Almost 90 percent of all Indian children were enrolled in school. Approximately half of these children attended public school; a little over a third of them were in schools operated by the Indian Bureau; and almost 10 percent were in private or mission schools. Of those who attended Indian Bureau schools, an equal number were enrolled in off-reservation and reservation boarding schools and a much smaller percentage were in day schools.

These statistics, however, were misleading. Although many children started school, a large proportion of them dropped out in the early years. On some reservations the average education level was fifth grade. Most students who attended Bureau boarding schools returned to their reservations, where they were unable to apply the training they had received. Course work in these schools was usually unrelated to the environment and culture from which the student came; on the other hand, vocational training was not sufficiently advanced to enable the student to find an urban job. Physical conditions in boarding schools were notoriously inadequate. Overcrowding, insufficient food, and improper treatment of sick children led to frequent epidemics. Since congressional appropriations were meager, boarding-school pupils, including a significant percentage of preadolescent children, were forced to provide almost all essentials by working long hours in the shops, the gardens, and the kitchens. In addition, they were subjected to harsh discipline according to the arbitrary will of the school superintendents.

These conditions encouraged the movement for reform of the Indian Bureau. Beginning shortly after World War I, the reform movement climaxed in 1928 with the publication of *The Problem of Indian Administration,* more commonly known as the Meriam Report. A critical analysis of the Indian Bureau, the Meriam Report was prepared by a team of experts employed by the Brookings Institution, an independent organization. The Indian Bureau has been analyzed a number of times, but no study has had a greater impact than the Meriam Report. During the administrations of Hoover and Roosevelt the recommendations of the Meriam Report often served as a guideline for the Indian commissioners. However, when Collier resigned in 1945, the Meriam Report was seventeen years old, and the two bodies that formulate Indian policy—Congress and the Bureau of Indian Affairs—were no longer in the mood for its style of reform. During the next fifteen years it received little attention, as few Bureau leaders considered its approach applicable to the postwar world. Not until the decade of the sixties was it again belatedly recognized by Congress and the Bureau. At this time new critics of Bureau education policy asserted that a number of the Meriam Report's recommendations were still as applicable as they had been in the 1930s. This meant that some of the problems pointed out by the Brookings Institution experts in 1928 were still uncorrected forty years later. The importance of the Meriam Report to an evaluation of Indian education during this period should not, therefore, be underestimated.

The Meriam Report suggested that education should be the primary function of the Indian Bureau. It advised that Indian education be geared for all age levels and that it be tied in closely with the community. It encouraged construction of day schools to serve as community centers and proposed extensive reform of boarding schools, including the introduction of Indian culture and revision of the curriculum so that it would be adaptable to local conditions. In addition, the report attacked the physical conditions of the boarding schools, the enrollment of preadolescent children, and the inadequacy of the personnel. It recommended that salaries and standards be raised and that a professional educator be appointed Director of Education.

Between 1930 and 1970 five persons served as Director of Education for the Bureau, and all but one were professional educators. The first two, Will Carson Ryan, Jr., and Willard Walcott Beatty, whose consecutive administrations ran from 1930 to 1952, were eager to implement the recommendations of the Meriam Report and made some progress in this direction during Collier's administration (1933–45). The last part of Beatty's term of office, however, as well as the administration of his successor, Hildegard Thompson (1952–65), witnessed the reversal of many of these efforts. It was not until the late 1960s, during the brief administrations of Carl Marburger and Charles N. Zellers, that the Education Division began to reconsider the recommendations of the Meriam Report. Thus, in spite of the changes instituted by Ryan and Beatty during Collier's administration, the period from 1945 to 1965 saw the earlier advances reversed, and in 1969 the Kennedy Report concluded that many of the recommendations of the Meriam Report were "yet to be accomplished."

Between 1928 and 1973, the educational policies of the Indian Bureau were formed under conditions that precluded any degree of freedom. Perhaps the greatest barrier was the number of outside pressures that shaped Education Division policy. The first of these pressures was federal Indian policy itself. Throughout the years of federal involvement in Indian education, the Education Division served as a barometer; whenever federal policy changed course, Indian education also changed. Thus, even during the late nineteenth century, education was a prominent feature of the policy of assimilation, which sought to absorb the Indian into the mainstream culture. In the 1920s Indian education was affected by the reform movement, which encouraged a return to Indian culture. In the late 1940s, it was subject to the policy of termination (an updated version of the old policy of assimilation). Finally, in the late 1960s, it responded to the movement for Indian self-determination by recognizing that Indians should have a voice in their own educational programs. The influence of federal Indian policy on the Education Division determined in large part the shape of Indian education.

The second pressure on Bureau education was the national educational scene. As new trends permeated public and private schools, they also affected Indian schooling. In the 1930s the Progressive Education movement saw its ideas adapted to Indian Service schools through the energetic efforts of directors Ryan and Beatty, both of whom were Progressive Education leaders. In the postwar period, as this movement declined in non-Indian education, it also lost strength in Indian Bureau schools. The demise of the community-school concept exemplified this change. In the 1950s, when the nation began to demand an educational system suited to a technological society, the reorganized Branch of Education shifted its high school curriculum toward academic rather than vocational courses and encouraged post–high school training. The early 1970s witnessed a renewed interest in Progressive Education concepts, newly labeled "open education." As the experimental stage of this movement began to affect public and private schools, it also reached into schools run by the Indian Bureau.

Education Directors for the Indian Bureau provided the third form of pressure on Indian education. Each director attempted to mold educational policy, but all of them discovered that it was necessary to administer within limitations imposed by the administrative structure of the Indian Bureau, the Commissioner of Indian Affairs, the Secretary of the Interior, the President, and federal bodies outside the Indian Bureau, including Congress and the Bureau of the Budget. Given these restrictions, the directors during the period from 1930 to 1970 found it impossible to shape Indian education in accordance with their own wishes. Every director found himself at odds with at least one of these limiting factors during his term of office.

Significantly, the greatest changes occurred when there was the least conflict between Director of Education and these restrictive factors. Ryan and Beatty, the two directors who served during the period that became known as the Indian New Deal, were more successful in implementing the Meriam Report recommendations than were any later administrators. The fact that Beatty accomplished more than Ryan did was due, in part, to the increased funds that became available when he took office. However, the changes also reflected his more dynamic personality. In contrast, between 1952 and 1965 Hildegard Thompson worked with severe restrictions, and as a result she was unable to implement the policy changes desired by the Indian people.

The year 1965, therefore, marked the end of an unusually frustrating period for Bureau Education Directors. Shortly thereafter, the Senate subcommittee began its research. One of the primary topics it chose to investigate was the federal funding program for Indian pupils in public schools. Although the Kennedy Report attacked this program severely, again it stressed results rather than causes. The failures of federal funding are more easily understood if they are traced back to the mid 1930s, when the Indian Bureau signed its first contracts with individual states for the education of Indian pupils in public schools. State contracts were legalized by the passage of the Johnson-O'Malley Act in 1934. Prior to this time the Indian Bureau had contracted with thousands of individual school districts for federal payment for Indian pupils. Carson Ryan had encouraged the legalization of state contracting because he foresaw that it would simplify the administration of this funding.

A few years later Willard Beatty discovered that state contracting for public school funds led to inferior education for Indian pupils in public schools. Beatty was well aware of the financial need of public schools at this time, and he surmised that state education systems would be far more interested in the additional funds than in the Indian pupils. His prediction proved to be correct. As the states began to assume administrative control of federal funds, they demonstrated a decided lack of interest in developing special programs for Indian pupils. Most federal funds, including both Johnson-O'Malley money and the money made available through legislation in the 1950s and 1960s, were used in the general school budgets and often affected non-Indian pupils more than Indians. Beatty fought this trend as long as he could. He attempted to retain Bureau educators in key administrative positions to direct the state programs. This, however, only served as a holding action. Within a few years state education systems forced his hand, and the Bureau gradually withdrew from direct administration of federal programs.

With almost autonomous control of federal funds for Indian students, the states were in an enviable position. Since they were held accountable only in a general manner, most states used the funds freely. By the late 1960s, the mishandling of federal funds for Indian pupils had become as notorious as the boarding school scandals of the 1920s. When the movement for Indian self-determination publicized the illegality of this procedure, Indian parents and leaders began to demand a voice in controlling these funds. The Kennedy Report helped to publicize the public-school issue and reinforced Indian efforts to achieve some change.

If the movement for Indian self-determination had begun earlier, abuses such as state misappropriation of funds might not have occurred. Unfortunately, however, the movement had no significant effect on Indian education until after 1965. Its origins can be traced back to World War II, with the formation of the National Congress of American Indians in 1944. While the war itself was a strong factor in encouraging the Indian people to improve their education, in the postwar years Indian leaders had little time for education problems. Their primary concern was preserving the status quo in the long fight against termination. During this time, however, these leaders learned to deal with the sources of power, and in the 1960s, when Indians actually began experimenting with running their own schools, the political education gained during termination stood them in good stead.

This book is a historical examination of the conditions that shaped Indian education in Bureau and public schools between 1928 and 1973. At the same time it is the story of the Indian people and their struggles to gain an education that will teach their children not only the fundamentals of mainstream society but also the contributions of their own cultural heritage.

2

BACKGROUND: FEDERAL INDIAN EDUCATION, 1870–1926

In the fifty years before the publication of the Meriam Report, the federal government pursued a policy of total assimilation of the American Indian into the mainstream society. Recognizing the vast difficulties in achieving this goal, Congress and the Indian Bureau adopted a plan to remold the Indian's conception of life, or what came to be known as his "system of values." If this could be changed, assimilationists reasoned, the Indian would then become like the white man. The Indian's system of values was expressed in the education of his children and in his attitude toward the land. Consequently, the assimilationists chose to attack these two concepts as the major targets of their campaign.

The land issue was easily resolved. If the Indian owned his own land, they reasoned, he would assume a responsibility for taking care of it and would thus become a good citizen. Land allotment was secured through the passage of the Dawes Act (more commonly known as the Allotment Act) of 1887, which provided for the allotment of lands in severalty of Indians on the various reservations.[1] The remolding of Indian education to conform to white cultural values could not be achieved by a single piece of legislation, but during this same decade the federal government began to assume responsibility for Indian education and provided the first significant federal funding for Indian schools.

During the first century of U.S. Indian policy, the federal government made provision for Indian education through legislation and treaties. In 1819, Congress established the "civilization fund," which provided for a small annual sum for instruction.[2] Between 1783 and 1871, when the treaty period ended, a number of Indian treaties set aside portions of tribal annuity payments for education, or included specific provisions for schooling.[3] Although the federal government funded these efforts, missionary groups administered most of the schools. Among the southeastern Indians, however, several tribes developed their own highly successful education systems.[4]

Although there had always been a small number of people who were convinced that the Indian could be civilized, the public generally believed that he was incapable of progress. This negative view was reinforced by attitudes on the frontier. Many frontiersmen were inveterate Indian haters, and as the frontier shrank in physical size this attitude seemed to intensify. Those who encountered the Indian under the often brutal frontier conditions had little respect for the humanitarian viewpoint of the easterner.

In the post–Civil War decades the public attitude began to shift, and within the space of a few years, in spite of the antagonism of westerners, assimilation became the popular approach. The impetus for this change of opinion was provided by reformers who responded to a national outcry against publicized incidents of white injustice. Events like the Nez Perce retreat, the Ponca removal, and the flight of the Northern Cheyenne, as well as the intrusion of white settlers into Indian Territory and the exposure of graft within the Indian Bureau, increased congressional concern and aided the reformers in their efforts to secure legislation to change the national Indian policy.

In this era of individual fortunes and economic dreams, the presence of idealistic reformers may seem somewhat strange. On the other hand, the American system had yet to be shaken by internal doubts. Consequently, these reformers, like many other Americans, held their society in such high esteem that they developed an almost imperialistic attitude toward cultures that responded to other values. Armed with this type of evangelistic fervor, the reformers stood a good chance of succeeding. By the late 1870s they had begun their campaign.

The first extensive federal funding of Indian education was stimulated by the efforts of Richard Henry Pratt, the U.S. Army captain who founded Carlisle Indian School in 1879.[5] Captain Pratt's most important contribution was to convince the public that the

Indian was educable. The success of Carlisle, which was acknowledged by a large congressional appropriation in 1882, led to a sudden expansion of off-reservation industrial boarding schools. Those that were to have the longest life spans included schools at Forest Grove, Oregon, established in 1880 (later known as Chemawa); Albuquerque (1884); Chilocco (1884); Santa Fe (1890—renamed the Institute of American Indian Arts in 1962); Haskell (1884—renamed Haskell Indian Junior College in 1965); Carson (1890—later known as Stewart); Phoenix (1890); Pierre (1891); and Flandreau (1893). By the turn of the century twenty-five off-reservation industrial boarding schools had been opened.

In spite of the rapid expansion, reformers were by no means unanimous in their enthusiasm for this type of school. Although critics recognized the merits of Captain Pratt's "acculturation policy," they soon began to question whether the negative features of the industrial training schools did not outweigh the positive. They argued that such schools trained too few Indian youths at too great expense. However, the most convincing criticism was that many Indians who attended the schools "returned to the blanket."

The problems faced by this minority of educated Indian youth did not lend themselves to an easy solution. When the pupils returned to the reservation, they often became objects of ridicule. This situation was complicated by the fact that the training they had received had little or no application to reservation life. Thus these pupils became the first victims of the "either/or" policy of assimilation. Their education forced them to choose either the culture of the white man or the culture of the Indian; there was no compromise.[6]

Despite this drawback, the off-reservation industrial boarding school became an entrenched form of federal Indian schooling during the assimilation period. Shortly before the turn of the century, however, other forms of education were introduced. The main alternatives were reservation boarding or day schools. Critics of off-reservation education supported this type of schooling because it offered several distinct advantages. In the first place, reservation schools were less expensive.[7] Day schools required little transportation or boarding, and transportation to reservation boarding schools was much cheaper than to off-reservation schools. Second, reservation schools were more acceptable to parents, who were generally hostile to the idea of having their children taken any distance from home. Incidents of enforced seizure of children to fill the quotas of off-reservation schools during this period have been reported too frequently to be considered mere exaggeration.[8] Although many parents objected to off-reservation schooling, opposition to education itself was by no means a universal phenomenon among Indians. However, those parents who did object may have "understood . . . that it represented the most dangerous of all attacks on basic Indian values, the one most likely to succeed in the end because it aimed at the children, who had known little if any of the old life."[9]

As an adjunct, then, to the off-reservation industrial boarding schools, the reservation schools were the second type of federal Indian education. Day schools in particular increased after the turn of the century. Many of those who promoted Indian assimilation, however, predicted that public schools would prove to be the best solution to the problems of Indian education. Early observers of the effects of public schooling on the Indian child concluded that separate Indian schools supported by the federal government would eventually become an anachronism.[10]

With the exception of eastern Indians not under the jurisdiction of the federal government, the first tribes subject to public schooling were those whose reservations were allotted. As whites responded eagerly to the newly available leases and surplus lands of these reservations, they brought with them demands for public schools for their children. By 1902 Agent Jay Lynch wrote from the Yakima Reservation that there were "so many white people renting land on the reservation . . . it was found necessary to have schools for white people renting Indian lands."[11] On reservations that were not allotted (including most reservations in the Southwest), public schooling did not become an issue. Where it existed, it encouraged assimilation. As Agent Lynch wrote, "Indian children progress much faster when thus thrown in contact with white children than they do when they are all kept together with whites excluded."[12]

By the turn of the century these three major forms of Indian education had become firmly established. A fourth form that should be mentioned was the mission school, the forerunner of both federal and public Indian education, which retained its foothold during this period. Although mission schools did not educate a significant proportion of Indian children, they were responsible for a consistently small percentage, with considerable variation from reservation to reservation.[13] One of the reasons for their continued existence was simply that not enough schools were built to take their place. However, mission schools continued to exist even after the Indian Bureau was able to report that the majority of Indian children were enrolled in some other type of schooling. Another reason for their tenacity may have been that they had become established institutions.

It appears more likely, however, that the hold of mission schools on Indian education was due to the persistence of both the churches and the Indians themselves. Dedicated educators within the churches fought hard to maintain their schools. They believed that Indian children who were unable to attend public school would receive a better education in a mission school than in a federal school. William M. Chapman, who was director of St. Elizabeth's School (Episcopal) on the Standing Rock Reservation for a short period, maintained that even though conditions at his school were by no means ideal, they were "better than in the big government **boarding schools which sometimes housed five hundred Indian** children." Chapman also suggested that the "church training" offered by the school "meant a great deal" to the children because they were "naturally devout."[14] A large portion of the budget for these schools came from tribal funds, and Indians were vehement defenders of sectarian schools threatened by closure.[15]

At the beginning of the twentieth century the status of the Indian was not only bleak, it was hovering on the edge of disaster. The dual inheritance of the assimilation policies of education and land allotment had already given some indication of their potential ability to damage if not destroy a majority of the Indian people. During the next three decades (1900–1930) the unchecked pursuit of these policies led the Indian to a point of no return. By the end of World War I he was suffering increasingly from disease and a short life expectancy, malnutrition and starvation, a diminishing land base, and a stagnant, unrealistic school system. In the early 1920s federal Indian policy was a notorious example of bureaucratic inefficiency and ineffectiveness, and the possibility of change from within appeared to be hopeless. The time was ripe for reform.

The decade of the 1920s witnessed the movement for reform; the decade of the 1930s saw the rhetoric of reform transformed into action. Reformers of the 1920s uncovered extensive mismanagement within the Bureau, which gave them ready ammunition for their attack on the administrative walls of the structure. Failures of the education system provided some of the most lethal ammunition. The reformers dwelt on the "plight" of Indian children through a direct emotional appeal that drew immediate response from an increasingly irate public.

Reform in the 1920s followed a pattern not uncommon to other reform movements in the United States. It was triggered by a *cause célèbre*, an incident that occurred when the climate of opinion was ready for reform. The Bursum bill of 1922, "an act to quiet title to lands within Pueblo Indian land grants," proposed to give potential legal rights to white men who had settled on Pueblo lands and force the Pueblo Indians to prove ownership of their lands. Establishing such proof would have been difficult if not impossible, for the Pueblos would have had to clarify ownership through three periods of occupation—Spanish, Mexican, and American. The Bursum bill and the Dawes, or Allotment, Act bore witness to the land hunger of those who lived near reservations. Although the Dawes Act had been encouraged in 1887 by reformers who were anxious for Indians to become independent, self-supporting citizens, it had also received a hearty push from westerners who were eager to acquire Indian land. However, in 1922 the Bursum bill served as a catalyst for change because it was proposed at a time when the increasingly disastrous effects of the Dawes Act had become apparent to advocates of Indian rights.

Serving as a target for these sympathizers, the controversial bill provided a focal point of discontent and thus led the reform movement to its second phase—development of dynamic leadership among the reformers themselves. During the 1920s a number of leaders emerged from Congress and from the new organizations formed to fight the Bursum bill. One man overshadowed all the rest. This was John Collier, the outspoken idealist whose life became intertwined with the fortunes and future of the Indians. Collier went on to become Commissioner of Indian Affairs from 1933 to 1945 under Franklin D. Roosevelt, holding that position longer than anyone else before or since.

Collier's interest in Indians dated from 1920, when he and his family came to Taos at the invitation of Mabel Dodge Luhan, a friend from New York City, where she had been best known for her salon. Like many other members of the "Lost Generation," Mabel Dodge Luhan had been depressed and dissatisfied with America after the war. Unlike her contemporaries who fled to Europe, she sought her new life in the American Southwest. For Collier, also, it was dissatisfaction that initially led him to the West, first to California and then to New Mexico. Among the Taos Indians he found a perfect example of the communal life he valued so highly. From these Indians his interest spread, first to the other Pueblos, then to tribes across the continent. The fight against the Bursum Bill propelled him into the forefront of the reform movement.

As the principal spokesman for the reformers, Collier was pushed into the limelight when he became Executive Secretary of the American Indian Defense Association. This organization, formed in direct response to the Bursum bill, became the strongest and most outspoken of the Indian reform groups of the 1920s. Although its directives (many of them Collier's) came from the main office in New York, California claimed four of the seven chapters that formed between 1922 and 1927. Many of the California reformers were also active in the Division of Indian Welfare of the General Federation of Women's Clubs. The goals of the two organizations were complementary.

The American Indian Defense Association was determined to reach the public. It published its own bulletin, *American Indian Life,* in the muckraking tradition established at the turn of the century by men like Lincoln Steffens, and it also had ready access to the press. Liberal magazines like *The Nation, Survey Graphic,* and *The New Republic* turned a sympathetic ear to the popular topic of Indian reform, but the issue was also covered in prestigious journals like *Current History* and *The Forum.* The magazine that became the primary voice for the reformers, however, was *Sunset,* a popular California publication edited by Walter V. Wohlke.[16] A prominent crusader, Wohlke wrote many of the articles that criticized the Bureau.[17]

Through this publicity the reformers launched the third phase of the reform movement—public response and encouragement. The level of the appeal was emotional; the crusaders often contrasted the appalling extent of Indian poverty with the general prosperity of the 1920s. Reader reaction to this approach indicated its effectiveness. One *Sunset* reader wrote, "I have been shocked and pained at the revelations brought out by these articles. I feel that in the name of humanity and to keep our great country from blackening its fair name any further, something should be done and that right soon. . . . I want to know what I can do to help."[18]

Public response led the reform movement into its final and most significant phase—action. In the 1920s, however, the action taken failed to satisfy the demands of the reformers, for it came primarily in the form of independent, private studies commissioned by the federal government. The twentieth-century reformer already had begun to learn that the results of such studies often lie neglected. This was what happened to the first study made in the 1920s, a report compiled by the Committee of One Hundred, a group of citizens who met in Washington, D.C., on December 12 and 13, 1923, to discuss the direction of Indian affairs and to make suggestions for their improvement. The recommendations of this committee, particularly in the area of education, were noteworthy, but they had little effect on the Bureau. Although the Indian Service began to encourage public-school enrollment and to reorganize its own schools in order to offer more advanced instruction, these steps did not radically alter its total education system. Few federal boarding schools had a high school curriculum, and none of those that did compared favorably in quality to the public schools.[19] Vocational training in Bureau schools remained inferior, and other courses continued to be unrelated to the reservation life that the pupil generally returned to when he left school. Although the Bureau recognized the existence of the report, its overall effect was negligible and it served only to point out that the work of the reformers was far from finished.

3

W. CARSON RYAN: FROM THE MERIAM REPORT TO THE INDIAN NEW DEAL

In 1924 and 1925 the clamor for reform rose to a second crescendo, and in 1926 Secretary of the Interior Hubert Work turned once again to independent experts, this time to the well-known Brookings Institution. Under the capable direction of Dr. Lewis Meriam, the institution spared no effort in preparing its report. Meriam relied on a team of experts and gave them adequate time to prepare their conclusions. This thoughtful, thorough approach produced one of the finest studies ever made of a government bureau. The recommendations of the Meriam Report were not designed as a lesson in tactful advice.[1] They pinpointed the glaring weaknesses within the Bureau and offered concrete cures for its numerous shortcomings. As one contemporary magazine concluded, the Meriam Report "was in effect a stinging reproach to a niggardly and exploiting government."[2]

Like the earlier report of the Committee of One Hundred, the Meriam Report relied on individual expertise. The education section of the report was prepared largely under the direction of W. Carson Ryan, Jr., an educator whose talents were well known to Lewis Meriam. Meriam recalled later that "when the time came for the Indian survey . . . Professor Ryan of Swarthmore, with his long record of constructive work on educational surveys, was the logical choice for the educational assignment." When the survey got under way, Meriam added, Ryan made a "contribution in every branch of the work."[3]

At the time of this assignment, Ryan was a nationally known

educator. He had worked for the U.S. Bureau of Education from 1912 to 1920. In 1918 he had received his doctorate from George Washington University. Shortly thereafter he had served for a year as educational editor for the *New York Evening Post.* Although he had been appointed professor of education at Swarthmore in 1921, this had not curtailed a broad use of his talents. As Lewis Meriam observed, by the time Ryan began work on the Meriam Report he was already recognized as an expert in educational surveys. Between 1917 and 1929 he conducted seven studies of education systems from Saskatchewan, Canada, to the Virgin Islands, including American Indian education (1926–27). At the same time he had served as American delegate to several international education meetings. These experiences kept Ryan in touch with current educational trends, and, like an increasing number of educators in the 1920s, he developed a professional philosophy that committed him to the new concepts of Progressive Education, an outgrowth of Progressivism that traced its origins to the educational ideas of John Dewey.

During his long and diversified educational career, Ryan also pioneered in guidance, mental health and hygiene, special education, cultural education, and international education. He achieved an international reputation as consultant for private foundations and organizations (for example, the World Federation for Mental Health) and as representative of the U.S. Department of State for the Fulbright programs in Europe and the Near East. His published works included, among others, *The Literature of American School and College Athletics* (1929), *Mental Health Through Education* (1938), and *Studies in Early Graduate Education* (1939).

In keeping with the rest of the Meriam Report, Ryan analyzed the education program of the Indian Bureau with an approach that was biting and penetrating. The nature of his criticisms made it quite apparent that they came from the pen of a man deeply concerned about the appalling failures of Indian education. Even more significant was Ryan's awareness of the potential of Indian education, untapped during the fifty years that preceded the Meriam Report.

Ryan viewed education not in the narrow sense of the word but in its overall application to living, a concept basic to Progressive Education. From this perspective, he believed that a new education program for the Bureau should affect the entire Indian Service. Furthermore, he asserted that "adequate, well trained personnel" were imperative to this new program because it would include "not only school training for children but also activities for the training of adults to aid them in adjusting themselves to the dominant social and economic life which confronts them."[4] What Ryan was suggesting was a total revamping of the education system. This was a revolutionary idea for the late 1920s, but it was in keeping with the increasingly vocal views of the Progressive Education movement.

In 1928 a little less than half of all Indian children who were enrolled in school were attending public school. Allowing for the 14 percent who were not in any school and the 14 percent who were in federal day schools and mission schools, out of a total of 78,377 children, 21,053 or almost 27 percent were enrolled in reservation and off-reservation boarding schools.[5] In spite of the fact that this was less than a third of all Indian children, it was still a significant number. Some of these children were away only during the school year, but those who did not see their parents during the summer were totally isolated from their homes and from the culture of their people.

It was for the sake of these children that the reformers attacked the education system of the Bureau. As their criticism intensified during the 1920s, they began to identify the boarding school as the symbol of all the evils of the Bureau education system. They were less concerned about the children who were not in school, and they paid little attention to those who were in Bureau day schools; nor did they publicize the fact that a large percentage of Indian children were in public school. What they sought to achieve was an end to the dreary existence of the Indian youngsters taken from their homes and placed in reservation and off-reservation boarding schools.

When the Meriam Report tackled education, therefore, it is not surprising that it concentrated its criticism on the boarding schools. Although Ryan was concerned with the total education program, the boarding school was the obvious place to begin. Food, overcrowding, medical service, student labor, teachers, curriculum, and discipline—all of these had been attacked by the reformers and all of them fell under the sharp criticism of Ryan's pen. He summarized their failures by stating "frankly and unequivocally" that "provisions for the care of the Indian children in boarding schools are grossly inadequate."[6]

During the 1920s the entire boarding-school system had been subjected to the stringent economic policies of the administrations of Warren G. Harding and Calvin Coolidge. In an effort to comply with the restrictive and unyielding position of the newly created Bureau of the Budget, both Indian Commissioner Charles H. Burke (1921–29) and Louis C. Cramton, Chairman of the House Subcommittee on Appropriations for the Department of the Interior (1921–30), permitted the Bureau budget to be maintained at a dangerously low level.[7] Cramton and his committee suggested that even the minimum standards of health and nutrition in the boarding schools were an extravagance. Stymied by the limiting recommendations of the Bureau of the Budget, Commissioner Burke did not press the issue. As Lawrence C. Kelly points out, Burke was "always the politician, temperamentally incapable of being a reformer. . . . he did what he could and never advocated what he believed to be the impossible."[8]

For the children in the Bureau boarding schools, this penury on the part of the government meant that they subsisted on a diet that was the equivalent of slow starvation. A Red Cross investigator who visited Rice Boarding School in Arizona in the mid twenties reported that the diet of the children consisted of bread, black coffee, and syrup for breadfast; bread and boiled potatoes for dinner; more bread and boiled potatoes for supper. In addition, there was enough milk for each child to have a quarter of a cup at each meal, but the big children received all of the milk and the little ones received none. This diet enabled the school to feed the children for an average of nine cents a day per child. Although the researchers for the Meriam Report described Rice as an "extreme example," the generally accepted minimum figure for feeding the children during this period was only two cents higher, or eleven cents a day.[9] Reformers pointed out that, according to nutrition experts, thirty-five cents a day was the minimum for "enough food of sufficient variety to keep a growing child healthy and vigorous."[10]

The effects of slow starvation were compounded by lack of medical care, dangerous overcrowding, and the excessive labor required of the children because of the lack of funds. Physicians who were acquainted with the conditions in the schools emphasized that widespread illness was encouraged by lack of space. It was estimated that schools were overcrowded by almost 40 percent, but some of them evaded this issue by not listing all of their pupils.[11] Epidemics swept through crowded dormitories and endangered new arrivals. The two illnesses common among Indians at this time

—tuberculosis and trachoma—struck many of the children. The tuberculosis death rate among Indians was estimated to be six and one-half times that of non-Indians. Although this illness was known to be highly contagious, children with TB were seldom isolated and sometimes were sent home to live within the close confines of a hogan or other dwelling. Trachoma, a disease of the eye that often results in blindness, was widespread. At this time there was no known cure for the disease; consequently the children who suffered from trachoma experienced little relief.[12] One doctor described the "truly pitiful" condition of the fifty or sixty girls whom he had observed. Since they were unable to attend classes, "they sat or lay about in the dormitory shading their eyes from the strong light."[13]

In spite of these threats to the children's well-being, boarding-school directors must have found some children whom they classified as "healthy," because without student help the schools could not have survived on their meager budgets. In 1928 the Meriam Report observed, "Boarding schools are frankly supported in part by the labor of the students," who, when they were as young as fifth graders, "work for a half a day and go to school for half a day."[14] The children were put to work in the dairy or in the fields, usually to raise crops for the school itself. Their clothes and shoes were provided for by their own labor through long hours in the laundries, tailor shops, and leather shops. The Meriam Report suggested, "The question may very properly be raised, as to whether much of the work of Indian children in boarding schools would not be prohibited in many states by child labor laws, notably the work in the machine laundries."[15] Finally, the report seriously questioned whether the "health of the Indian children warrants the nation in supporting the Indian boarding schools in part through the labor of these children."[16]

The children were awakened between five and six in the morning and went to bed between eight and nine at night. In between there was little time for recreation. The daily routine was very much like that of a military school. "You are drilled back to the dining room for breakfast and go back to the dormitory and then you are drilled to the school yard," a Santa Clara Pueblo woman recalled of Santa Fe boarding school.[17] During the Sunday dress parade at Albuquerque Indian School, each student carried a "dummy rifle" and was "dressed up like a regular army."[18] At Haskell Institute the military organization was even more rigorous. Every student at this school was in a regular military outfit, and in 1922 eighty of the older students were in a special machine-gun company, which had undergone two weeks of training with the Kansas State Militia the previous summer. At Haskell the military organization was considered as essential for "control of the students."[19] Other schools used the same rationale.

Nonetheless, the discipline issue continued to plague the boarding schools. Part of the blame for both this issue and the related weakness in teachers and staff lay in the lack of funding. The highly criticized disciplinary method of the boarding schools was directly related to the fact that the Bureau was simply unable to compete with public schools in hiring teachers and staff members. Since the "Indian Service is handicapped by low salaries," the Meriam Report observed, it "must accordingly adopt low standards for entrance." As a result, Indian Service teaching was "not up to the standards set by reasonably progressive white communities."[20]

This is not to say that harsh discipline imposed upon children was a problem throughout the entire Indian Service. In spite of the noncompetitive salaries, the Bureau managed to attract some qualified educators. Often, however, teachers or staff members who sympathized with the children were quietly transferred by less sympathetic directors. Testimony given at the Senate Hearings (Survey of Conditions of the Indians) between 1928 and 1933 revealed that the type of discipline as well as its severity was determined by the director of each school. That some of these individual directors persisted in using their severe methods after antidiscipline directives were issued in response to the Meriam Report was a measure of the directors' power. Although these directives specifically forbade unjust punishment, as late as 1934 (after four years of Bureau leadership by the Quaker humanitarians Commissioner Charles J. Rhoads and his assistant, Henry J. Scattergood, and one year of leadership by Collier) a highly publicized incident of harsh school discipline rocked the Indian Service.[21] Until the level of salaries was improved and the Washington office was able to impose more uniform and humanitarian standards of discipline, the conflict between Old Guard disciplinarians and new, better qualified employees would continue.

Those who were most informed about the power of the Old Guard—the Indian pupils themselves—were seldom given the opportunity to reveal how it affected them. Boarding-school students may have written a number of letters in the 1920s and 1930s but few of them ever reached the Bureau's Central Office. The absence of such correspondence in Bureau records serves as testimony to the thousands of unspoken complaints and silent sufferings. That they did oppose an authority which at times failed even to recognize them as human beings can be seen by a short letter from a Flandreau pupil in 1930. Protesting the treatment of Indian pupils, she said, "When they write to Washington, Superintendent alway[s] think we tell lair [lies]." Too many people, she went on, feel that the Indian students "don't know nothing." But they were very much mistaken in this "because they human and we human too."[22] Repressed emotions such as these often forced pupils to seek the only avenue of escape—running away.

The runaway was one of the chronic features of the discipline issue. Within the Bureau itself this problem was openly recognized. At least one superintendent was encouraged to include in his annual expense account the fees charged by cooperating local police departments to return the runaways. The superintendent at Chilocco was advised that "where the boys themselves have money sufficient to cover these bills they must be met out of their individual funds."[23] Superintendents were encouraged to return the children rather than expel them because of the fear that expulsion would merely invite an increase in desertions and that in addition the government would be charged with neglect of its duty to educate and civilize the children for their own future welfare.[24]

Although punishment of children who were brought back was left to the discretion of the superintendent, reformers suggested that even if children were not punished, they would not want to return to the conditions from which they had fled. Surely, the reformers argued, there was no more obvious evidence of dislike than a runaway child, and some youngsters ran away not just once but again and again.

The Bureau was on the spot when it came to defending its school system against the destructive effect of this problem. Loyal administrators suggested that desertions occurred "not usually because of punishment nor because of any oppressive or uncomfortable living conditions but because certain boys or girls simply do not want to remain in school."[25] Reformers countered that the fault lay with the schools themselves, which anthropologist Oliver La Farge, with typical reform gusto, labeled as "penal institutions—where little children were sentenced to hard labor for a term of years to expiate the crime of being born of their mothers."[26]

Reformers insisted that the boarding-school system should be terminated, but Ryan argued that complete closure was unrealistic. If these schools ceased to operate, he asserted, many children, particularly those who lived in remote areas of reservations, would not receive any education. It would be better, he suggested, to change the format of the schools themselves.

The first point of attack was the boarding-school curriculum, which, according to Ryan, was ill suited to the needs of the child. Course material was based on two erroneous assumptions: first, that it should follow a uniform curriculum; second, that it should stress only the cultural values of the white. Ryan lashed out at the Uniform Course of Study. This program prescribed a single regimented curriculum for all pupils in federal boarding schools in order that all children might study "the same thing at the same time of day."[27] The Meriam Report stated quite flatly that "routinization must be eliminated." It recommended that the differences among tribes be recognized by the use of classroom material from the "local Indian life, or at least [from] within the scope of the child's experience."[28] It stressed that "Indian tribes and individuals vary so greatly, that a standard content and method of education . . . would be worse than futile."[29] Anthropologists and students of Indian culture had been aware of the fact for some years, but the burden of the assimilation policy had made it insignificant in the eyes of the Bureau. What difference did it make that Indian cultures were varied, if all Indians were going to adopt the white man's civilization? In theory, the introduction of cultural values into the curriculum was admirable. In practice it proved to be complicated, and Ryan found in his short five years in office that he could take only a few stabs at what would later become known as cross-cultural education. Nonetheless, he remained hopeful that the concept of teaching the children about their culture would be adopted throughout the boarding-school system.

The second point of attack was the age level of boarding-school children. The Meriam Report recommended that boarding schools be reserved for the education of older children. "One of the definite objectives of the Service, vigorously pursued," it counseled, "should be the elimination of the pre-adolescent children from boarding schools."[30] The proper school for young children was a community school near their homes. The community school would serve a dual purpose—first as a day school for young children and second as a community center to strengthen local concern through involvement of the entire community. When the child was old enough to attend boarding school, then he would leave home for that period of time and learn a trade that would enable him to find a job.

The report also criticized the vocational training of the boarding schools. Industrial training that was not geared to meet the job market was simply unrealistic. Some trades taught in the boarding schools were already vanishing; others were not taught at a level sufficiently advanced to enable the student to get a job. Moreover, despite its inadequacies, the industrial training program discouraged graduates from returning to the reservation. If the recommendations of the Meriam Report were put into effect it would not be as difficult for the graduate to return. The community-school experience of his elementary years and the boarding-school emphasis on his cultural heritage would prevent him from being alienated from his people.

The Meriam Report suggested that the duty of the Indian Service was to provide both the youth and his parents with the tools to adapt to two worlds—the white and the Indian. Thus, the primary task of the Indian Service was viewed as education. In the years of reform that followed its publication, the Meriam Report became the symbol of definitive response to the failure of fifty years of assimilation policy.

The first Indian commissioner to tackle the recommendations of the report was Charles J. Rhoads, who was appointed in the spring of 1929 by President Hoover. His selection seemed calculated to suit the demands of the reformers as well as the business-oriented mood of the public. Rhoads was a wealthy Philadelphia banker, well known for his philanthropy. Faithful to the Quaker tradition, he had expressed a personal concern for the Indian that had led him to become president of the Indian Rights Association, an organization founded in 1882. Rhoads's appointment was fully approved by Ray Lyman Wilbur, Hoover's new Secretary of the Interior, whose interest in the Indian was also well known. The eagerness with which the press responded to the appointment was caught by the *New York Times,* which suggested that it was time to reorganize the old Bureau with its "obsolete traditions, methods and standards [and its] obfuscated Washington officials." The *Times* admitted that even though "part of the red tape" probably never could be removed, a "competent" Indian commissioner and a "fearless and upright" Secretary of the Interior could certainly "improve the lot of the Indians."[31]

The attitude in the spring of 1929 was optimistic. The prosperity of the twenties still dominated the economy and the election of the new President during the "Hoover bull market" of November 1928 symbolized the national ethos. But, it was Hoover's misfortune to become President at a time when the boom of the 1920s was about to collapse. Within a year after his election a crisis unprecedented in the nation's history was thrust upon him. Although Hoover did begin to use the new tools of economic aid, his action was too little and came too late and he lost the election of 1932. Hoover's Indian commissioner was forced to combat some of the same problems that the President faced. Indeed, the actions of the two men were bound together by the overbearing pressures of the nation's economy as it sank into the morass of the Depression. The last act of this play of the 1920s seemed to be an ironic comment on the temporal nature of America's lust for material success; and the men who sought to guide the government during this time seemed unable to control the whims of the vast machine.

The enthusiastic reception that Rhoads received in 1929 was a sharp contrast to the criticism that hounded his office a year later. As with his chief executive, the longer he was in office the more difficult it became for him to appease the insatiable appetite of the critics. In 1929, however, the reformers were eager for action. The publication of the Meriam Report and the resignation of their archenemy, Commissioner Burke, had whetted their appetites. At a conference in Atlantic City in January of that year they asserted, "Today is the accepted time, the psychological moment. Reform is in the air. People want it."[32] In the spring of 1929 when Rhoads's appointment was made public, the reformers were delighted. Harold L. Ickes, future Secretary of the Interior, predicted that Rhoads would "humanize and vastly improve the efficiency" of the Indian Bureau. The joint appointment of Rhoads and Scattergood has "heartened friends of the American Indians everywhere," he added, for "Mr. Rhoads will write a new and fairer chapter in the terrible history of our treatment of the Indian."[33]

That year the reformers kept their peace, but their silence did not mean they had relaxed their vigilance. Continually alert, they kept their eyes on Congress as well as the Bureau, anxiously watching the progress of reform. In the year after Rhoads took office they returned to the attack.

In the summer of 1930 *American Indian Life* asserted that although Rhoads and Scattergood had been in office for ten months, "their accomplishment has been practically nothing." The bulletin went on to say, "They have not rectified the extreme abuses in the treatment of the Indians . . . nor have they put into effect a single constructive plan. . . . The Indian Bureau is, if anything, in worse plight now than under their predecessors, Burke and Meritt."[34] This became the theme of the reformers and was the thesis of a work by Robert Gessner entitled *Massacre* (New York, 1931), an emotional piece of anti-Bureau (and anti-Congress) muckraking that probably surpassed earlier productions of the Progressive period. Gessner had gone on a "fact-finding" tour of reservations before writing the book and drew on this experience, along with some erroneous historical background, to describe the plight of the Indian.

At this time spokesmen for the Indian people were seldom Indians themselves. Even though Indian leaders and tribal groups frequently voiced their opinions during the decade of the twenties, their point of view was rarely publicized unless it was reinterpreted by self-appointed muckrakers, such as Gessner, or by the reform groups. Thus, in 1932, when a number of Indians attacked the Bureau through a critique sent to Senator William H. King (Democrat, Utah), the Indian signatures were followed by those of members of the American Indian Defense Association, including Collier. As a congressional spokesman for the Indian people, King was already well known for his sympathy toward the Indians. In 1928 he had introduced the resolution for the Senate investigation of Indian affairs.[35] The critique that he read before Congress denounced the Wilbur-Rhoads-Scattergood administration for breaking its "promises," and for setting up "new evils of far-reaching kinds."[36]

Senator King's action provoked a sharp reply from Secretary Wilbur, who had little sympathy for the leading critics of the Bureau: Collier, Senator King, and Senator Burton K. Wheeler (Democrat, Montana), an influential member of the Senate Investigating Committee. In the heated debate that followed, Secretary Wilbur complained that "constant badgering of faithful and devoted men who are working hard in the national service is pretty poor business." Those responsible for this badgering, he noted, reminded him of "David Harum's observations on the need of some fleas for every dog."[37] Nonetheless, the attack on these administrators did not subside until Rhoads submitted his resignation.

One of the difficulties of the Rhoads administration could be traced to the commissioner himself. Rhoads was a businessman, inexperienced in the administration of federal bureaucracy. He later admitted that he was "appalled by the intricate nature of the Indian situation and the mass of detailed information necessary to arrive at even a reasonable understanding of all of its complexities."[38] Combating the bureaucracy, which he described as "a wilderness of past misadventures,"[39] demanded a stronger personality than he possessed. Rhoads, who was genuinely interested in reform, might have been more successful if he had been supported by the Secretary of the Interior and the President; there were many strikes against him, not the least of which was being part of the Hoover administration.

Despite these problems, Rhoads's administration laid the groundwork for Collier's Indian New Deal. While it lacked the dramatic overtones of Collier's administration, it was an improvement over Burke's commissionership. The period from 1929 to 1933 should be viewed as a time of transition, marked by Rhoads's efforts to apply the suggestions of the Meriam Report, particularly in the area of Indian education.[40]

One of the first actions of the new Bureau directors was to persuade Congress that the boarding-school budget should be increased. This concession was not secured without the encouragement of President Hoover, and even the President's request for more money was followed by several months of debate in Congress. If the appropriation for Indians had increased, Congress asked, why had their status not improved?[41] The increase was finally granted in 1930, and for the first time children in boarding schools were guaranteed enough food and clothing. Thus one of the major issues fought by the reformers in the 1920s was resolved as the decade ended.

Rhoads was also responsible for improving general conditions in the boarding schools, including the publicized issue of child labor. The problem of discipline in the schools was not so easily solved. School superintendents who had been in the Bureau for many years had achieved a large degree of autonomy. Some of them practiced the old forms of discipline, labeled by Collier as "medieval." One of the last acts of Commissioner Burke in January 1929 was to forbid the use of flogging, a widely used form of boarding-school discipline. This restriction was obviously directed at the autonomy of the "medieval" superintendents. But Commissioner Rhoads spent several months studying the effects of Burke's directive and concluded that it had made control of the students in some situations almost impossible. At the beginning of his second year as commissioner, on March 20, 1930, Rhoads issued a new directive, a carefully worded statement that said, in effect, that severe punishment would be permitted in "emergency" situations. He cautioned, however, that any action of this nature would have to be reported to the Central Office.[42]

Rhoads succeeded only in arousing the wrath of the reformers, who up to that point had been reasonably tolerant of his administration. The first to attack the directive was John Collier, representing the American Indian Defense Association. In an address before a conference of Camp Fire Girl executives, he accused Commissioner Rhoads of restoring the principle of flogging and then went on to criticize Rhoads for all the problems he had failed to correct during his first year in office. Although Rhoads had not specified the type of punishment that should be inflicted as an "emergency measure," Collier had immediately concluded that he meant flogging. Rhoads, who was appalled by this interpretation of his new policy, had underestimated the ferocity of the reformers. The furor raised by the reformers led Rhoads to confess privately, "If the circular is going to be interpreted as Mr. Collier interpreted it, I shall, of course, take steps to redraft it so that its meaning cannot be misunderstood."[43] Publicly, however, he continued to defend his stand, suggesting that Collier's statement was a misinterpretation and an exaggeration.

In his address before the Camp Fire Girl executives, Collier laid the blame for many of Rhoads's failures on what he called the "pressure of the Old Guard," Education Division employees who were a carry-over from the "dark ages" of Burke's administration. Chief among these offenders, according to Collier, was Hervey B. Peairs, Burke's Director of Education, who had not yet been replaced. During the controversy Rhoads pointed out that he was looking for a new Education Director, and when W. Carson Ryan was chosen the punishment issue seems to have died down.[44]

By the time Ryan became Director of Education, the requirements for education positions in the Indian Service, including that of superintendent, had been raised. Unfortunately, this change did not affect those who had been hired during the pre–Meriam Report era and who were still responsible in part for the ignominious reputation of the Bureau. It would prove to have increasing effect, however, on the quality of the new education staff, who became fully professionalized during Ryan's administration.

Upgrading of Indian Service personnel was not restricted to lower grade employees. On March 30, 1931, the Bureau announced a major administrative reorganization. Under the new system education would be moved from its former subordinate status under the nonprofessional division of Administration to a more prominent position. The new plan provided for five field divisions under the guidance of two assistants to the commissioner, one for human relations and one for property. Education would be one of the five divisions; the others included Health, Extension, Forestry, and Irrigation. Each of these divisions would be directed by "trained and technically qualified executives."[45] This system was a watershed in the history of Bureau education, for it meant that Indian education was given new stature. For the first time it was considered of sufficient importance to be placed under the direction of a professional educator, which implied, in effect, that its standards might be raised to meet national education levels.

When the position of Education Director was vacated in July 1930 by Peairs, *American Indian Life* asserted that the "Director of Indian Education is the most challenging position in the American school field."[46] The new director would be faced with the problems of administration, personnel, "education substance," and politics. In addition, with the exception of a "few Indian day schools," the entire Indian school system would "have to be revolutionized." In order to achieve this, the director would have the "burden of handling Congress," a Congress whose members were not amenable to closing boarding schools that brought "$300 in local trade for every child." For these reasons, the journal declared that the position of Education Director was "next in importance to that of the Commissioner himself."[47]

One month later, on August 19, 1930, when Secretary Wilbur announced Ryan's appointment, the reformers were exultant. *American Indian Life* declared that he was not only at the top of the list of candidates but the only "eligible" individual at the time.[48]

When Ryan accepted the position he was a professor of education at Swarthmore. By this time the college had become accustomed to sharing his talents. At the time of his Indian Service appointment, he was president of the National Vocational Guidance Association, a member of the executive committee of the National Education Association, and active in the Progressive Education Association. Ryan's appointment meant that another Quaker committed to the concept of service to humanity was added to the Rhoads-Scattergood administration.

Although the new commissioner had already begun to apply some of the proposals of the Meriam Report, Ryan gave them such force and direction that even the outspoken critics of the time admitted that his appointment was the "one incontestable forward step" in Rhoads's administration. Ryan envisioned a threefold program: (1) the development of a community school system, which would be oriented to the needs of existing population centers on the reservations; (2) federal-state education contracts, an increasingly popular concept, which would rapidly accelerate the number of children attending public school; and (3) the gradual phasing out of the boarding schools. In the interim he sought to make the boarding schools more responsive to the needs of the students.

In developing these concepts Ryan reflected the rather detached outlook of professor and analyst. During his years as administrator he discovered that it was much more difficult to convert them into realities. As Education Director, Ryan was a transitional figure. Since he was not appointed until a third of the way through the Rhoads administration, he actually served about the same length of time under Rhoads and under Collier. The fact that he remained in office during the early years of Collier's administration indicates that Indian education reform began not with Collier but during Rhoads's commissionership.[49]

Closure of the boarding schools was a necessary counterpart to the growth of the community school. This program was begun during Rhoads's administration and continued under Collier. The number of schools closed during these years indicated the pervasive influence of the Meriam Report. Rhoads was as strongly affected by the Meriam Report as was Collier. The obvious contrast in the administrations of the two men was due not only to the length of their respective terms in office but also to the difference in their personalities. Collier's administration made more of a splash and in the long run accomplished more partly because of the dynamic force of his personality. But Rhoads, like President Hoover, introduced reform to a greater degree than critics were willing to acknowledge.

The issue of boarding-school closure exemplified the difficulty of accomplishing reforms. From 1928 to 1933, the number of boarding schools decreased from seventy-seven to sixty-five. Some of these schools merely changed from boarding schools to day schools, but a total of twelve stopped caring for children away from home entirely. In 1930, when Ryan assumed responsibility for the program, he cautioned against haste: "We make no secret of the fact that we hope to eliminate gradually practically all the Government boarding schools," he wrote, "but we do not intend to do this until a real study is made of each school and the necessary guarantee of follow-up of the child is obtained."[50] In 1931, his first full year in office, three boarding schools were closed; in 1932 one was closed and two were changed to day schools. In addition, children in the lower grades were gradually being transferred to day schools or public schools.

In spite of this beginning, liberal magazines claimed that boarding-school closure had been insignificant. In terms of numbers, they had a point. Even though twelve schools were closed from 1928 to 1933, the Indian population continued to grow and the number of children in boarding schools was greater in 1933 than it had been in 1928. Part of this increase was due to the pervasive influence of the Depression. As Commissioner Rhoads observed in 1930, "during the current year . . . the drought and economic conditions will impose a heavy demand upon boarding school facilities."[51] Further boarding-school closure also hinged upon construction of a large number of day schools, which were not significantly funded until Roosevelt's administration.[52]

One of the most effective barriers to closure, however, proved to be those congressmen who represented districts containing boarding schools. Aware of the boost that these schools gave to the local economy, they were determined to prevent the Indian Service from interfering with "one of the things the Chambers of Commerce all boast about."[53] Nonetheless, Ryan pursued the closure campaign to the extent that in the early years of the Depression few schools escaped its threat.

Early in 1933, both Haskell Institute and Chemawa, two of the oldest off-reservation schools, were informed that they would be closed. Adverse reaction to the Chemawa closure came not only from the local community and its representative in Congress. For some fifty years Northwest tribal members in Oregon, Washington, Idaho, and Montana had been sending their children to this institution. The school had assumed a traditional place in the educational needs of the Indians, and they saw no justification for the closure. As the Warm Springs Tribe pointed out in their protest letter, "Such action is utterly unjust to us and to other Indians of the Northwest . . . and it will deprive Indian youth of our reservation of higher educational advantages."[54] By the fall of 1933, the order to close Haskell and Chemawa was rescinded, but the enrollment for each school was severely cut for the 1933–34 school year and Chemawa was reduced to the status of a two-year vocational school.

While few schools were actually closed, most felt the effects of proposed curriculum changes. One of Ryan's first objects of attack was the Uniform Course of Study. In part, this meant that courses that were not pertinent to the Indian's cultural background, such as English classics, algebra, geometry, and ancient history, were gradually removed from the regular course of study, and a serious effort was made to introduce subjects more suited to the children's needs.

The Uniform Course had assumed that Indians would adopt white culture. Ryan's second step was to introduce courses that were part of Indian cultures. He felt that it was vital for these children "to understand something of the precious nature of the heritage they have as Indians."[55] The diversity of this heritage precluded teaching it through a Uniform Course. Ryan recognized, too, that it would not be possible for whites to teach this heritage. This was before the Bureau began to use anthropologists in its programs to help educate white teachers, and in only a few isolated instances were any whites familiar enough with Indian culture to adapt it to the classroom.[56] Consequently, when the new program began, it relied on Indian help whenever possible, particularly in reservation day schools or boarding schools where teachers could come from their homes. On the Navajo Reservation experienced artists began to teach rug weaving and silver making in reservation boarding schools. Pueblo youth attending Santa Fe boarding school were returned to their nearby pueblos regularly for instruction in pottery making. The famous Maria of San Ildefonso took part in this program in the early 1930s. In Oklahoma, a small number of Indians, some of whom had been educated at Bacone College, taught in Bureau day schools scattered about the state.[57]

In spite of these beginnings, a significant time lapse separated the initiation of proposals by the Central Office and any progress in the field. While Lewis Meriam praised the fact that a Nevada Indian child in 1931 was no longer forced to recite the verse,

> What do we plant
> When we plant the tree?
> We plant the ship
> That sails the sea,[58]

ninth graders at Pierre Indian School (South Dakota) in 1932 still found *Julius Caesar* and *Lady of the Lake* on the required reading list.[59] Change in any given school was dependent on both the administration and the teachers. A preponderance of Old Guard teachers almost guaranteed a stultifying atmosphere of status quo. While one Indian Service observer praised the new teachers for their willingness to change, he commented about the Old Guard, "It is practically impossible to change their habits and attitudes. . . ."[60]

As partial remedy for this situation, Ryan encouraged decentralization among Indian Service schools. Moving away from the traditional system in which each school depended on the Central Office for subject matter and approach, he urged Bureau schools to begin meeting state curriculum requirements and standards. This change went hand in hand with Ryan's push toward state control of Indian education.[61] Ryan was a firm believer in the principle of decentralization and foresaw the day when states would accept total responsibility for Indian children who attended public school. State orientation in Bureau schools reflected a growing concern with local needs in preference to a curriculum chosen by bureaucrats in Washington, D.C.

The new attitude was summed up in 1931 by the National Advisory Committee on Education. Selecting Indian education as an example of the detrimental effects of federal control, the committee observed, "Our sad experience with centralized supervision of education for the Indians should forever warn the American people away from centralized control of their own education from Washington."[62] The conclusion of this committee, published a scant three years after the Meriam survey, served to emphasize the recommendations of the earlier report. It also lent support to Carson

Ryan who, at this time, was fighting an uphill battle to implement his policy plans.

Ryan's emphasis on the community school was sometimes at odds with state education standards. Since he viewed such schools as rural education situations, he felt that the "local needs" of the curriculum were necessarily rural needs. This concept had already begun to achieve popularity among Progressive educators. State curriculum standards, however, usually lagged behind the latest trends in educational thought and, as a result, state criteria for schools did not differentiate to any degree between urban and rural curricula. When the Indian Service began to develop a special rural school program, oriented to specific area needs, some state educational administrators "expressed the hope that their own public schools might eventually achieve a similar freedom."[63] In a sense, therefore, Ryan was using the Indian Service as an experiment to test his interpretation of Progressive Education, and the Indian Service for the first time in its history was serving as the avant-garde in school change.

Ryan wrote in 1928 that the "Indian Service has not appreciated the fundamental importance of a family life and community activities in the social and economic development of a people."[64] Four years later, in 1932, John Collier observed that the Mexican approach to the rural school "has lessons to teach the United States." Collier suggested that the "school in Mexico exists only incidentally as a school; it is rather the promotion center for a multitude of community activities."[65] Ryan's concept of the rural school as the center of community activities foresaw not only a healthy developmnet of the community itself but a specific place for the Indian child in that community.

Development of the child's role in the community was part of Ryan's aim of ensuring a fulfilling future for the Indian child. If he remained in his community for the first and most impressionable years of his schooling, then he would be able to relate to his own environment if he chose to return there after high school. On the other hand, if an Indian youth determined to stay in the white man's world, Ryan deemed it imperative that he be prepared for this kind of life. Consequently, one of Ryan's strongest priorities was vocational education. His own experience as a specialist in vocational education for the U.S. Bureau of Education had engendered an interest that continued into the 1920s and was reflected by his recommendations in the Meriam Report. Certainly Indian Service education had not accomplished its goal of teaching the students skills that would enable them to find jobs.

The Senate hearings on Indian affairs that began in 1928 supported this conclusion. Senator Wheeler, a member of the subcommittee that conducted the investigation, frequently expressed his exasperation with the Indian Service, and Bureau employees often found it difficult to defend themselves against his relentless questioning. His summary of the Bureau's failure with vocational education left little doubt as to where he stood. "It seems to me," he remarked to the superintendent of Indian schools in Oklahoma, "that where the Indian Service has fallen down in dealing with the Indian children has been that they have not given this vocational training." The superintendent's defense was dismissed by Wheeler, who asserted that Indian children were not "any further ahead than they were twenty years ago. You turn them out of your ninth grade schools," Wheeler continued, "and they go back, most of them, to the reservation and to the blanket."[66] Several months later, at a hearing in Arizona, subcommittee chairman Lynn J. Frazier (Republican, North Dakota) carried this criticism even further: "If you cannot instill into them [the Indians] the idea that it is necessary for them to go out and hold jobs and take their place in the world," Frazier observed, "then it seems to me the spending of money on them is more or less of a loss."[67]

Ryan, on the other hand, saw Indian education as an opening of a wider range of opportunities for the young Indian. If practical vocational training were included in the schools, he reasoned, the student would have more freedom of choice. Ryan's attempts to establish a new program were hampered by the increasingly defeatist attitude of Rhoads's administration, the reluctance of Congress to increase the budget of the Indian Bureau, and, finally, the deliberate style of Ryan himself. Once described as a "pacificator" who ranked with Henry Clay,[68] Ryan was no radical, and he never hastened into a new project without careful planning.

In spite of budget problems, in 1932 he was able to secure a new Bureau position for the director of vocational guidance. The first duties of this individual would be to make a thorough study of the needs for vocational education within the schools and to ascertain what kinds of jobs would be feasible for the Indian students. Ryan's background of educational studies was again guiding his actions as

Education Director: first a study, then action. In addition, he named department heads to direct each of the vocational departments in the schools, such as industrial training, economics, and agriculture. Since all of these changes would affect the often isolated boarding school, Ryan also created a new liaison position whose holder would work outside the schools, contacting potential employees. All of these steps were crucial to the development of a strong vocational program. Again, the foundation was laid by Ryan under the commissionership of Charles Rhoads.

As the traumatic years of the Hoover administration ground to a halt, Ryan might have looked back on his two and one-half years of leadership with some degree of satisfaction. Most of the changes that he considered crucial to Indian Service education had been initiated. Certainly there had been no overwhelming successes, as reformers were quick to point out. Conditions of the time as well as the measured tempo of Ryan's nature contributed to the generally conservative results. However, in each of Ryan's major goals—development of community schools, improvement in federal-state relations, and change in boarding-school curriculum to meet student needs, as well as some boarding-school closures—there had been progress.

4 | JOHN COLLIER AND WILLARD WALCOTT BEATTY: NEW DEAL ARCHITECTS OF EDUCATION

Despite Ryan's efforts to improve education, the accomplishments of the Rhoads administration failed to satisfy Bureau critics. Determined to achieve the goals they had set for Indians, they increased their barrage of criticism as the 1932 election drew closer. In the Novemer 5 *Nation* John Collier wrote, "The system of 1929 is the system of today." Even though Rhoads and Wilbur "knew the fact and the truth" of the Burke regime when they took office, before the end of the first year the Wilbur administration had "reversed itself." The result, Collier concluded, was "old evils continued and new evils set up."[1]

Although the most widely publicized attacks on the Bureau were made by congressmen or prominent Indian reform leaders, other people also helped to keep Secretary Wilbur on his toes. In the campaign year of 1932 Mary Austin, a well-known southwestern writer and friend of Indian causes, wrote to him to complain of the Bureau's failure to construct day schools in the Southwest. Austin's complaint was typical of a reformer's analysis of the Rhoads administration. She pointed out that Rhoads had promised day schools at the beginning of his term; that Congress had allocated funds; that both Rhoads and Ryan wanted more day schools; but that little or no action had been taken. "It will be a great annoyance to the friends of the Indian," she concluded, "if we have to make another appeal, and thus stir up public antagonism toward the department. Could you not manage to get something in motion immediately. . . ."[2] This threat was not taken lightly by Secretary

Wilbur, who replied within a month to the effect that there was more progress than Austin apparently was aware of.[3] Repeated pressure of this type made it all too clear that critics of the Bureau were eager for a change.

In 1932 the American people were in the throes of one of the most frightening experiences in their history. In the three and a half years following the Great Crash, the national economy had plunged into a seemingly endless downward spiral. The bravado of 1920s prosperity, which had swept Hoover into office, was a thing of the past. In electing Roosevelt the nation indicated its need for action and direction, two things that the people now believed President Hoover had failed to provide. Those concerned with Indian reform expressed a similar disenchantment with Rhoads's commissionership.

A new administration meant that the reformers had the opportunity to advocate a reform-minded candidate for Commissioner of Indian Affairs. On hearing of Roosevelt's victory, a number of concerned people, including Collier, sent a petition to the President-elect with more than six hundred signatures. Although many of the signatures read like a Who's Who of American Indian reform in the 1920s, leading educators, physicians, churchmen, and social workers had also added their names. The petitioners did not mince words: "So great is the Indian distress in many tribes, and so rapid is the shrinkage of Indian property held in trust by the Government," they wrote, "that we do not believe we are exaggerating when we suggest that your administration represents almost a last chance for the Indians."[4]

Although the reformers tended to dramatize events, in this instance they had a point. FDR's victory was the most significant event for the Indian people since the Dawes Act. The net effect of Roosevelt's election, at least until the impact of World War II, was a reversal of the policy of assimilation. Nonetheless, it still offered no guarantee to the Indian people that it would outlast the leadership of the men who initiated it. As long as this leadership was divorced from the Indians themselves, it was not directly responsible to them. The fundamental problem with the Indian New Deal, like that of all earlier administrations, was that it maintained a paternalistic control over the lives of the Indian people.

President Roosevelt's search for a new Commissioner of Indian Affairs was crucial to the education reforms of the 1930s. The changes initiated by Ryan could easily have been reversed by a commissioner who was a proponent of assimilation. Although Collier was one of the foremost candidates for the position, the final choice was not made without deliberation. During Collier's decade or so of reform crusading he had made enemies as well as allies. His ideas aroused strong emotion and his extremist techniques encouraged a polarized response—one either loved or despised the man. Thus, when his nomination was made known to the Senate, Collier was opposed not only by the supporters of the other chief contender for the office, Edgar B. Meritt, former assistant commissioner under Burke and a prime target for the anti-Burke crusaders, but also by some senators from states with large Indian populations, such as Elmer Thomas, a member of the Senate subcommittee investigating Indian affairs, and Thomas P. Gore, both Democrats of Oklahoma. As the *New York Times* put it, "some opposition developed among those who did not share his views regarding Indian welfare."[5]

Indian reaction to Collier's nomination was also mixed. The All Pueblo Council sent a special message to President Roosevelt recommending that Collier be appointed.[6] Collier's closest Indian friends were among the Pueblos; other tribes, such as the Navajos, regarded him with considerably less affection. In addition to the limited support of Indians and of Congress and the full backing of reformers, Collier's greatest asset was his friendship with Harold Ickes, Roosevelt's newly appointed Secretary of the Interior and a well-known supporter of the Indian cause. Ickes's insistence on the choice of Collier guaranteed the position for his friend.[7]

Collier became Commissioner of Indian Affairs on April 21, 1933, seven weeks after Roosevelt became President. Already the New Deal was beginning to move, and those who had hurried to Washington, D.C., to catch the swell of the new wave felt the surge of its motion. The excitement was contagious. Oliver La Farge, the well-known anthropologist and writer whose most famous novel, *Laughing Boy,* appeared at this time,[8] described the mood of 1933 as he recalled it two years later:

> Beginning with a shake-up of the top personnel, the new administration flew at it . . . it meant upsetting more than a century of tradition. . . . And then, one must consider the atmosphere of the New Deal. The Indian Bureau . . . since March, 1933, has reflected the tone of the Roosevelt administra-

tion. It has been plagued by bright young men, attached to the various departments, who found in this microcosm a chance to imitate what they conceived to be roles of Brain Trusters in the larger government. If a Brain Truster has drawbacks, a sub-Brain Truster is almost indescribable.[9]

News of Collier's appointment brought an exuberant response from liberal publications. *The Nation*, which had published a number of his articles, suggested that there would be "rejoicing on the reservations, at least among the Indian inhabitants. . . . For the first time in many years," it concluded, "the Indians have a right to expect justice and sympathy from their guardians in Washington."[10] Even the more cautious *New York Times* conceded that Collier was "rated as an outstanding national leader in Indian welfare."[11]

As Commissioner of Indian Affairs, Collier provided the forceful leadership necessary for change. This proved to be of inestimable value to the Education Division during the New Deal. Although Ryan and Beatty were responsible for formulating and directing the new education programs, in the long run they too were dependent upon Collier's determination and conviction. Initially, therefore, it was Collier who made the educational changes of the 1930s possible, for it was he who created the climate necessary for educational reform. Within the Bureau he ruled with the firm conviction of a man who knew he was right. Within the delicate framework of Bureau relations with Congress he secured the legislation and the funds that were the lifeblood of his programs. Finally, within the context of the reform direction sought by Ryan and Beatty, he supported their new ideas because they coincided with his own convictions.

In his dealings with Congress, Collier relied heavily upon the rapport he had established with congressmen and the press. In these areas he had labored extensively. His testimony at congressional hearings during Rhoads's administration and his voluminous writing, which attested to a ready access to the press as well as favorable press coverage, had convinced several influential congressmen that Collier was not a man to be underestimated.[12] With their support at a time when the New Deal was moving rapidly, Collier was in a favorable position to secure legislation to support his goals. That these goals had been in his mind for some time was confirmed later when he admitted that by the time President Roosevelt took office, the "basic, and in large measure the detailed change-over needed in Indian administration had been spelled out and agreed upon by the Indians and their friends."[13]

Shortly after his appointment Collier outlined his objectives to the Indian Bureau. They included "economic rehabilitation of the Indians, principally on the land; organization of the Indian tribes for managing their own affairs; and civil and cultural freedom for the Indians."[14] These goals were dealt with in the Wheeler-Howard bill, which was introduced in February 1934, only ten months after Collier became commissioner. Education was less directly affected by legislation, with the exception of the crucial appropriation bills. In the Indian Reorganization Act (IRA)—the amended version of the Wheeler-Howard bill that was finally passed—education was addressed only in Section 11, which provided that $250,000 annually be made available for Indian children who sought special vocational or trade-school education. The primary concern of the IRA was with improving the economic condition of the Indians and facilitating political effectiveness at the tribal level. Consequently, its most significant measures were prohibition of further allotment of Indian land, and other features to enlarge the depleted land base; establishment of a revolving credit fund; development of methods for conservation of Indian resources; waiving of restrictions for Indians who sought civil service jobs; and establishment of provisions for tribal organization and incorporation.

The IRA was the first major piece of legislation to counter the policies established in the late nineteenth century. Its primary aim was to reverse the pattern of Indian economic destruction begun with the Dawes Act in 1887. But education, which was the second major thrust of the assimilation policy, could not be determined by legislation; rather, it was subject to the mercies of the Bureau educational directors and congressional funding.

If the Education Division had been restricted to the funding available through the Indian Bureau budget, it would not have been able to get its new programs under way. In the first years of the New Deal the budget for the Bureau of Indian Affairs hit the lowest point for the decade. In 1933 total federal funding for the Indian Bureau was approximately $22 million, in 1934 it dropped to approximately $18 million, and in 1935 it was about $19 million. This contrasted sharply with the budget at the end of the decade, which was about $33 million in 1939.[15] The amount budgeted for education within the Bureau fluctuated less. At $9 million in 1934, it was about half of the total Bureau budget; at $10 million in 1939, it was less than a third of the total.

The impact of New Deal emergency funding was of far greater importance than the annual operating budget. In 1933 the $19 million allotted from Public Works appropriations for Indian Service projects was almost as much as the entire Indian Bureau budget for that year. Public Works funds were allocated to numerous projects—hospitals, irrigation and drainage, water and sewers—including large amounts earmarked for education. Construction of long-needed school buildings, including new community day schools and dorms, and building of roads were directly funded by Public Works appropriations.

The establishment of the Civilian Conservation Corps (CCC) in the spring of 1933 provided another important boost to Indian education. Shortly after the CCC was formed it placed at the disposal of the Indian Office $5,875,200 for a separate Indian CCC, which became known as the Indian Emergency Conservation Work (IECW) program. The IECW was not part of the Education Division, but it typified the practical education made possible by the New Deal. Like its parent organization, the IECW was aimed at land conservation and management. The Indian CCC was geared to the unique needs of Indians and reservations and, consequently, it provided a tremendous opportunity for vocational training. IECW workers learned to be carpenters, truck drivers, radio operators, mechanics, surveyors, and engineers. The Indians responded overwhelmingly; some 85,000 served during the nine-year life of the program (April 1933–July 1942).[16]

This funding had far-reaching effects that went well beyond the limited capacity of the Indian Bureau to directly affect the Indian people. The combined funds of the WPA, the PWA, and the CCC provided jobs as well as job training, income, and vast improvements on the reservations, not only in construction of buildings and roads but in conservation of land, streams, and forests. The Indians thus were direct beneficiaries of the Depression. Although the economic conditions of the Depression were scarcely new to the Indians, the fact that they affected the mainstream society finally moved the federal government to action. The Indians benefited not because their plight was unique but because they were part of a national plight.

The acquisition of funds and, to a lesser degree, favorable legislation were the first steps in the new education program for the Bureau. Collier also gave his support and encouragement to the major ideas developed by Ryan and Beatty. Collier did not approach Indian education from the same perspective as did his Education Directors. They were educators, while he had been a social worker. Nonetheless, these three leaders had shared the framework of Progressivism that had dominated the decade before World War I, and the pervasive influence of this earlier reform movement molded a good part of the Indian education program of the 1930s. While Ryan and Beatty reflected the educational concepts of this period, Collier exemplified the Progressive concern with community.

In the years preceding World War I, Collier had found his niche among the Progressive idealists by becoming a community worker. Like many of his colleagues who fought the battles for better government, improved cities, the beginnings of conservation, and aid for immigrants, Collier believed that man could achieve a better world. In order to help bring this about, he went to work with the urban masses, a hitherto-neglected segment of the population. Employed by the People's Institute, an organization founded to give voice to this group, he spent over a decade (1908–19) struggling with the problems of the heavily immigrant population of New York City's Lower East Side. One of the chief programs that he encouraged was the People's Forum, which held a series of lively debates at Cooper Union, the social and meeting center of the area. This and other programs convinced Collier that the People's Institute was a success. Not only was it developing a feeling of involvement in community, but also it was creating a viable public opinion, which, in Collier's view, was the "true culture of the nation." This was the "soul of American democracy," he wrote in 1912, and it was "not confined to any dogma or party."[17] Some years later Frederick C. Howe, one of the directors of the People's Institute in this period, wrote in retrospect that all of them had believed that the "political renaissance was now surely coming"; it would not "stop with economic reform; it would bring in a rebirth of literature, art, music and spirit . . . it would call forth the impoverished talents of the immigrant and the poor."[18]

As Howe admitted, World War I and the ensuing peace at Paris were the dividing line for those who had believed they could turn ideals into reality. Although Henry F. May suggests in *The End of*

American Innocence (New York, 1959) that the disintegration of values, which he saw as the theme of the 1920s, began as early as the turn of the century, the influence of World War I was enormous. The disillusionment that followed in its wake was directed against the mainstream society and, although it affected only a small minority, those individuals often sought to recapture their ideals through another culture. Thus, Collier's involvement in Indian culture served as an outlet for his personal disillusionment. Initially he was attracted to Indian culture for its intrinsic qualities, but when he became aware of the need for champions of the Indian cause, the attraction became even stronger.

Similarly, disillusioned Progressives in Congress who sought new crusades also turned to the Indian. When the 1920s began, most of these congressmen knew very little about the condition of Indians, but under Collier's enthusiastic guidance, they acquired sympathy and respect for the Indian people. At the same time, Collier was gaining allies who would be very useful in passage of legislation when he became commissioner.[19]

The disillusionment that characterized the 1930s was no longer the prerogative of an exclusive minority. The Depression brought about a widespread dissatisfaction with mainstream culture. For some, this meant an honest flirtation with the concepts of socialism or communism. As the popularity of Huey Long of Louisiana attested, the roots of faith in the American form of government were seriously shaken by the fact that, despite politicians' rhetoric, things just didn't seem to improve. Throughout this time, however, Collier retained his faith in the culture of the Indian people. From his first interest in the Indian until his death, he was probably one of the most verbal spokesmen for their cause throughout the history of Indian-white relations.

Collier's faith in the Indian way of life flowed as a theme through all of his writings. In his letters, his articles, and particularly in his editorials in *Indians at Work,* he developed the following argument. The American way of life, he felt, was based on a "shallow and unsophisticated individualism," which had allowed itself to become subservient to the goals and means of a technological society. As recently as the 1920s the "white race" had thought that this way of life was unquestionably superior to that of other cultures. The Depression had demonstrated that this was not true, and now in the 1930s Western civilization was on the verge of collapse. Collier urged the nation to turn for advice to the ancient culture of the American Indian. Unless it adopted some of the primary values of Indian culture—living in and through a community, living in harmony with nature, and stressing spiritual rather than material values—the white race might not survive. Collier wrote in 1934 that the white race had become a "shattered race—psychically, religiously, socially and esthetically shattered, dismembered, directionless."[20]

One of the unique aspects of Collier's long administration of Indian affairs was his ability to view the government's involvement with Indians from a broad perspective. Collier viewed his administration in a historical context. How, he asked, does our treatment of the Indian compare with that of earlier administrations? By reprinting policy statements of earlier commissioners in *Indians at Work*, he illustrated vividly the contrast between the policy of the late nineteenth and early twentieth centuries and the Indian New Deal. The following quote was from the Report of the Superintendent of Indian Schools in 1898: "In our efforts to humanize, christianize and educate the Indian we should endeavor to divorce him from his primitive habits and customs. . . . We want the power of the Latin expressed . . . as well as the intellectuality of the Saxon . . . we must recreate him, make him a new personality. . . ."[21]

Collier also viewed his administration from an international perspective. He never lost sight of the fact that American Indian policy was being observed by nations, as well as native groups within nations, that had been or were subject to colonialism. As these people began to throw off the yoke of subjugation they became more critical of the American system, reasoning that the nation that was supposed to be the cradle of freedom and democracy should also have an enlightened Indian policy. Did the United States still practice paternalism toward the American Indian? Did the Bureau education policy discourage the Indian from maintaining his cultural heritage, or was he encouraged to preserve his ways in recognition of the diversity possible in a democracy? These questions became more relevant to Collier as he attempted to develop an exchange of ideas among Indians of the Americas and their respective governments, and as he became personally interested in the Indian policy of Mexico.

As a result, Collier brought a perspective to the Education Division that went well beyond his Progressive background. His conviction that Indian education should be rooted in the community and should, in turn, stress the values of native culture was reinforced by his awareness of the international implications of this policy. Moreover, as Ryan had written in the Meriam Report in 1928, education was the primary purpose of the Bureau. Consequently, the direction of the Bureau could be gauged both nationally and internationally by its attitude toward Indian education. It was Collier's intention that this attitude should undergo major changes in the 1930s.

The far-reaching significance of education made the position of Education Director one of the most critical appointments in the Indian Service. It was important that the men who held this position be personally dedicated, professionally qualified, and gifted at leadership. Carson Ryan clearly fulfilled the first two categories, but as a leader Beatty was the stronger of the two. Both men entered the education position with a commitment to Progressive Education, and both enlarged that commitment to include a deep involvement in the education of Indian children.

Ryan was perhaps the less fortunate of the two, because he had to work under the crippling effect of the Rhoads administration. Although he himself had definite plans for the Education Division, he was unable to do any more than begin them while Rhoads was commissioner. On the other hand, it was he who started the program that, with the advent of Collier's leadership and the dynamic input of New Deal energy and funding, was fairly well established when Willard Beatty became the new director.[22]

Willard Walcott Beatty was born in 1891 and was raised in Berkeley, California, just across the water from San Francisco. Undoubtedly the cosmopolitan character of the city influenced his youth. In the prewar years education was in a state of tremendous flux, and the Bay Area was one place in the nation where avant-garde ideas were being pushed. As John Dewey's ideas on educational change in an industrial society began to filter out to the country, education became one facet of the tumultuous and short-lived era of Progressivism. The Progressive Education Association was formed in 1919.

While John Collier and others were working enthusiastically in the People's Institute in New York City, Dr. Frederick Burk was redirecting the educational concepts of the teaching staff at San

Francisco State Normal School, and Willard Beatty was taking a B.S. in architecture at the University of California, Berkeley, in 1913. Beatty's first teaching job was at Oakland Technical High School, but within a few years he also became director of the training school at San Francisco State Normal School, where he met Burk.

Burk was one of the major influences in Beatty's career. It was through his association with Burk that Beatty became directly involved in one of the first successful Progressive Education experiments in the country. At San Francisco State, Burk developed the new concept of individualized teaching, wherein the child received "individual instruction and promotion." His method was so well received that educators began to visit him from all over the world.

In the early 1920s when the first public-school system in the country adopted Burk's system, Beatty was invited to be a member of the staff. Thus in 1922 he went to Winnetka, Illinois, a wealthy suburb of Chicago, to become principal of Skokie Junior High School; later he became Winnetka superintendent of schools. The new teaching method proved to be very successful, and educators soon began to refer to it as the "Winnetka technique." In Winnetka it won the enthusiastic approval of parents, students, and faculty.[23]

When the school system of Bronxville, New York, decided to experiment with the Winnetka technique, it engaged Beatty because of the reputation he had helped to establish at Winnetka. Beatty inherited a system that was overcrowded, short on funds, and beset with problems, not the least of which was uncooperative parents. With his Winnetka background to aid him, however, he overcame these obstacles and earned the appreciation of the community. When he accepted the position of Education Director with the Indian Bureau, the *Bronxville Press* described him as the "master builder," and noted proudly that he "was putting Bronxville on the map."[24]

The ten years that Beatty devoted to the Bronxville schools were dramatically successful. They made him a national figure and illustrated the potential of Progressive Education concepts. His standing in education circles was so high that in 1931 the General Education Board asked him to take a survey of all Progressive private and public schools. A year later he was chosen as vice president of the Progressive Education Association, and in 1933 he assumed the presidency of this organization, a position that he held until 1937, several months after he became Director of Education for the Indian Service.

Beatty's prominence as a leader in Progressive Education was seized upon by the press as an indication that the Indian Bureau was going to adapt these new methods to Indian education. *Time* magazine suggested that Beatty, as the "titular leader of U.S. Progressive Education," was now in a position "to dispense the blessings of his faith to 81,000 Amerindians." The appointment "indicated a new attempt to develop some sort of education to which the Indians will respond," *Time* concluded,[25] failing to note that Carson Ryan had also been deeply involved in Progressive Education and had already begun to use its principles in Indian education.

Collier, Ryan, and Beatty provided the stimulus for a vast improvement in Indian education during the New Deal. Strong leadership gave the impetus to construction and change: to a curriculum more suited to the needs of the child; to community day schools and a decreased emphasis on boarding schools; and to a better qualified faculty and staff. When the money available through the early years of the New Deal made these plans feasible, the result was the most dynamic program of Indian education in the history of the Indian Service.

Between 1936 and 1952 the program reflected the character of its chief architect, Willard Beatty, a top administrator and a remarkable individual. As Hildegard Thompson, Beatty's successor and Director of Education from 1952 to 1965, pointed out, "he did not fit any ordinary mold."[26] Others who knew him have suggested that what set him apart from most administrators was a sense of vision.[27] Beatty was dynamic and imaginative. He had a brilliant mind and a quick grasp of not only all of the aspects of an issue but the potential outcome as well, and often he was several steps ahead of everyone else. Hildegard Thompson wrote that Beatty had the "unusual skill of motivating people to work in team fashion toward common objectives"; "he could discover talents in others, that they themselves did not realize they had."[28] Another employee wrote to Beatty during his second year of office, "Your talks on human relations coupled with the human element practiced as you are inaugurating it will go farther to make an effective cooperative organization out of education than anything else that can be done."[29] In spite of the constant harassment directed toward him as Education Director, Beatty maintained his belief that the people with whom he worked as well as those whom he was serving were more important than the organization itself. Those who worked with him knew this.

Beatty, like Collier, was critical of the culture developed by the white Western world. However, he never acquired the bitterness that led Collier to an almost antiwhite, racist attitude. Beatty's chief criticism of whites was of their failure to put human before material values. His attack on their concern for money exemplified this. Pointing out that whites had attempted to "corrupt" Indian thinking by persuading them that the "activities by which countless previous generations of Indians won their livelihood" might be "too difficult for the modern Indian," he concluded, "we people of the United States have allowed our respect for money to outweigh our recognition of the fact that human effort and human will existed before money and may perpetuate the race after money ceases to be important."[30]

Finally, Beatty had one quality which was exceptionally important in the field of Indian education. He was sympathetic and understanding of the customs and heritage of other peoples. As he wrote in a letter of advice to an employee, "Look out you don't get yourself into the natural difficulty that all of us new to the service are in danger of doing and that is of jumping to too many conclusions. Watch for deep-rooted customs that represent what is being done without necessarily being talked about very much."[31]

All of these qualities were needed for Beatty to achieve the level of success that he managed. As John Collier wrote in retrospect, the directorship of Indian education was "one of the most demanding jobs in the world." For "geographical size" and "variety of problems," Collier pointed out, there was no other school administrative unit in the United States that could match it.[32] During the most significant years of the Indian New Deal, Beatty brought to this position a unique blend of talents. As a Progressive educator, humanist, and dynamic leader, he remolded the Education Division as far as was humanly possible in a brief decade of experimentation.

5

NEW DEAL INNOVATIONS: PROGRESSIVE EDUCATION AND ANTHROPOLOGY

As the dominant figures in education in the Indian New Deal, Ryan, Beatty, and Collier were responsible for the introduction and adoption of at least two new approaches to Indian education. The first of these, which was introduced by Ryan and Beatty, was Progressive Education; the second, which was encouraged by Collier, was the recognition of anthropology as an aid in understanding Indian cultures.

When Beatty, like his predecessor Ryan, began to apply Progressive Education concepts to Indian education, he was formulating one of the earliest programs of cross-cultural education. Beatty and Ryan envisioned this program as one in which the Indian child would learn through the medium of his own cultural values while also becoming aware of the values of white civilization. This would not be an easy task, but it was the goal that Beatty personally set for himself when he became Director of Education.

Both Ryan and Beatty were caught in the swell of the Progressive Education movement in its strongest years. They were introduced to it during the formative period and they had the opportunity to apply its principles during the height of its popularity. However, the vigor of the movement in the 1930s was deceptive. By the time World War II ended, it had lost its strength and vitality. Critics of the movement were no longer willing to hold their peace, and "long smouldering criticisms" of "its optimistic humanitarianism, its essential naturalism, its overwhelming utilitarianism and its persistent anti-formalism suddenly burst into flame in the popular press."[1]

The serious shortage of schools, which was accelerated by the impact of the war babies, added to the frustrations within this short-lived cause, but the roots of its decline lay even deeper. Although the movement supposedly reached its zenith in the years just before World War II, even then it was fighting one of its chief problems—increasing professionalization, a trend that tended to dissociate educators from parents and community. Ironically, this was the antithesis of one of their original goals, that of being closely associated with the community. In addition, Progressive educators were narrowly intent upon feuding among themselves.

By the early postwar years the movement had failed as a viable, living force. The tremendous influence that its ideas had exerted on educators and, to a lesser extent, on the public in the 1930s had dwindled. Even theorists whose concepts had led to its founding had turned against its recent manifestations. John Dewey foresaw the death of the Progressive Education movement even before the war: ". . . any movement that thinks and acts in terms of an 'ism,' " he wrote in 1938, "becomes so involved in reaction against other 'isms' that it is unwittingly controlled by them." Then it becomes a defense mechanism, rather than a "comprehensive, constructive" force.[2] But despite the death of Progressive Education as a structured movement, some of those who had believed in its basic ideas (for example, Beatty) did not radically alter their concepts. As an "ism," Progressive Education may have been dead, but as a source for approaches to education, it had not been destroyed.

The ideas that spawned the movement are less easily grasped than the history of the movement itself. Beatty suggested that Progressive Education was a "point of view or an attitude of mind."[3] He might well have agreed with Lawrence Cremin's analysis of the term. Cremin posed the hypothetical question What is a "capsule definition of progressive education"? and responded, "None exists, and none ever will; for throughout its history progressive education meant different things to different people; and these differences were only compounded by the remarkable diversity of American education."[4] Educators like Beatty were aware that their apparent unwillingness to define the term was, in itself, a partial definition; one of its most appealing qualities was that it permitted the teacher to adapt his or her interpretation to the situation at hand. Built into the term, therefore, was the principle that education must adapt to the environment.

Progressive Education developed as a direct response to changes in American society. John Dewey foresaw that the America emerging in the late nineteenth century would require a new approach to education. The traditional three Rs that had been satisfactory for Thomas Jefferson's idealized nation of farmers would not suffice for an urban-industrial nation; "the time-honored education of the agrarian household and neighborhood," Dewey wrote in 1899, could no longer meet the needs of a transformed society. With the influx of immigrants who swelled the cities and the migration of rural Americans to urban jobs, society in America was losing the familiar teachings of home and community. Instead of growing up on farms children grew to maturity on streets and vacant lots surrounded by rows of apartments, brownstones, or tenements. Industrial growth and urbanization were tearing American life from its roots. According to Dewey, in this new America, the school itself "would have to assume all the educative aspects of traditional agrarian life." In other words, each school would develop an "embryonic community life," which would not only "reflect the life of the larger society" but would also encourage the children to improve upon that society until it could become, in Dewey's visionary terms, one which is "worthy, lovely, and harmonious."[5]

Dewey's school would be directly connected with reality, with "experience," as he was fond of saying. This would enable the child to relate to his environment and community while he was in school and would prepare him to deal with life when he had completed his education. Traditional education, said Dewey, failed because it was divorced from reality. As if in anticipation of Carson Ryan's criticism of pre–Meriam Report Indian education, Dewey attacked nineteenth-century mainstream American education for its failure to deal with the real world. In traditional education, he concluded, "the subject-matter in question was learned in isolation . . . in a water-tight compartment . . . and hence is so disconnected from the rest of experience that it is not available under the actual conditions of life."[6]

Leaders of the Progressive Education movement remolded Dewey's ideas according to their own interpretation of changing society. Implicit in their understanding was the concept of freedom for the individual child to develop according to his own abilities, level, and speed of attainment. In the first experimental programs such as Winnetka, responsibility for learning was given to the child. Within a short time the success of these experiments led to a rapid expansion of the individual learning method, and this aspect of Progressive Education became one of its most harshly criticized features. During the vehement public attack on the movement in the 1940s, I. L. Kandel, professor of education at Columbia University and author of numerous books on education, lashed out at the encouragement of rampant individualism. The lack of traditional values, Kandel asserted, was a "menace" because it forced the individual to find "his own salvation without the guidance of values other than those that he creates for himself through his own limited sphere of activities."[7] With his usual foresight, Dewey had anticipated such an attack, and several years earlier had redefined individual freedom: "The ideal aim of education," he wrote, "is creation of power of self-control"; it is, therefore, a "sound instinct which identifies freedom with power to frame purposes and to execute . . . purposes so framed." He concluded, "Such freedom is in turn identical with self-control. . . ."[8] Admittedly, achievement of freedom thus defined would not be an easy task, but it was typical of the high standards that Dewey established for education. Although Dewey frequently expounded on the merits of relating education to reality, often his own ideas tottered on the edge of unreality, postulating a form of education so idealistic that it never came into existence.

Dewey was the type of thinker whose ideas provide the impetus for movements, and in the 1920s and 1930s thousands of educators took his words to heart. Among these were Ryan and Beatty, who saw their potential for the field of Indian education. The journal of the movement, *Progressive Education,* also recognized the possibilities of adapting Progressivism to Indian education, and often printed articles on the subject. In February 1932, it devoted its entire issue to the education of Indians and primitive peoples, an occurrence that delighted people who believed in the interrelatedness of the two forms of education.[9] Familiar names dominated the list of contributors: John Collier, Oliver La Farge, Mary Austin, and even Julian Huxley, who wrote an article entitled "The Education of Primitive Peoples." Carson Ryan and Rose K. Brandt coauthored the lead article, "Indian Education Today." According to Ryan and Brandt, the "best opportunity" to apply Progressive Education ideas was among certain Indian groups, which already sustained the "ideal" conditions. "A mere 'three R's' type of education is sufficiently absurd anywhere," they concluded, "but nowhere more so than among the Pueblos, where life itself provides genuinely the elements that many progressive schools can only reproduce artificially."[10]

Throughout the 1930s ideas were exchanged freely between the Progressive Education Association and the Indian Service. Carson Ryan observed that the Indian Service had been "notoriously lacking in the past in its contact with modern education movements," and thus he encouraged the exchange in order to keep Indian Service employees in touch with current trends.[11] When Beatty became Education Director he was still president of the Progressive Education Association, and although he soon resigned, his continuing interest meant that contact between the two organizations was maintained.

Indian Service teachers and administrators were the chief beneficiaries of this increased exposure to Progressive Education. As one of them acknowledged to Collier, "We are isolated and far removed from educational centers and leadership. There is considerable danger of professional regression. . . ."[12] Beatty's primary aim was to overcome this problem. Since Indian education could improve only to the degree that the teachers and staff improved, he considered them his first concern. His long-range goal, therefore, was to find a method by which he could introduce the theories of Indian education to new teachers and yet enable other teachers and staff to keep up to date on changes.

The major new approach that Ryan and Beatty tried to develop was one that would meet the Indian child in his own milieu. One of their basic criticisms of pre–Meriam Report Indian education was not unlike Dewey's attack on traditional American education —namely, that it was taught in a "water tight compartment." In both cases, what the child learned was unconnected to the reality of his life. A child taken from a nomadic, home-oriented life of herding sheep on the Navajo Reservation could make no connection between this and the white middle-class stories of "Dick and Jane" he read in school. A child who had hunted wild horses or ridden after cattle in the hills of the Yakima Reservation could not comprehend why he should learn to distinguish between a noun and a verb or why he should study American history when all it discussed was what the whites had done. Nor did this education enable the child who chose an off-reservation life to support himself adequately. Beatty cautioned against this approach. When we encourage a child to go to boarding school or college, he said, "let us be sure that the experience won't unfit him for return to life among his own people, while failing to fit him for making a living anywhere else. . . ."[13]

This was the fundamental thesis of Indian education during the New Deal years. But, like Dewey's dream for an ideal American education, the goal set up by Ryan and Beatty ran into numerous hurdles and was never realized. Even so, the leadership of these men during this decade of change was important, because in spite of their long-range failures they did achieve a number of successes.

The success of the cross-cultural education program for Indian Service teachers, one of the most innovative ideas developed in the 1930s, was partially due to the addition of anthropologists to the Indian Bureau staff. John Collier's decision to employ anthropologists was revolutionary. Prior to the 1930s the Indian Bureau had seldom bothered to acknowledge the existence of this profession. The first issue of *Indians at Work* asserted that the Indian Service not only had ignored the research of the Bureau of American Ethnology but also had been "so tacitly hostile" to the "knowing branch" of the "Government's Indian organization" that the "public mind has forgotten one of the main reasons why the Bureau of American Ethnology was established and has ignored the important practical findings of that Bureau."[14] The article went on to point out that one of the *raisons d'être* of the Bureau of American Ethnology was to "obtain knowledge" about the tribes so that the other branches of government could administer both intelligently and sympathetically. That this goal had not been achieved was patently obvious to John Collier and the leaders in his administration.

Collier considered close ties with anthropologists and their representative government bureau necessary to an Indian Service administration that sought to understand Indian culture and to encourage the Indian to develop his communities in accordance with traditional culture patterns. Thus, in the 1930s and 1940s, Collier attempted to cooperate with the Bureau of American Ethnology and nongovernmental organizations in carrying out some of the recommendations for practical research and study found in the *Handbook of American Indians North of Mexico.*[15]

In the early years of the administration, when generous funding was made possible by Collier's good relations with Congress and the general impetus of the New Deal, a working relationship was established with the Bureau of American Ethnology. As early as 1934 Dr. Duncan Strong of the Bureau of American Ethnology was named liaison officer between the two bureaus. Shortly thereafter, in January 1935, Strong was succeeded by Dr. H. Scudder Mekeel, who became director of the Applied Anthropology Unit. Mekeel, who had received his Ph.D. from Yale University and was a member of the Harvard faculty when he joined the Indian Service, was assisted by Dr. Julian Steward (Ph.D., University of California, and ethnologist at the Bureau of American Ethnology), and a number of anthropologists who were sent out to the field to gather data for the research projects. However, the Applied Anthropology Unit had a short life. In 1937, due to lack of funding and possibly also to internal bickering between anthropologists and Indian Service administrators, Mekeel left the Indian Service, and the unit went out of existence.

This did not mean that Collier had ceased to look for sources of anthropological assistance. By September 1941 he had secured a new program based upon a contract between the Indian Bureau and the University of Chicago Committee on Human Development.[16] This project, which was under the direction of anthropologist Laura T. Thompson, undertook in-depth studies of Indians, both as tribes and as individuals, in order to analyze the effectiveness of the long-range programs of the Indian Bureau, in particular the functioning of the Indian Reorganization Act (IRA). Field research of a total of eleven communities within five tribes (Hopi, Zuni, Navajo, Papago, and Pine Ridge Sioux) was completed under the contract with the University of Chicago, and under a subsequent contract with the Society for Applied Anthropology the research was analyzed and published in a series of monographs.[17] The project was terminated after Collier resigned as commissioner, according to Collier because it criticized the Indian Service. His successors, Collier said, were not prepared to confront the "disconcerting" nature of the project's conclusions and to make the difficult administrative and political adjustments it called for.[18] Consequently, practical implementation of the research, which had been projected as the third phase, never occurred.

Although the Bureau's experiment in working with anthropologists failed to achieve the long-term goals that Collier had envisioned, there were successes in the 1930s. When Collier began to contact social scientists in 1933–34 he received an almost overwhelming response. Collier's plans for cooperation with anthropologists were published in the first issue of *Indians at Work* and elicited an immediate affirmative reply from Dr. Charles T. Loram, chairman of the Department of Race Relations at Yale University. "I am sure you are right in planning for the training of your officials," he wrote; "be assured of our interest and willingness to cooperate with you."[19] Loram was one of many scholars who contributed to the sudden flurry of meetings held to exchange ideas among educators, anthropologists, and Bureau administrators. Enthusiasm was so contagious in the first months that the accelerated pace of interbureau and cross-discipline relations became almost frenzied. It was as if anthropologists had suddenly achieved official recognition after decades of neglect, and from the musty halls of the Smithsonian the most respected members of the profession emerged to offer their ideas.

Early in the new administration Collier conferred with officials of the Bureau of American Ethnology, who helped him formulate the initial plans and "loaned" him the services of Strong. On May 28, 1934, the commissioner held a conference with several anthropologists and other scholars, including Lewis Meriam. This group concentrated on suggestions for teacher and staff education and discussed a number of possibilities, including a lengthy training program of perhaps a year, a summer-school session, and a short field institute, which would be held in several areas. It is significant that this meeting, as well as later ones, witnessed an exchange of ideas on methods used by colonial powers such as the Dutch and the British. Collier's awareness of international interest in U.S. Indian administration was shared by these scholars, and this multicultural perspective added a dimension to the Indian Service that had hitherto been lacking.

In December of 1934 during a national anthropological meeting Collier gave an address on the new Indian program that was received with "enthusiastic" approval.[20] During this conference a special meeting was held for a number of distinguished anthropologists and members of the Indian Service staff, including several education leaders, where even broader issues were raised: How could anthropologists aid in the organizing of Indian communities under the IRA? How could anthropologists aid in the training of Indians and whites already in the service, as well as those who would be employed later? How could anthropologists continue to cooperate with the Indian Service?[21]

By early 1935, therefore, the background work in anthropology and the Indian Service had been done, and Scudder Mekeel, as the new liaison officer between the two bureaus and field representative in charge of the Applied Anthropology Unit, had accepted the tremendous responsibility of turning these ideas into reality. Mekeel's primary work involved direction of field research in preparation for the adoption of the IRA by individual tribes. He also became involved in the in-service training program that was established shortly after Beatty became Education Director.

Despite these extensive projects, the experiment of cooperation between the Indian Bureau and the Bureau of American Ethnology and other organizations fell heir to the tensions and misunderstandings that often plague the relationship between administrators and scholars. There was no lengthy tradition of cooperation to fall back on, and there seemed to be an innate distrust on both sides. Each in a sense saw the other as a trespasser in an area where he had neither training nor authority. The bureaucrat was convinced that the social scientist simply lacked the experience to administer; the anthropologist believed that the administrator lacked the knowledge of the subject to administer wisely. In addition, the administrator had some (not illogical) doubts about the objectivity with which the anthropologist viewed his subject. "The failure of the anthropologist to consistently segregate technical recommendations from personal convictions," wrote H. G. Barnett, "has not strengthened his claims to scientific detachment. . . ."[22]

This conflict may have contributed to the dispute that arose between Collier and Mekeel. Several years after he had left the Indian Service, Mekeel worte an article in the *American Anthropologist* evaluating the IRA. One of his chief criticisms of Collier's administration was the experimental use of anthropologists. Mekeel asserted that the gap between the "scientific staff" and the administration was "too wide" to achieve any degree of success. "Eventually in the Indian Service," he wrote, "there may be a group of social scientists who are thoroughly familiar with administration, and executives who have a grounding in the social sciences."[23] Collier's reply, argumentative as usual, was calculated to put his opponent on the defensive. He implied that since the entire Indian Service had supported Mekeel's Applied Anthropology Unit there had been little divisiveness. With a parting barb, he observed that the "effectiveness" of anthropological work had "decisively increased" after Mekeel's position with the Indian Service had been terminated.[24] The vehemence of Collier's rebuttal suggests, however, that Mekeel had hit a sore spot, and that there may have been some grounds for the criticism. As far as the Education Division itself was concerned, there was more cooperation than bitterness between anthropologists and educators. Perhaps this was because anthropologists felt there was more chance for success in educating teachers than in changing bureaucrats.

The aid given by anthropologists in training Indian Service teachers in the years before World War II should not be shrugged off. Much of the success of Beatty's cross-cultural education program was due to the new perspectives introduced by anthropology and Progressive Education. Through these concepts Indian Service teachers were taught to be sensitive to Indian cultures and to consider teaching methods adapted to the unique characteristics and needs of Indian children. Thus, anthropologists and Progressive educators helped to shape the approach of Indian Service teachers as well as the format of the education program. Their importance in the 1930s was largely due to the persistence of Collier and Beatty, who made them part of the new Bureau policy.

6

THEORY CONFRONTS REALITY: CROSS-CULTURAL EDUCATION

Progressive Education and anthropology provided guidelines for educational policy during the Indian New Deal. The concrete changes initiated by the Education Division in this period, therefore, were in accord with one or both of these influences. Major policy changes of the 1930s included opening of community day schools, closure of some boarding schools and curriculum changes in those that remained, and education of Indian Service teachers. Ryan had begun to work toward these objectives under Rhoads's administration, and the New Deal witnessed extensive progress in these areas as Beatty continued the effort. Nonetheless, when World War II brought an abrupt end to many of the educational innovations, there was still a wide gap between Beatty's goals and reality.

Closure of the boarding schools was a good example of the limited success achieved. This issue was the subject of more publicity than almost any other aspect of Indian education. Collier knew the value of favorable publicity, and when he began closing boarding schools, he made sure that everyone knew about it. Twelve schools were closed between 1928 and 1933; Collier obtained maximum effect from the statistics by pointing out that during his *first year* in office a total of ten schools were "either abolished entirely or changed to community day schools."[1] During the rest of the thirties the decline was less dramatic, and by 1941 there were still forty-nine boarding schools with a total enrollment of about 14,000 children.

The construction of community day schools was more successful. Whereas boarding-school enrollment declined by only a third during this period, between 1933 and 1941 the number of day schools jumped from 132 to 226 and enrollment almost tripled. With 15,789 children in day school in 1941, more children were attending day school than boarding school.[2] The capacity of the new schools did not begin to meet the need, and in 1941 there were still thousands of children in remote areas who were not in school,[3] but due to the leadership of Collier and his two Education Directors, Ryan and Beatty, the decade of the thirties at least saw the first dynamic effort to improve the situation. These three men approached the issue of community education from different directions, but they agreed that a strengthening of community was of crucial significance to the Indian people.

Collier had been concerned with the concept of community as far back as the Progressive era preceding World War I. His search for community was not an uncommon quest in late nineteenth- and early twentieth-century America. The widespread uprooting of the traditional American pattern of living had also led Charles S. Peirce and Josiah Royce, leading philosophers of the time, to seek some form of community. Their search was a response to the dilemma of man in modern America,[4] for concern with community values had been generally absent from the American scene since the demise of Puritanism.[5] After the seventeenth century when the Puritan experiment with community had dissolved, there had been few successful attempts to achieve a true community. Not until the turn of the twentieth century, therefore, had the search become a serious one, and even then it was short-lived since the advent of World War I once again altered the mood of the nation. When this search failed, Collier found himself more and more attracted to a culture that recognized and accepted the value of community.

Although the commissioner developed a deeper feeling for the concept, attaching mystical values to its significance, like Ryan and Beatty he also saw its practical side. The Education Directors themselves were primarily concerned with its potential impact on Indian education. Since community values were so important to the Indian, Ryan and Beatty felt that it was imperative for their program to encourage these values. Their plan for community schooling was to help the child achieve a secure position in his community by teaching him in a local school for his first years of education, and to strengthen the community feelings of the immediate area by molding this local school into a center for the entire community.

While these Indian Service leaders developed the major thrust for community schooling, their concern was no greater than the commitment of a number of Indian tribes. Most Indian parents preferred local education for their children. In part, this was because they wanted to keep their families together. "We want our children to live in their homes as white children do and to have day school education as white children have," wrote the Council of New Mexico Pueblos in a 1930 resolution.[6] Some parents also preferred day schools to public schools because they wanted their children to be educated with Indian rather than non-Indian children. In 1934, when Fort Bidwell (California) Indians heard that their day school would be closed, they protested to the Bureau, "We would rather our children be in a school by themselves."[7] Indian preference for day schools, particularly for younger children, was expressed frequently during the thirties. While their requests were not always heeded, the fact that they were made at all indicated that there was a measure of favorable response to the new day-school policy.

Ryan's encouragement and keen interest had set the idea in motion as early as 1930 and prompted the rapid pace of building that began in 1933. As Beatty wrote three years later, the "foundation stone" of the "new educational policy" is the "establishment of community day schools."[8] Between 1933 and 1941 almost one hundred day schools were constructed on reservations. The schools were scattered from the Pima and Papago reservations to Oklahoma and north to the Sioux reservations, but the largest number was on the Navajo Reservation.[9]

In the 1930s schooling on the Navajo Reservation was totally inadequate. Spread across portions of three states, although primarily in Arizona, the reservation presented difficult problems for schooling. It had few roads, and those were almost impassible during much of the year. The rainy season turned them into a thick gumbo and winter cold froze them into hard, icy ruts. The life style of the people also militated against establishing permanent schools. Dependent on herds of sheep as their primary source of food and income, families moved as units from season to season in order to find grass and water for their livestock. "Community" was important to the Navajo, but it was often a very small group with a fluid character.

In 1928 only a little over a third, or about five thousand, Navajo children were enrolled in school. During the 1930s the federal government constructed between forty and fifty day schools on the Navajo reservation. Despite Navajo opposition, which was based in part on the argument that boarding schools offered a more realistic solution, and the additional challenge of locating adequate water supplies in areas with sufficient population to justify construction, building was pushed ahead, primarily with the use of Navajo workers.[10] By 1940 Navajo school enrollment had jumped to six thousand—a deceptive figure, because the population increase during the decade meant that this was still only a little over a third of the Navajo children.[11]

The enthusiasm of Indian Service employees who taught in these new community schools was symptomatic of the spirit of the New Deal. Eager to introduce new concepts of Indian Service education, they devoted long hours to their jobs, traveling over rough roads to isolated hogans in order to introduce innovations such as the sewing machine and attempting to communicate with whatever techniques of sign language they could initiate on the spot.[12]

The schools themselves became community centers partly because they offered services that were otherwise unavailable. Since they were built near a source of water, they provided a place to wash clothes and to bathe—a significant attraction in an environment so arid that families often had to travel several miles to fill their water barrels. For the men, the schools had equipment for shop work and repairs. On some reservations libraries were built up at the schools for community use; on others, traveling libraries visited each school on a scheduled run. On the Sioux reservations community gardens were a common feature of the day schools. In this way the school served as a focal point for entire families, and hence the community became involved in its activities. However, the learning process proved to be a two-way street, and Indian Service instructors developed a tremendous admiration for the families whom they served.

The community schools had built-in advantages that could not be duplicated in boarding schools. Ryan and Beatty saw no immediate alternative to the boarding schools, however, so they sought to modify living conditions within them in order to narrow the gap between the home and the institution.

Due to the lag between the issuance of Central Office directives and their implementation, no drastic changes within the boarding schools took place in 1930, when Ryan took office. By the middle of the decade and the beginning of Beatty's administration, however, boarding-school conditions had been considerably altered. The military routine that had characterized schools of the 1920s and earlier had largely disappeared. Henry Roe Cloud (Winnebago), the new superintendent of Haskell Institute in 1933, determined to transform Haskell from a pseudoprofessional athletic and military institution to one that would train Indian leaders of the future. Cloud fired the football coach and terminated the close ties with the National Guard that had dominated the school for a number of years. At Albuquerque Indian School the boys' advisor observed in 1935 that with the military abolished, "We find a different atmosphere throughout the entire plant, there is more home life and more student participation . . . as compared with the old military days."[13]

As boarding schools gradually shifted away from the military policy they began to relax other restrictions. By 1936, a former Santa Fe boarding-school student recalled, the school was "more tolerable," there was more "social life," and students were permitted to go into town to shop.[14] In the late thirties Beatty attempted to relieve the institutional nature of the dormitories by constructing cottages for living quarters at some schools, a project that was short-lived. The completed cottages were popular and were the envy of other schools, but further construction was discouraged by the Bureau of the Budget and Congress.

In spite of these changes, most boarding schools in the 1930s continued to be supported in large part by student labor. The Depression made it necessary for them to become partially self-sufficient and imposed standards that later served as guidelines during the lean years of World War II. Grains, truck gardens, and orchards supplied much of the food, which was then canned or dried. Many schools also had their own milk cattle and sheep. With the aid of the staff, the students did the laundry and much of the mending and cleaned the buildings and grounds. They assisted in the kitchens, where they baked breads, prepared meals, and washed dishes. As self-sustained units, these boarding schools were almost anachronisms, reflecting conditions of nineteenth-century rural America. Yet the routine necessary to support this system lent an atmosphere to the schools that was maintained as long as the system itself existed. At a few schools, notably Chilocco and Carson, the superintendents attempted to combine with the work pattern a purposeful instruction in late-nineteenth-century Christian ethics. Generally, however, this unusual approach did not survive beyond World War II.[15]

While the self-supporting system was in part a matter of necessity, some kinds of school labor also served as training for students who were to return to their reservations. During the 1930s both Ryan and Beatty, with the firm approval of Collier, attempted to develop a vocational program to teach the students skills that would be of use "especially on their own reservations or in Indian villages or communities."[16] In 1935, his last year in office, Ryan created a committee to determine policy for nonreservation trade and vocational schools (such as Chilocco, Haskell Institute, and Chemawa), and one of the major directives of this committee was that training be geared toward reservation life. The administrators assumed without question that most graduates of Indian Service schools would return to their reservations or communities. In 1940 directors at Chemawa pointed out that 90 percent of those Indians who left home for education and jobs returned to the reservation after a few years and remained there the rest of their lives. For this reason, they argued, the students should be given courses that would "meet their needs on the reservation."[17]

The Depression gave added impetus to this policy. In 1931 Indian Service schools were specifically directed to admit "as many older boys and girls as possible" due to the pressures of the "unemployment situation."[18] Under these circumstances it was considered unadvisable to train students for nonexistent jobs in urban areas. As Beatty pointed out, most of the nation's unemployed were the "wage earners of our cities." Thus, he concluded, "The man with a good farm is better off than the man who depends upon a weekly pay check." While the boarding schools might continue basic courses in "woodworking, metal work, automobile mechanics, dressmaking, and cooking, these, in many instances, should be supplementary to more fundamental training in land use."[19]

Beatty's goal was to replace inadequate industrial training with course work oriented to the "long-range economic purposes of each reservation."[20] Thus the type of training was varied according to the needs of the area. Its success depended in large part on the interest of the students. At Chilocco and Chemawa, administrators complained that students failed to respond to the extensive opportunities offered in agriculture. In spite of the administrators' conviction that these pupils should want to become farmers, enrollments remained small. Elsewhere response was more gratifying. In the Pine Ridge Sioux area the pupils were managing a herd of beef cattle of almost a thousand head by 1940. At Carson the students raised a variety of grains and also had a herd of cattle. On the Cheyenne River Sioux Reservation pupils at the boarding school went ahead with a beef-cattle program when the Tribal Council gave them permission to use certain tribal lands for grazing purposes. At the Phoenix school pupils learned how to operate heavy farm equipment. For girls, most schools still stressed practical courses in cooking, sewing, home nursing, and child care.[21] It was assumed that the majority of them would become wives and mothers in reservation communities. In this decade only a few schools continued to offer training for urban jobs; for example, Haskell Institute retained its secretarial training program, and Sherman Institute taught shop courses for pupils looking for jobs in the Los Angeles area.

Through this shift from urban to rural job training, Ryan and Beatty sought to maintain a link between student and home. Less successful, though equally ambitious, was their effort to introduce aspects of Indian culture into the boarding-school curriculum. While in theory this had merit, in practice it proved to be extremely difficult.

Edward Sapir, professor of anthropology and linguistics at Yale from 1931 to 1939, framed what has become a classic definition of culture: "Genuine culture is . . . the expression of a richly varied and yet somehow unified and consistent attitude toward life, an attitude which sees the significance of any one element of civilization in its relation to all others."[22] Anthropological descriptions of culture may not, however, have practical applications, and the Education Division had to prepare for concrete situations. Bureau educators in the 1930s therefore approached Indian culture by breaking it into components: history, customs and traditions, religion, art, language, philosophy, societal structure and regulations, and a system of values. Only three of these areas were introduced into the curriculum of Bureau schools—history, art, and language.

With the exception of religion, the other aspects of culture were ignored. Religion, however, fell under the broader category of

Bureau policy change. Before Collier's administration, when Indian culture was regarded as barbarian and decidedly inferior, assimilationists viewed religion as a focal point of attack. During the 1920s, such treatment of Indian religion was high on the list of reformers' grievances, and when Collier became commissioner he did not delay many months before issuing a directive to all superintendents decreeing "No interference with Indian religious life or ceremonial expression." In the field of education this meant, in effect, that Indian children in federal schools should no longer be forbidden to practice their native religion. In some schools this was enforced promptly. At Santa Fe, for example, Pueblo youths were permitted to return home to participate in the ceremonial training of their Pueblos.[23] (This opportunity meant little, of course, to those who did not have the means to get home; children who lived as far away as Acoma seldom returned during the school year.[24])

In spite of Collier's directive, a change in attitude toward Indian religion was slow in coming. Like so many of the commissioner's revolutionary concepts, the directive on religion ran into hard-core resistance molded by more than a half-century of assimilation rhetoric and legislation. While in school at Santa Fe, the children were required to attend church.[25] At the national level, antagonism to Collier's directive arose from those who continued to believe that there was no inherent value in Indian religion. The issue prompted a lively debate in *The Nation* between Commissioner Collier and Elaine G. Eastman, a white woman who had married a full-blooded Sioux doctor. Eastman had published in the *Christian Century* and was, at the time, completing a biography of Richard Henry Pratt, founder of Carlisle Indian School. Collier, in a gesture of tolerance, pointed out that there was some value in Eastman's article because it revealed the "peculiar presumptions which the discrimination of the past years have been based upon, and repeats a number of the factual errors . . . used to sanction the old policy."[26] Thus the commissioner discovered early in his term of office that Bureau directives alone were unable to sway long-held prejudices.

In the Bureau schools themselves the new approach to Indian culture sometimes elicited an enthusiastic response. In 1935, Chilocco decided to offer "for the first time" a course in "Indian history and lore." Ironically, the Central Office was no better prepared for this action than the school itself. For some reason, admitted A. C. Monahan, Acting Director of Education, there is "comparatively little material in the Indian Office to help you in your course. We are, however, asking our librarian to send you what there is."[27] After attending to Indian needs for almost a century, the Indian Office discovered somewhat belatedly that it had very little information on Indian culture or history.

At Chilocco this failed to dampen the enthusiasm for the new course. Almost three hundred students, or a little less than half the student body, enrolled in Indian History, and many completed individual projects that ranged from drawings of Plains costumes, to maps of lands ceded by the Five Civilized Tribes in Oklahoma, to sketches and biographies of famous Indian leaders including Crazy Horse, Gall, and Roman Nose. One student even wrote an analysis of the Indian Reorganization Act.[28]

This course clearly struck a responsive chord among seventh- to twelfth-grade pupils who were separated from their homes for a large part of each year. In the day schools, where pupils remained within their cultural milieu, a course of this nature had less significance. "The culture life is always around you there," a Pueblo Indian remarked. "You just automatically learn it. You hear it, you see it, you feel it and you do it."[29]

Proximity to home was a definite advantage for a number of the art students at Santa Fe boarding school. Since many of these pupils came from nearby pueblos, they were able to augment their courses at school with instruction from artists among their own people. The art courses introduced at the Santa Fe school in the early 1930s owed their existence not only to the new cultural emphasis of the Collier administration; they also reflected a growing national interest in Indian art.

In December 1931 an Exposition of Indian Tribal Arts opened in New York City and then went on a two-year tour throughout the nation, appearing in Venice as well. Although a number of earlier shows had been arranged by Santa Feans in the 1920s, this was the first exhibition to capture the public imagination. Response to the New York show indicated that white Americans had been almost totally unaware of the unique beauty of Indian art. Federal Indian policy, which had failed to recognize the merits not only of Indian art but of its culture as well, bore the major burden of this national ignorance.[30]

Shortly after Collier became commissioner, efforts were made to remedy this situation. In 1934 Secretary Ickes appointed a committee to study the protection and marketing of Indian arts and crafts, and the following year saw the formation of the Indian Arts and Crafts Board, a body which sought to improve quality as well as marketing of Indian arts and crafts. In order to facilitate this process, the board established trademarks for Indian-made objects. These served to set standards of "genuineness and quality" and also provided a guarantee for a piece of art.[31] One of the most successful projects of the board was its work with craft guilds on the reservations. With the board's aid the newly formed guilds served as "training centers" for local artists and craftsmen and also provided a direct market outlet that bypassed the well-established middleman. According to J. J. Brody, these guilds were the board's "most significant contribution . . . to the economic welfare of the tribes."[32]

The Indian Arts and Crafts Board organized art classes in the federal schools, but these were not the first of their kind; other classes had been started, even before Collier's term began, as part of Carson Ryan's initial program. Ryan had recommended in the Meriam Report that Indian arts and crafts be stressed, and the first art classes to be offered in a federal boarding school were begun in 1931 at Santa Fe.[33]

It was logical that the Santa Fe boarding school should become the leader in art training for boarding-school pupils. Although a number of other schools eventually began to offer courses in crafts such as weaving, silverwork, and Plains beadwork, none of the other regions of the West had the advantages of the Southwest. First, this area had been out of the general path of conquest and annihilation by Anglo-Americans, and the years of Spanish control had served more to blend Spanish and Indian cultures than to destroy either one. Consequently, these Indians may have modified their traditions, but they had not severed the link with their cultural past. Second, in the two decades before World War I, the Southwest had witnessed a period of reawakening in Pueblo and Navajo art, a revival that came into full bloom in the 1920s and 1930s.[34]

The revival of Southwest Indian art was strongly influenced by Anglos. Whether as individuals, like the traders on the Navajo Reservation who revived the art of rug weaving or the anthropologists who encouraged the revival of prehistoric designs for pottery and painting, or in groups, like the New Mexico Association on Indian Affairs (founded in 1922) or the Indian Arts Fund (founded in 1924), the Anglos put their stamp on the revival.[35] Like the reformers of the 1920s, they thrived on publicity and action. During this period they were as influential in promoting the rebirth of traditional Indian culture as the American Indian Defense Association was in promoting the general cause of Indian reform. Although the nature and the purpose of these two movements were not identical, their fervor and enthusiasm for reform gave them a common cause.

Although Collier was more closely identified with the general reform movement, he was also a champion of traditional Indian art. Through his years of studying Indian culture, Collier had come to believe that the Indian who maintained his traditional relationship to the universe held the key to a fulfilling life. This was possible, he believed, only through continued reinforcement, which was provided through the unity of ritual, often expressed through art, and the reflection of solitude. "Man, both in solitude and in tribal ritual," Collier wrote, "draws upon the cosmos and yields back that which the cosmos requires for its own life or fulfillment . . . through ritual art. . . ."[36] Thus, Collier concluded, traditional art was a vital link to maintaining the creative life force of these people. Although Collier directed part of his Indian Bureau program toward off-reservation Indians, he believed that most Indian people would retain this traditional approach to life.

Dorothy Dunn, director of the first program of Indian painting at the Santa Fe boarding school, sought to encourage traditional Indian culture through the medium of art. A young Anglo art instructor who had taught at Santo Domingo, one of the most conservative Pueblos, Dunn completed her studies at the Art Institute of Chicago. On her return to New Mexico, she established the painting program in 1932 and, although she received little encouragement from the Indian Service, which was suffering from budget cuts because of the Depression, she managed to convince her superiors that the program was worthwhile. By 1933 she had received official sanction from the Bureau in the form of a civil-service appointment as "Teacher of Fine and Applied Arts," and in the next few years she developed a highly successful course in painting. Dunn prefers to describe her role at the Santa Fe school as "an artist-researcher and guide rather than as teacher in the formal sense."[37] Nonetheless, the encouragement she gave the young artists in treating traditional subject matter based on their tribal culture had a significant influence. As Brody points out, most of the Southwest as well as many Plains artists from the mid-thirties to the sixties came under the influence of Dunn's program, or what he terms the "Studio" style of painting. After Dunn left the school in 1937, her students took over and under their direction her general approach was maintained for over two decades.

Although Carson Ryan supported Dunn's program, he had serious doubts about the feasibility of either teaching Indian languages or using them in class. "We do not attempt to use the local language as the medium of instruction," he wrote in 1932, for "the practical difficulties are probably insurmountable."[38] Given the conditions of the time, Ryan's appraisal was probably a realistic analysis of the problems that would confront the Indian Service if it attempted to introduce bilingual teaching.

First among these was the traditionally negative attitude toward Indian languages that had prevailed throughout American history. Before the Meriam Report was published, Indian Service education had reinforced the general disdain for Indian culture by opposing any suggestion of bilingual education. All instruction in boarding schools was in English, and the children were forbidden to speak their own language, even outside the classroom. This unnatural restriction only served to widen the chasm between boarding-school pupils and their own people when they sought to return home. The attitude of cultural superiority was summarized succinctly in the remarks of Commissioner J. D. C. Atkins, who observed that the language "which is good enough for a white man or a black man ought to be good enough for a red man." Atkins also suggested that "teaching an Indian youth in his own barbarous dialect is a positive detriment to him."[39] Although this attitude was modified during the two administrations that followed the Meriam Report, it was by no means eradicated. Those who promoted the mainstream theory for the amalgamation of the Indian into the dominant culture saw no reason to postpone the inevitable by encouraging native languages. During Collier's term of office this point of view, which was dominant among older employees, made implementation of each of the new programs a continuing challenge.[40]

A second, more concrete problem for bilingual teaching was a general lack of competent Indian Service instructors. Before Ryan became Director of Education most instructors not only were poorly qualified teachers, they also knew very little if anything about Indians. Although qualifications for Indian Service teachers were raised under Rhoads's administration, these standards failed to include culture awareness and language training. In 1935, for example, an experienced teacher who passed the civil service exams was theoretically eligible to teach Indian children even if he or she had never seen an Indian. Although Ryan began to change the curriculum to meet the special needs of the students, little consideration was given to teacher training.

The problem of poorly qualified Indian Service instructors might have been solved if there had been a sufficient number of trained Indian educators. Before Beatty took office, however, few Indians were employed even to assist Indian Service teachers except in the narrow area of arts and crafts. As a result, they remained an untapped resource. Given the opportunity, they could have provided crucial assistance to Anglo teachers floundering with classses of first graders who spoke little or no English.

A third problem was the lack of bilingual books. In the early 1930s they simply did not exist. The books that Indian children were forced to read described an alien culture in what was often an alien tongue. It was not at all surprising that when Indian pupils in federal schools were tested, the results were almost invariably lower than those of white children in comparable grades.

Carson Ryan recognized the immensity of these problems, but if Ryan saw them as "insurmountable," Beatty interpreted them as a challenge. The reaction of the two Education Directors to this issue illustrates the contrast between them. Ryan, the thoughtful analyst, was more cautious about attacking a difficult situation. He was, perhaps, the more practical of the two. Beatty was so confident he would find some answers among the endless number of possible solutions that he was undaunted by the complexities of the situation. He may have been less practical, or, as one of his leading experts in bilingual education concluded, "Beatty was . . . in many areas, somewhat ahead of his time."[41]

Beatty met head-on the difficulty of working without bilingual texts. If they don't exist, he reasoned, then we will write them, and by the end of the decade he was ready to start. Securing the aid of white educators like Ann Nolan Clark and linguists like Robert Young and Edward A. Kennard, he began publication of a number of bilingual pamphlets entitled the Indian Life Series, most of which appeared between 1940 and 1945. Although the stories were based on legends or everyday incidents of the tribe described, they suffered one serious drawback—they were composed in English and then translated into the native language. Their subject matter was appealing, but their vocabulary, which was well suited to the primer and preprimer level in the English version, became ill suited to this level when translated. Ideally, these bilingual books should have been written in the Indian language and then translated into English, but at this time there were few if any trained Indian elementary teachers who were equipped to tackle this job.

Despite these drawbacks, the project was a first stab at meeting the needs of the non-English-speaking Indian child. Not all of the pamphlets were bilingual, but even those written solely in English told stories to appeal to children of the tribes included in the series: Sioux, Navajo, and Pueblo. Some of the titles included *Singing Sioux Cowboy* and *The Hen of Wahpeton* (Sioux), *Field Mouse Goes to War* (Pueblo), and *Little Man's Family* (Navajo). Each of the stories was translated by a tribal member and illustrated by an Indian artist. Some of the illustrators were graduates of the "Studio" classes at Santa Fe boarding school, including Andy Tsihnajinnie and Gerald Naylor. Other stories were illustrated by Andrew Standing Soldier, a young Sioux artist.

Perhaps Beatty would have expanded the series to other tribes if the war had not curtailed the project. If so, of course, he might have encountered further difficulties in working with written Indian languages. Aside from the basic problems of finding qualified people to write and translate the stories, one of the chief difficulties in developing bilingual texts was the lack of written Indian languages. Of the approximately 230 surviving Indian languages in the United States, a significant number had remained oral. Written Navajo, for example, had come into existence only during the 1930s. Although a number of translations and vocabularies had been written previously, they were generally inadequate and inaccurate. After the language was written, the few persons who had mastered it were in demand for their ability to teach adult Navajos to read well enough to understand a newspaper. Severe criticism of Collier's conservation program of livestock reduction on the reservation made the Bureau almost desperate to find bilingual Anglos who could explain the program to the Navajos (in spite of these efforts, however, the Bureau failed to persuade many of the Diné that the drastic program was necessary).

The innovative value of bilingual texts did not solve the problem of bilingual education, however. As far as Beatty was concerned, it was merely one aspect of his program. Of equal importance was the education of Indian Service teachers in the techniques of bilingual teaching. That this was one of the earliest problems Beatty faced is indicated by a letter he wrote during his first month in office, in which he described the difficulties encountered in teacher recruitment for the large number of new day schools in the Southwest. Even though the teachers were selected from the government civil service register for elementary teachers and community workers, he explained, "a large proportion of them are encountering problems which are totally outside their previous experience." He pointed out that the major problem was that of adjusting to non-English speaking students: "Approximately ninety five per cent of the Navajoes in our new elementary day schools come from families in which English is not in general use. . . ."[42] The necessity of training teachers to approach children for whom English was a second language was a strong factor in encouraging Beatty to develop an intensive teacher-education program.

A structured program on how to reach children who spoke another language had never been developed in the Indian Service. Much of Beatty's effort in this direction, therefore, broke new ground. Earlier administrations had assumed that the child would absorb the language simply through regular exposure. That this was not true was illustrated graphically in Ruth Underhill's novel, *Hawk over Whirlpools,* the story of a Papago youth's disastrous encounter with boarding school. The boy described English as "a language with many words for the same things so that you were never through learning them. These words were placed backwards so that, before you knew what a mouthful of them was about, the teacher had gone on to the next."[43]

Beatty developed one of the earliest bilingual training programs in the country. He recognized that the language problem was one of the greatest barriers for Indian children. If they stayed in school, generally teachers passed them each year in order to get them through, but their reading comprehension remained well below their grade level because they had failed to grasp the essential concepts of the English language in their first years of school. For this reason, Ann Clark advised Indian Service teachers in the primary grades to "take a half year, a year, a year and a half before you begin formal reading instruction but make that preparation time

rich in activities, experience, participations, and associations. . . .
Spoken English must be a living part of every child before written
English can be made alive."[44]

Although the major portion of the bilingual program was directed
toward correcting the handicaps of the Anglo teacher, Beatty also
attacked the problem of Indian teachers in federal Indian schools.
He turned first to the resource already at hand. On reservations,
such as the Navajo, where little English was spoken, he saw the need
for tapping the potential value of Indian assistance, and with his
customary gusto he began to search for Indians who could aid in the
schools. As Collier reminisced later, Beatty "scoured" the Navajo
Reservation for teachers and assistants and even brought translators
into some of the schools.[45]

Next Beatty began a program for professionally trained Indian
educators. Through congressional funding, he was able to award a
number of teacher apprenticeships to Indian college graduates who
had chosen to teach in the Indian Service. This program, begun in
1936, established a two-year training period for the apprentices,
during which time each of them would work with an experienced
Indian Service teacher who served as a general supervisor for the
student. In addition, the superintendent of the school, the Indian
agent, and the in-service training supervisor for the Education
Division maintained a close watch on the student's progress. Beatty
expressed his deep concern for these young Indians in a sixteen-
page mimeographed letter that was both a comprehensive analysis
of their role—their aims and what was expected of them—and a
personal interpretation of the aims and methods of ideal Indian
education. "You have the possibility," he wrote, "of being better
prepared to work in Indian education and to serve the Indian race
than many Indian Service employees who have entered the service
at any earlier date."[46] Only fifty students participated in the
program and, like so many of Beatty's innovations, it was canceled
during World War II.[47]

Beatty watched the progress of the bilingual teaching program
with an anxious interest characteristic of the type of directorship he
gave to the Indian Service. Although linguistics was not one of his
primary interests, he developed his own understanding of it by
consulting experts, and persuaded some of them to experiment with
their ideas through the Indian Service. After the program was
started he maintained an enthusiastic interest in its progress. One of

his linguists described him as a man of "enormous energy" who "was always on the move,"[48] and Hildegard Thompson wrote of him in retrospect, "No one worked with Beatty without catching his spirit of urgency and enthusiasm."[49]

Beatty himself wrote editorials in *Indian Education* that covered almost all areas of education. He developed his own ideas about language through this medium, pointing out that the educator who is teaching English to a child is at the same time teaching him the cultural values of the English-speaking society. The error of the teacher, Beatty said, was in assuming that the child already held those concepts when he entered first grade and, consequently, in speaking to him with the broad vocabulary upon which those concepts are based. The "average teacher," Beatty said, addresses first-grade Indian children with the "same language she would use with public school first graders who enter school with a spoken vocabulary of several thousand words."[50]

Despite the pervasiveness of monocultural instruction, Beatty still believed that it was possible for the Indian Service to pursue a bicultural approach to education. It should be the "task" of Indian Service teachers, he asserted, to conserve the "original background of native culture when it exists," and "to introduce . . . an economic and cultural understanding of . . . white neighbors and associates."[51] This dream was also shared by Commissioner Collier. Although Collier walked the thin line between proponents of assimilation and proponents of preservation of heritage, he too believed that the Indian could achieve a balance between these two seemingly contradictory ways of life.

Beginning in his days as a reformer, Collier dedicated himself to defense of this principle. Three years after he took office, he wrote, "Assimilation and preservation and intensification of heritage are not hostile choices, excluding one another, but are interdependent through and through."[52] In concurrence with this statement, one of the staff members at Haskell Institute described Collier's program as one that looked "both forward and backward." In other words, he said, "It looks backward and utilizes customs, tribal lore and history and looks to the future for an integration of these into the world of science and industry."[53] Both Beatty and Collier recognized that their aims conflicted with almost all of the earlier goals of the Indian Service. However, at least in the 1930s, they did not seem to regard their goal—that the Indian child choose the best of both worlds—as unattainable.

One of the greatest difficulties they faced was shortage of time. The transition from the traditionally negative approach to Indian culture could not be accomplished in a decade; it demanded continued experimentation and change over a long period. Although Ryan and Beatty concentrated on only the most obvious areas of culture and those that might have the most significant effect on the learning process—art, history, and language—even these restricted attempts were short-lived. The bilingual text project did not begin until just before World War II and it effectively ended before the war was over. The introduction of Indian history in the schools was considered novel when it was first suggested but the novelty soon wore off. An effective cross-cultural program would have required significant change in federal school curriculum. At the very least, this implied teaching a large number of classes in one or more Indian languages, as well as instruction in the languages themselves for children who had learned only English; rewriting many textbooks in order to stress Indian culture and the Indian contribution to American history; teaching Indian poetry and philosophy, as well as art; and using Indian teachers for many of these courses.

Beatty was fully aware of the gaps that his programs left in the cultural spectrum. As he pointed out, when classes were taught in English, the only value system imparted was that of the English-speaking civilization. Consequently, what might be called the core of a culture, that is, its system of values, was ignored. In areas of the country where Indian tribes had been able to maintain their ways as "cultural islands" because the traditional value system was taught within the home and the tribal society, this gap in federal school education was less important. Many children in boarding schools, however, did not come from such favorable environments, and the boarding-school curriculum tended to change their cultural outlook.

Anthropologists have consistently pointed out that culture is a total system with interlocking parts that depend upon each other for the maintenance of the whole. In writing of their experience with the Navajos, Clyde Kluckhohn and Dorothea Leighton concluded that "every way of life is a structure—not a haphazard collection . . . but an interdependent system. . . ."[54] Many years earlier Edward Sapir had written that a "genuine culture" is one in which "nothing is spiritually meaningless, in which no important part of the general functioning brings with it a sense of frustration, of misdirected or unsympathetic effort."[55] In a comment directed specifically toward administrative bodies such as the Indian Bureau, Mekeel wrote in

1936, "It is not yet appreciated by administrators of peripheral peoples that culture is a delicately balanced mechanism, a part of which cannot be tinkered with, without in some degree affecting the whole."[56] Mekeel pointed out that the efforts of previous Indian Bureau administrations to destroy the value system of an Indian child by educating him according to white standards had a serious effect on the child's effort to reestablish himself in an Indian community after his schooling. By the same token, the efforts of the Bureau in the 1930s to teach some Indian culture in the federal schools, while much better than the previous approach, did not begin to solve the problems of adjustment for a disoriented Indian child. A course in silverwork or in Indian history did not answer the child's question: Who am I?

The polarity between Indian and white cultural values was so great that the teaching of white values to a child raised in a traditional home often had a shocking effect, and such a child found it difficult to retain his tribal view of the world without periodic reinforcement. Thrown into a world that directed him to be aggressive and fiercely competitive in order to achieve the white man's version of success, which generally meant a good job and the accumulation of material possessions, the Indian child faced the antithesis of his own cultural goals. If he came from a traditional home, he had lived close to the earth and had been taught to respect nature. In the Tewa Pueblos of the Southwest he might have heard this song:

> O our Mother the Earth, O our Father the Sky,
> Your children are we, and with tired backs
> We bring you the gifts that you love.
> Then weave for us a garment of brightness;
> May the warp be the white light of morning,
> May the weft be the red light of evening,
> May the fringes be the falling rain,
> May the border be the standing rainbow.
> Thus weave for us a garment of brightness
> That we may walk fittingly where birds sing,
> That we may walk fittingly where grass is green,
> O our Mother the Earth, O our Father the Sky![57]

Yet his boarding school experience quickly taught him that the white man was vain of his ability to subdue nature. The transplanted European had been striving to conquer nature and the Indian from the moment he first set foot on the continents of the Western Hemisphere but in both cases he had been less than successful. (It was not until the 1930s and later, however, that he belatedly discovered the extent of his failure.)

The trauma for the Indian child of this particular cultural conflict was reinforced by hundreds of smaller, more subtle ones, which varied according to the tribal heritage of the youth. Conceptions of time and of space countered the white man's notion of progress. In the view of the Hopi, ancient people of the Southwest mesas, time is viewed as a "duration, a storing up of change. . . . Everything that has ever happened, still is—though in a different form."[58] Among the Salteaux, durations "are interwoven with, and experienced as, events in all their individuality. Night is darkness, the stars and their movements, sleep, quietness. Day is light, the journey of the sun across the sky, the round of domestic duties. . . ."[59] The Saulteaux, A. Irving Hallowell explains, "lack the more exact frame of temporal reference that we possess which permits time measurement."[60] This deliberate existence is also described by Frank Waters, who suggests that " 'I have no time' . . . is the despairing cry of the twentieth century man, panicky with unrest, as he rushes ever faster from the past to the future over the knife-edge of the unlived present."[61]

The traditional Indian view of time as a motionless, boundless element caused the Indian youth to puzzle over the white man's preoccupation with haste. Yet the Western or European man knew that he must hasten because time, in his view, was an unwinding scroll. In this, the Indian reflects his culture no more and no less than does the white. The twentieth-century white American is, in the long-range view, the product of a major change in attitude toward time that dates back to early Christianity. As Lynn White, Jr., points out, the early Christians could not accept the "pagan belief in purposeless temporal undulation," because it countered his new-found belief in the "uniqueness of the Incarnation." When the Christian church became an "exclusive cult" within the Roman Empire, the break from a cyclical view of time was complete; as White suggests, "no more radical revolution has ever taken place in the world outlook of a large area." During the Middle Ages and Renaissance this Christian concept of time gradually evolved into the secularized and modern notion of progress. White points out, however, that within very recent years Western man has begun to question this long-term idea of progress.[62] In the United States this questioning began with the disillusionment with World War I and was accentuated by the Depression, which appeared to be a disturbing indication of failure.

The child in boarding school during the decade of the 1930s had to grapple with the bits and pieces of Indian culture that might be included in his curriculum, interspersed with the primary course work. The curriculum had improved, but often it lacked the cohesiveness that might have given the child the security that comes from simply knowing who one is. Sapir described this state of cultural insecurity as one of "bewildered vacuity," the tragic confusion that results when one "has slipped out of the warm embrace of a culture into the cold air of fragmentary existence."[63] When, in Sapir's terms, the "unified and consistent attitude toward life" becomes jumbled and broken, the child no longer knows who he is.

From this perspective, therefore, it must be concluded that the prodigious effort of Beatty and Ryan to develop a cross-cultural education program in the federal boarding schools was a failure. The program in the day schools was more successful simply because of daily cultural reinforcement in the home and community. The goals of these educators were noteworthy and in many areas they achieved some individual successes. But the task was far greater than the time, energy, and money that were allotted to it in the brief span of years from the early thirties to the early forties.

7

TRAINING TEACHERS FOR
CROSS-CULTURAL EDUCATION

Although the successes of the Education Division in the thirties were in many cases short-lived, even its modest accomplishments were largely dependent on the personnel involved. Both Ryan and Beatty sought to upgrade the educational staff during the decade. They recognized that Indian Service teachers and other education employees would need new skills and greater adaptability. Unless those who worked in the Indian Service schools could apply the ideas of these two directors, there would be no change.

Beatty was well aware of the need for in-service training because of the lengthy discussions held by anthropologists and Indian Bureau employees prior to his appointment. These exchanges produced numerous suggestions for different types of in-service training programs, and Beatty himself had made some preparations for the eventuality of in-service training. As he pointed out many years later, he did some of his homework for the Education Division even before he took office. Consequently he was able to plan for the immediate introduction of programs such as the summer sessions. In retrospect it was very important that he was able to do so, because the time period of generous funding by Congress for his new programs was no more than five or six years.

In-service summer training was not a totally new idea to the Indian Service. Sporadic summer training courses had been taught before, some in the late nineteenth century. In the immediate years before Beatty became director, courses were taught in Alaska (Nome, 1934; Eklutna, 1935) and in the Southwest. At Fort Wingate on the Navajo Reservation, a week-long conference was held in the summer of 1935 for Indian Service employees to discuss the development of an education program in that area; in the summer Dr. Gladys Reichard[1] taught the Navajo language in the "Hogan School" at Ganado; in Santa Fe, Ruth M. Underhill[2] taught a six-week anthropology course for Indian Service employees; at Yale University, Loram directed a summer education seminar on social, religious, and educational problems in mixed cultural areas. The variety of these courses was evidence of the upsurge of interest in summer training.

An altogether different type of training was offered to teachers throughout the Indian Service in the summer of 1935. During this year's vacation the Indian Service held a number of summer schools for Indian children. The locations of these schools demonstrated the wide range of summer work that drew many Indians from their winter homes in an annual migratory cycle. In the Northwest, one site was at the salmon fishing village of Celilo Falls on the Columbia River. Each summer Plateau Indians from several states gathered here to set aside a winter food supply and to sell that which they did not need. In the north-central states, a school was held near the blueberry fields, close to Washburn, Wisconsin, where Indians came to harvest the berry crop each summer, and near the wild rice fields on the Kakagon River near Odanah, Wisconsin, where others gathered the rice crop. In Oklahoma, thirty-five summer schools were held in small Indian communities scattered throughout the state.

When Collier sent his first queries about the summer program early in the year no one knew how the teachers would respond. In the first place, it was a new program. Second, those who were asked to volunteer were not day-school teachers who had been living near their pupils on the Navajo, Sioux, or other reservations. Rather they were off-reservation boarding-school teachers who, in some cases, had never been on a reservation. Thus the Central Office expressed delight and surprise when the response surpassed all expectations. The applications pouring in were so numerous the office admitted that it was "somewhat astonished at the enthusiastic requests . . . from teachers . . . who seem anxious for the opportunity of getting firsthand information concerning Indian life in Indian communities and on reservations."[3]

During the summer, as the teachers began to send in their reports, it became clear that their anticipation had not been unfounded. One of the unexpected results was their discovery that they were learning as much as their pupils. Part of the reason for this was the lack of class structure. None of them was given as much as a course outline. "We are giving you a real opportunity to break away from any formalized type of work," the Education Division wrote to the prospective instructors, "and to develop something that will be of genuine value to the children in their actual lives and which will be educational in the broadest sense of the word."[4] The teachers took these instructions to heart and, as a result, they developed programs as diversified as the places where they taught. Some spent much of their time harvesting and canning wild and cultivated foods, a project that involved mothers as much as children. Others taught the girls to sew and encouraged the boys to practice their carpentry skills. Many became involved with the environment, taking long walks and going for picnics. One teacher wrote, "All the children are teaching me the different kinds of trees in the neighborhood."[5] By encouraging an interest in tribal history and craftwork, some of the teachers themselves became acquainted with local culture. As the summer progressed, they discovered, perhaps for the first time, that teaching Indian children could be a two-way learning process. The eagerness of their reports indicates that a number of them regarded this summer as one of the highlights of their careers with the Indian Service.

Unfortunately, the summer-school program was of short duration. The following year, under Beatty's directorship, the Education Division turned to in-service training, which, while it had its merits, did not offer the unique experiences available in the reservation summer schools. However, summer schools for Indian children did not serve Beatty's purposes. His goals could be met only by intensive training sessions that would enable Indian Service teachers to become aware of Indian cultures and of special techniques adapted specifically to teaching Indian children.

Beatty pointed out that his in-service training program had benefited from the cooperation between anthropologists and Indian Service staff before he joined the service. However, it was his unique administrative ability that funneled these ideas into a concrete plan for the summer of 1936. Previous individual courses had been taught, but the 1936 session marked the first time that a broad spectrum of courses was made available. These sessions, which were held in two locations, at Fort Wingate, New Mexico, and Pine Ridge, South Dakota, offered a diversity of subjects, including philosophy of Indian education, rural sociology, Indian school administration, observation and applied techniques in the elementary school, weaving, racial psychology, general agriculture, the Sioux language, the Navajo language, Indian reorganization, anthropology, health, and mental hygiene. The range of instructors was equally wide, including a number of experienced Indian Service staff members as well as prominent anthropologists. Ruth Underhill taught the anthropology course on the Southwest at Fort Wingate and Mekeel taught the popular anthropology course at Pine Ridge. Beatty lectured in the evening classes on the philosophy of Indian education. Those who heard these lectures described him as a dynamic, "spellbinding" speaker. As Hildegard Thompson put it, "He could dramatize the most dry subject and make it interesting and educational."[6]

Some Indian Service teachers were attracted to the summer courses because they could be taken for university credit. In the first year of in-service training the University of Arizona, the Colorado State College of Education, and the University of New Mexico offered credit for specified courses at Fort Wingate; at Pine Ridge, credit was offered by the University of South Dakota at Vermillion and the Colorado State College of Education at Greeley. Soon the list of cooperating colleges and universities had expanded to more than fifty schools. University credit for course work was not important to all the teachers; one participant commented, "I do not need the credit, I am here to find out how to improve my work."[7]

In 1936 the total enrollment at the two schools was 489. Beatty and all those involved in planning and instructing felt as though the first two sessions had more than met their expectations. Their chief concern in analyzing the program was that they should add additional locations for future sessions. In 1937, in response to the "urgent request of workers in the field," the number of schools was increased to four by adding Sequoyah and Chilocco, Oklahoma. Attendance at these schools appeared to justify the expansion. At Fort Wingate there were about 400 students (90 of whom were Indian assistants brought in for a two-week period); at Pine Ridge, a little over 300; at the two Oklahoma schools, approximately 250.

In 1938 the number of locations was cut back to two: Sherman Institute, California, and Salem Indian School, Chemawa, Oregon.

The Chemawa location was chosen to encourage attendance by employees in Alaska, but of a total of 78 students at the session, only 20 were from Alaska.[8] The total number in attendance at Sherman Institute was 300, a figure that startled those who had estimated another record response. It appeared that the number who would attend had leveled off and that plans for ensuing years should be made accordingly. In 1939 two four-week sessions were held at the original sites, Pine Ridge and Fort Wingate. In 1940 the courses moved to Chemawa and Santa Fe; in 1941 sessions were returned to Fort Wingate.

Courses in the later decades never achieved the unusual blend of ideas and enthusiasm that were the propelling force of the programs held during the 1930s. Part of the motivation for this early period may have been the insularity of a decade that lacked the rapid communication and mass media of, say, the 1960s. When most communication was still by letter rather than telephone and most contact with the more populous parts of the country was by radio rather than television, a gathering with other teachers to exchange ideas and observe innovative classes had tremendous appeal. An equally significant reason for the success of these sessions in the thirties was the pressure exerted on the Education Division by Progressive educators and anthropologists. They contributed a significant number of ideas to a government bureau that had been long in need of new blood.

Beatty's close relationship with the Progressive Education Association enabled him to rely on it as a source of ideas as well as more concrete forms of aid. In the initial planning stages of in-service training, he requested financial aid and also depended on the organization to provide instructors who could teach summer courses on Progressive Education methods. In this instance Beatty found himself at odds with the Old Guard, teachers in the Bureau who were generally critical of the new methods and particularly of their application to Indian education. They were convinced that instructors outside the Service could contribute very little to the specialized nature of Indian education. Criticism of these outside teachers became so intense that Homer Howard, an education consultant who was to become supervisor of in-service training, felt compelled to write an explanation. Before the second summer of courses began, Howard wrote to a number of superintendents, pointing out that the Progressive teachers were chosen because their experience

in "forward looking classroom practices" contributed to the "desire
to continue to modernize" the federal schools. These teachers "may
not know much about Indians," Howard admitted, but "they do
know ways and means of dealing with educational problems." In
conclusion he advised the superintendents to discourage any
opposition. "It is worthwhile," he wrote, "for you to help break
down, at the very beginning, the resistance which many teachers
feel in regard to the presence of outsiders."[9] Beatty's ideas thus were
not without criticism, but, as Hildegard Thompson wrote, "The few
who disliked him were those who couldn't accept the changes he
initiated or who couldn't adjust to the rapid pace he set."[10]

In addition to course instruction and the anticipated writing of
new texts, these Progressive teachers were also anxious to introduce
to the Indian Service the standard studies of Progressive Education.
Book lists for summer-school libraries included works by John
Dewey and other well-known names in the field along with the
complete file of *Progressive Education*. Their broadly based attack was
aimed at both the old and the new, for if the new teachers in the
Service were somewhat aware of Progressive Education concepts,
this certainly was not true of the Old Guard. As Homer Howard
lamented, many of them had been trained in the "traditional
education set-up," and consequently it was considered necessary to
reeducate them.[11]

The distress of Progressive educators at the lack of books
available to Indian Service teachers was shared by anthropologists,
who were amazed at the dearth of material on Indian culture. One
of their first suggestions was that the central library be strengthened
by the addition of "available anthropological information." As one
anthropologist pointed out, the Indian Bureau library was "more or
less isolated from the rest of the Bureau" and "frequently" was not
even consulted for the information that it did have.[12] Despite its
inadequacies, however, the central libary was better equipped than
the libraries in the Indian Service schools. On more than one
occasion, Ruth Underhill, who taught anthropology courses for a
number of years, commented on the meager supply of books on
anthropology; for example, in 1936 she wrote, in "preparation for
summer I ought to get out a bibliography quite soon for I know
there are no books at Fort Wingate and I suppose arrangements will
be made to have them sent."[13]

Anthropologists viewed the lack of books on Indian culture as merely one indication of the general ignorance of Indian Service teachers with regard to the children whom they taught. Most anthropologists were eager to correct this defect and found an equal enthusiasm among the teachers, who "would read widely about Indians if we let them know what to read."[14] But sometimes the failures of the Indian Bureau in this area were so painful to an anthropologist he could not conceal his reaction. Such was the case with Frederic H. Douglas, the well-known specialist on Plains Indian art and curator of Indian art at the Denver Art Museum. After Douglas taught a course on art of the Plains Indians in the summer of 1937, Homer Howard wrote to him asking if he could teach again the following year. In his reply, Douglas commented on his experience of teaching for the Indian Service. "Any dissatisfaction I may have felt was not with the students," Douglas observed, "who seemed to be capable and interested, but with the system which, after 100 years of dealing with the Indians, had found out so little about them! If I ever do teach for you again," he added, "it will be in the light of this information."[15]

The anthropologists, Progressive educators, and experienced Indian Service teachers who taught summer classes had their work cut out for them. Their effort to correct years of traditional education, which had chosen to treat Indian pupils as if they were middle-class white children, could not be accomplished in a decade. Nonetheless, this was a noteworthy and prodigious project and was not without merit. As Collier commented two years after the program began, "For the first time, teachers and others feel that they are being offered professional help designed to meet their special needs."[16] Teacher response also indicated that they saw much more value in course work offered on a reservation than in special classes taught in an urban university.

Beatty's concern for educating the Indian Service teachers also led him to publish a bulletin for Education Division employees. Summer-school courses were one step toward developing a new philosophy of education among the teachers, but their effectiveness was limited by their short duration, the lack of carry-over during the long school year itself, and the fact that not all of the teachers attended the sessions. Beatty hoped that the bimonthly bulletin, *Indian Education*, would fill these gaps. Initiated shortly after Beatty took office, the bulletin did not take long to prove itself.[17] Although Beatty wrote a number of the articles, he followed his usual technique of leaning heavily on experts to cover their own fields. Thus he was able to introduce ideas of Progressive Education that were adaptable to Indian education; to keep his teachers up to date on new theories in education philosophy; and to give them practical advice on specific problems. Shortly after the bulletin began publication, one of Beatty's staff observed that the more he visited Indian schools the more he realized the importance of *Indian Education.* He wrote to Beatty about how much the teachers looked forward to each issue and how "seriously" they took each word. "Talk of safety," he observed, "and every reader of 'Indian Education' becomes doubly careful about his youngsters." He pointed out that many of the teachers felt the bulletin was helping them learn about "this mysterious thing called 'progressive education.' "[18]

As Director of Education, Willard Beatty worked with many restrictions. In the first place, his dynamic program sought to change in a short period of time a philosophy of education that had dominated the Indian Bureau for almost a century. Criticism by the Old Guard during his tenure demonstrated the firm hold that pre–Meriam Report education had on the Indian Service. Second, progress in his program was restricted to the years before World War II. The changes brought by the war gave Indian education a different theme by 1945. Third, many of his programs were introduced in a period that simply was not ready for them. For example, few Indian teachers were available to offer bilingual instruction or to translate tribal stories into English. Yet his goals often proved to be an accurate forecast of the future.[19]

Beatty's own abilities were not among the limitations he faced. As a leader, a thinker, and a source of inspiration for people and for the Education Division, he was unequaled. As one staff member wrote early in Beatty's administration, "Personally, I believe firmly that if they [Indian Service teachers] and you stick together long enough . . . you'll have most of them doing a pretty good job."[20] They did "stick together," but more powerful circumstances prevented the achievement of many of Willard Beatty's aims.

8

THE JOHNSON-O'MALLEY ACT: INDIAN CHILDREN AND PUBLIC SCHOOLS, 1928–1945

Although some Indian children attended public school before the end of the nineteenth century, the federal government did not begin to contract for this type of education until 1891. In the first years that contracting was done, Bureau leaders were not convinced that the transfer of pupils to public schools was practical. After ten years of contracting, they admitted that "notwithstanding the incentive of $10 per capita offered by the government . . . indifferent results were obtained." Public schools for Indian pupils, they concluded, are valuable "only when they are located in sections favorable to the coeducation of the races."[1] Given the difficulty of contracting during this early period, this conclusion was realistic. Nonetheless, public-school enrollment began to climb after the turn of the century. By 1928, the year of the Meriam Report, public schools had already surpassed federal schools by a significant margin in number of Indian students enrolled.

The forty years between 1930 and 1970 witnessed the greatest increase in public-school enrollment in the history of Indian education. In 1930 federal schools accounted for 39 percent of total enrollment of Indian children in school, while public schools accounted for 53 percent. By 1970, public schooling had jumped over three times, from 38,000 in 1930 to 129,000 in 1970, which meant that 65 percent of all Indian children in school were attending public school. Those who attended federal schools in 1970 accounted for only 26 percent of Indian children in school, or a total of about 51,000.[2]

During much of this period the Education Division played a prominent role in the transition to public schools. From 1930 to 1953 it was the sole federal agency responsible for funds allocated to public schools for their Indian pupils. Carson Ryan had recognized the trend toward public education as early as 1928. In the Meriam Report he observed that the policy of placing Indian children in public schools was to be "commended."[3]

When Ryan became Education Director he retained this attitude. His quarrel with public-school enrollment was not with the theory but with the method of funding by the federal government. Funds were provided to school districts for their Indian pupils to the extent that the districts incurred a loss of revenue from nontaxable Indian lands. Almost all of the states with significant Indian populations financed their public schools principally from the property tax (New Mexico was one exception). Since Indian land was exempt from this tax, school districts with significant portions of Indian land suffered from the loss of this potential revenue. Therefore, the tuition paid for Indian pupils served as an offset for loss of taxes. Although the federal government did not "contemplate paying the entire cost for the education of Indian children," it was willing to make up the loss that their enrollment would entail.[4]

However, the system of payment was unnecessarily complex. Rather than contract with each state for a single annual tuition payment to cover all of the Indian children in the state, the Department of the Interior went through the tedious process of dealing with each school district. This meant, in effect, that it was negotiating hundreds, even thousands, of contracts each year. Ryan thought this was not only "administratively absurd" but also a "violation of every right principle of Federal-State relationship in education." The federal government "should not be dealing directly with local communities in this fashion," Ryan said; "it should be dealing directly with the states."[5]

As soon as he took office, Ryan began to implement this idea. Within a matter of weeks he began negotiating with a number of states on the Bureau's plan to consolidate its public-contract operations in several states. Ryan suggested that in each of these states the Bureau appoint a supervisor who would serve as a liaison between the Indian Service and the state department of education. In September 1931, he wrote to the superintendents of public instruction of Oregon and Washington, exploring the feasibility of this plan and pointing out that it had already been adopted by Oklahoma. His suggestion was worded as diplomatically as possible, but the undercurrent of constraint revealed the inherent awkwardness of the relationship between federal and state administrators: "If you wished a supervisor to be with you there at the State Capitol," he wrote to the Washington superintendent, "and could provide an office for him, we should, of course be glad to have that arrangement made but we would not insist upon this unless it was something you yourself wished to do."[6]

Despite the awkwardness of the arrangements, those states that cooperated with the Bureau's Education Division during this early period were among the earliest to sign state contracts with the federal government. The difficulty of reaching a compromise that suited both levels of government gave an advantage to states that had some experience in working with the Bureau. The situation within the state itself, however, also contributed to the early completion of some contracts. In both Washington and California, for example, by 1934, Indian education was already controlled by the state divisions of instruction.[7] This situation had shifted the responsibility for Indian education to state officials and had forced them to develop a state policy as well as a system of revenue. One of the last states to sign a contract with the federal government was New Mexico, which had been unable to direct the education of its Indian pupils since it had a large number of federal schools. On the other hand, Arizona, which had an even greater Indian population, was one of the first four states to sign a contract. The great majority of Arizona's Indians lived within the Navajo Reservation, which meant that they could not attend public schools in any case. Consequently, Arizona moved quickly to form a state plan for educating the small number of Indians who lived within access of the public schools, and sought a federal contract to implement this plan.

The diversity of conditions among the states with significant Indian populations was compounded by an even greater diversity among school districts within each state. Although the Bureau was fully aware of the problems this created, Congress was extremely slow to pass the necessary legislation, and it was not until April 16, 1934, that the Johnson-O'Malley Act was passed.[8] J-O'M, as the legislation came to be known, established the legality of state contracts by authorizing the Secretary of the Interior to enter into contracts with any state or territory that had the legal authority to do so for education, medical attention, agricultural assistance, and social welfare.[9] Thus, after providing funds to public schools for some forty years, the Bureau was finally given the authority to centralize its contracting on a federal-state basis.

The year 1934 marked the high point in good relations between Congress and Collier's administration. In the first six months of this year, two of the most important pieces of legislation of this administration were passed: the Indian Reorganization Act (IRA) and the Johnson-O'Malley Act, both of which would have a profound effect upon the Indian people. However, the net effect of the two measures was neither the sudden separatism feared by some nor the rapid assimilation feared by others. The heritage of Indian-white relations and of federal Indian policy served as an effective barrier to change, and change was also slowed by the critics of the new policies, who became increasingly vocal in the years leading up to World War II. The IRA received the most attention because, to a degree, the reputation of the Collier administration hinged on its success. J-O'M, while not as heavily criticized, was subject to the increasing parsimony of Congress. Although the federal government had been supporting Indian education for more than fifty years, Congress still begrudged these appropriations. In 1935, for example, debate in the House of Representatives raised the question of the legitimacy of appropriating funds for Indian children when general school funding was in dire need because of the Depression. Supporters of special funding for Indian children pointed out that the need of the public schools made it even more necessary to give them added funds for the new pupils. The increased Indian enrollment had already overcrowded the schools beyond the capacity of local or state funding. To turn back to boarding-school education was unrealistic, however, for the per capita cost would be "more than trebled" should the government "build Indian schools and attempt to run them on a departmental basis."[10] Thus Congress was committed, albeit unwillingly, to an expanding aid program for public-school education.

The J-O'M program was predicated on the assumption that state and federal administrators could work together toward a common goal. Even before the act was passed, however, Bureau education leaders were concerned about this relationship. When state administrators became aware of its built-in difficulties, they hastened to establish independent control, a hostile reaction that forced Bureau leaders to relinquish their aid and direction much earlier than they had originally planned.

Bureau educators were very dubious about the motives of the state public-school systems. Principally they feared that public schools were more interested in the money that Indian enrollment would add to their school budgets than in the Indian pupils themselves. They knew that many schools were in serious financial difficulty and were all too eager to receive additional funds. The challenge for Bureau educators was twofold: Could they retain sufficient control over the funding and administration of public-school programs to insure that the type of education needed by Indian pupils would be provided? Given the trend of increasing state control of J-O'M programs, could they teach state administrators the unique approach necessary for Indian students before the states took over? The history of the J-O'M program, from its inception to the 1950s, is, to a great degree, an account of the Bureau's failure to cope with this challenge.

The first few years of state contracting were a time of experimentation for everyone concerned. The Bureau had to contend with the willfulness of state educators, and the state had to accustom itself to including Bureau educators. Diplomacy was the unwritten guideline for Bureau communication with state departments of public instruction, but the tone of the correspondence made it apparent that Bureau educators felt they were in control of the situation. Their extensive experience in administering a system spread over a vast area and compounded by a multitude of tribal situations bred a superior attitude on their part. In most cases, the state appeared to them to be a novice, which with proper guidance might emerge as an able director of its own Indian education. Although Bureau leaders attempted, rather unsuccessfully, to conceal this attitude from state administrators, they expressed it quite frankly in their correspondence with each other. In the second year of J-O'M programs Samuel Thompson, the ubiquitous supervisor of Public School Relations, wrote a private analysis of the two contracts in existence, California and Washington. "These two states are doing as well as could be expected when all conditions are considered," he observed, "but if any of us think they can run alone we are badly mistaken. . . ."[11]

Despite this assumption of superiority, Bureau education leaders soon discovered that they also were learning things. Administration of Bureau schools, which had offered a significant challenge in the pre–J-O'M days, appeared, if not less complex, at least less frustrating than the process of negotiating with states. One of the chief advantages of running Bureau schools was that there was no other authority involved. If a superintendent displeased you, he could theoretically be transferred. State conditions seemed to exist in an infinite variety, and each had to be dealt with individually. Variety itself was not a new phenomenon for the Indian Bureau, but variety compounded by the administration of a separate bureaucratic entity was.

When the J-O'M program was only two years old and had only two contracts to its credit (although others were pending), the Bureau indicated that it was already impressed with the diversity of problems encountered. In the 1936 *Annual Report* Collier listed the most important controlling factors: type and quality of schools actually maintained; amount of money needed to maintain a suitable school adapted to the needs of Indian and white children; amount and value of nontaxable Indian lands; methods of taxation; amount of state support for education; basis of distribution of state support; maintenance and capital outlay costs; changing legislation affecting school finances; distribution of Indian children; and attitudes of whites toward Indians. Collier frankly admitted that these factors created the "ever-changing problem" of "determining what part the Federal Government should assume in support of public schools."[12]

During this experimental period of the middle and late 1930s, the Education Division repeatedly stressed the importance of recognizing the varied conditions within the different states and handling them in appropriate ways. In contract negotiations it was imperative that the Bureau be well informed about each of these conditions in the state concerned. In some states with large Indian populations, such as Arizona, few of the Indian children attended public school; in Oklahoma, on the other hand, more than three-fourths of the Indian children were enrolled in public school. At least one state—Oregon—derived about 60 percent of public-school revenue from local funds, which enlarged the responsibility and authority of local school districts,[13] while others depended almost entirely on state income.[14] Sources for state income also varied tremendously, from poor states like New Mexico where the property tax accounted for less than one-fourth of the state revenue, to more wealthy states where it provided a significant portion of state income. If the budget was dependent upon property taxes, the amount of nontaxable Indian land within a community was a determining factor in the ability of the school district to raise money for the schools. In such cases, the amount of Indian land was in direct proportion to the financial need of the school district: the greater the amount of nontaxable land, the greater the need of the district. However, if most of the school funding came from the state and most of the state funding came from sources other than property tax, then theoretically the impact of nontaxable Indian land on the school budgeting should be less significant, and, in turn, J-O'M funding would be proportionately smaller.

Many of the problems that arose in the federal-state relationships were present in the initial contracts. Between 1934 and 1941 four states negotiated contracts with the Department of the Interior: California (1934), Washington (1935), Minnesota (1937), and Arizona (1938). With the exception of Minnesota, all of these states experienced difficulties either in their contract negotiations or in the implementation of their contracts. In each relationship the circumstances were different, but there was a common thread through the discontent—that of the federal government asserting too much authority over a system that had already developed a jealously guarded autonomy. The federal bureaucracy might be older and more extensive, but it was being duplicated on a smaller scale by the expanding bureaucracies of state governments. The clash was intensified because Bureau education leaders had an unshakable faith in their ability to determine the nature of Indian education and how to administer it properly. Diplomacy notwithstanding, this attitude was clearly recognized by state education administrators, and it is not surprising that antagonisms developed.

California served as the advance guard by completing its contract in the same year that the J-O'M program went into effect.[15] The state department of public instruction had been preparing for the transferral of responsibility, but this did not guarantee a harmonious administration of J-O'M within the state. California's J-O'M program was one of the first to be terminated, a gradual process completed in 1958; one of the first to be placed back under J-O'M funding (in 1970, it was the only state that had returned to J-O'M after terminating); and one of the stormiest administrations of J-O'M of any of the participating states. There were a number of reasons for California's many problems, not the least of which was the response of the Indians themselves.

The concern of California Indians developed as a direct result of the actions of Purl Willis, a man who claimed to be an Indian. With his small group of followers, which reputedly ranged from 50 to 300, Willis roused the wrath of a large percentage of Indian parents in San Diego County by attempting to persuade state officials to withhold J-O'M funds from San Diego County for the school year 1940–41. Appearing before state education administrators, he tried to convince them that he represented the majority of Indian parents in the county and that these parents opposed J-O'M funding because of their fear that this money would be used as an offset against the claim money that California Indians would receive for loss of their lands.[16]

Although Willis's attack was unfounded, the methods he used were so unscrupulous that they provoked Indians throughout the state, and encouraged many California Indians to become interested in J-O'M funding. Those who wrote to defend their need for J-O'M funds also welcomed the opportunity to launch a counterattack on Willis, who was accused of getting a large portion of his funds from old-age pensioners among the Indians. As one Indian wrote, "while he sheds 'crocodile' tears supposedly for the down-trodden Indian, he has his hand out in the meantime to gather in funds from the poor misled Indians."[17]

The extensiveness of this correspondence indicated that many California Indians were satisfied with the J-O'M program. But if this was the case with the Indians, it certainly was not true of some of the state administrators who found it necessary to work with Mary Stewart, the Bureau appointee who held the position of Superintendent of Indian Education for the state. An experienced educator, Mary Stewart had been with the Indian Service for seven years when she received the California position. That Beatty found her work highly commendable is indicated by their correspondence. He wrote to her in California, "There is no one in the Indian Service who should be better qualified than you to work out cordial and enthusiastic cooperation with the state office in California."[18]

Despite Beatty's support, a number of factors combined to make this experience perhaps the most difficult in Mary Stewart's career with the Indian Service. One of the reasons she encountered so much antagonism may have been her approach, which Beatty later described as both a "frank and fearless presentation of the facts" and a "quiet but firm insistence that steps be taken to correct irregularities."[19] Her forthright attitude was not calculated to ease the problem of state autonomy, which in any case was blown up out of all proportion by egoistic state administrators. This combination of circumstances led Stewart to request a transfer after she had held the position for less than a year. Beatty refused to consider this course, pointing out that it would be a "confession of failure." He advised Stewart to use her "diplomacy to the fullest" and suggested that it was important to understand that the state directors were "anxious that their actions give every appearance of being voluntary on their part and not due to pressure from us."[20]

Beatty, with his customary perceptiveness, understood the dilemma of state education administrators who found it necessary to maintain, at any cost, the image of independence (even to the point of making a Bureau liaison appointee like Stewart feel like a "clerk"). Despite his support, however, the strain of the relationship must have proved too great. By 1941 Mary Stewart had retired from the Indian Service and by 1942 the Bureau position of Indian superintendent in California had been abolished. The Indian Service continued to maintain a watch over its "interests" in the state, but it no longer took an active hand.

The personalities of officials at both the state and the federal level undoubtedly influenced these relationships, for good or for bad. In Washington State and in California the respective harmony and friction that resulted reflected directly on the Bureau appointee and the state superintendent of public instruction. During the first five years of the state contract in Washington difficulties were few, particularly when compared with California. Homer L. Morrison, a Bureau employee and Superintendent of Indian Education, developed a good rapport with state and county administrators. Washington's Superintendent of Public Instruction, who had been on good terms with Bureau educators for a number of years, handled the situation without excessive demands for autonomy. When a new state Superintendent of Public Instruction was elected, however, the relationship suddenly became strained. The close cooperation between Homer Morrison and his superintendent had been so successful that when this political regime was ousted, Morrison himself was on the spot to defend his allocation of J-O'M funds to the school districts during the previous five years. As a result, the Bureau found it expedient to appoint a new Superintendent of Indian Education. The new superintendent was forced to step into the "rather delicate situation" of appeasing both the critics of the old policy and the demands of the new Superintendent of Public Instruction, who was anxious for the state to assume full direction of J-O'M funds.

Again, Willard Beatty's diplomacy was called upon to smooth over the situation. He was aware that the newly elected Superintendent of Public Instruction based her argument for autonomous control of funding on the situations in California and Minnesota. In each of these states the director of Indian education was appointed by the state, and the Bureau had assumed the capacity of advisor. In Washington State, however, Beatty had little confidence in the ability of the person whom the state superintendent wished to appoint. Although he modified his stand to the extent that he granted further control of the program administration to the state appointee, he saw to it that the reins of control remained in the hands of the Bureau employee. Within a few months, the beginning of the war, the resignation of this second representative of the Bureau, and the cutback of federal budgets enabled Beatty to transfer the direction of the Washington contract to the Bureau superintendent in Oregon. The latter was then responsible for a more economical district, which included Oregon, Washington, and northern Idaho.

In spite of Beatty's deft handling of the question of Bureau control, he predicted that assumption of state control in Washington was merely a matter of time. In 1941 he wrote, "We have looked forward to a gradual diminution of the total federal contract and its ultimate elimination as the state aid payments to districts reach a point of adequate support."[21] Beatty's primary concern was that the state be fully prepared for the total commitment, once it was made. At least one state—California—still was not prepared when termination of J-O'M went into effect. Despite the shortcomings of federal control, it might have been advantageous to maintain federal supervision in some states, even if only in an advisory capacity.

Minnesota proved to be an exception to the pattern of uneasy rapport established between the first two contract states and the Bureau. From the early thirties, Minnesota had had an exceptionally well run Department of Education. When Samuel Thompson visited the state for contract negotiations, he quickly decided on a positive recommendation and wrote to Beatty, "There is no state within my knowledge where the head of the state school system and his right-hand man have either the knowledge or the interest in the education of Indian children as is to be found in the State Department of Public Instruction in Minnesota."[22] When a state had already attempted to plan its education program around the needs of both Indians and whites, the Bureau reasoned, there was no necessity for Bureau control. Therefore, the Indian Service fully supported the state's choice of O. R. Sande as administrator, of the J-O'M contract. As an experienced education administrator, Sande was praised by Samuel Thompson, who observed that he had "always been interested in the Indians and for a number of years has given a large part of his time to looking after the Indian children."[23]

In the estimation of Bureau leaders, the early years of Minnesota's contract proved to be as successful as the Education Division had expected. In 1941, when Collier summarized the four state contracts then in existence, he concluded that the Minnesota J-O'M program was the "most efficient." The program "has produced greater advantages to the Indian people," he pointed out, "and as a result has furnished a better educational program to the white children also in attendance at these schools."[24]

The Arizona contract was much smaller than the others and consequently was less of a burden for the Bureau,[25] which could brush aside the usual dispute over who should manage and distribute J-O'M funds. The Education Division would keep in "close touch" with the state, Beatty advised the Superintendent of Public Instruction, but "your office would take over . . . the distribution of tuition funds to the several districts."[26] Thus one of the basic causes of conflict was avoided.

Nonetheless, during the initial contract negotiations, the Arizona Department of Public Instruction exhibited some common signs of frustrated state autonomy. At one point an overdue reply from Beatty and some hesitation on the part of the Bureau to complete the contract prompted H. E. Hendrix, the state superintendent, to send off a bristling letter, intended to reach the ears of the Education Director. "There seems to be plenty of money in the Office of Indian Affairs," he wrote, "for their administrators to jump hither and thither, by airplane, over the nation, into Alaska and elsewhere, but, when it comes to the matter of providing funds for the education and care of children, those for whom the program is intended, there is the cry of 'no funds.' . . ."[27] Beatty managed to smooth things over by assuring Hendrix that funding would be made available despite the absence of an immediate contract, but his defense of Bureau activities suggested that his patience was wearing thin. "The implication," he wrote to Hendrix, "that there has been plenty of money for field supervision and other activities but not for tuition, is not quite fair." The only program of the Indian Office that had not "suffered from curtailment of funds," Beatty pointed out, was public-school contracts.[28] Within the following year the contract was signed and Arizona was launched on the J-O'M program.

By the end of the 1930s the precedent for state contracting was well established. The Bureau had negotiated four contracts and others would soon follow. Bureau education leaders nevertheless remained skeptical of state control. Since they viewed public schooling for Indian children as a compromise at best, they regarded the independence of state educators as stretching this compromise. Some years later Beatty admitted that in many ways Bureau education was superior to that of public schools. Ryan had also questioned the advisability of transferring Indian students to public schools without extensive follow-through on the part of the Bureau. In the Meriam Report he recommended that the Indian Service "supplement the public school work by giving special attention to health, industrial and social training and the relationship between home and school." He concluded, "The transition must not be pushed too fast."[29]

This attitude was a significant comment on the esprit de corps of the Bureau in the 1930s. During the Indian New Deal the infusion of new leadership introduced a fresh approach. In the case of Ryan and Beatty, it may have been more optimistic than it was realistic. Under their guidance the Education Division began to demonstrate a concern for the value of Indian cultures and for the possibility of modifying the Bureau school system to meet the needs of those cultures and, consequently, of the individual student. When these ideas began to be implemented in the 1930s, the Education Division reasoned that Bureau education was geared more to the needs of Indian students than was public-school education. A number of education administrators who worked with the states were deeply concerned about the weaknesses of the public-school systems. Their experience convinced them that most public-school administrators had very little background in developing special programs for a unique group such as the Indian students, and they feared that the students would be seriously affected by this lack of understanding.

This concern was sufficiently great to reach the level of policy statement. In the 1934 *Annual Report* Collier indicated that the Bureau was fully cognizant of the poor condition of the schools where Indians would probably be enrolled. These were the schools that were "especially hard-hit by the depression," and as a result they tended to drop the newer courses—"health and physical education, shop work, home economics, art, music"—which, according to Collier, were the "real fundamentals." Since the Bureau had already begun to include these courses in the curricula of its schools, it was "naturally reluctant" to transfer Indian children to public schools without some assurance that a "modern type of education" would be provided. Collier concluded, however, that public schools offered other advantages that made the transfer advisable.[30] This was the dilemma of education leaders confronted with giving up students to an inferior system.

During the next few years Bureau education employees who worked directly with public schools continued to weigh the values of public-school education against those of Bureau education. They were in a position to observe the built-in faults of the public-school system, but the awkward nature of their divided responsibility—as liaison between the state systems, with their competing local districts, and the Bureau of Indian Affairs—made it exceedingly difficult for them to improve the existing structure. As one employee who had recently been transferred to a superintendency of state Indian education wrote, "I have been . . . almost completely baffled for answers to the problem of needed corrections for evident weaknesses."[31]

One aspect of public schooling that cried out for improvement was the attitude of teachers and administrators, particularly in rural areas. Whereas Bureau educators suggested that new Indian pupils might need individual guidance, rural teachers who had to conform to the attitudes of the local populace often found it difficult to regard their Indian pupils with even ordinary civility and kindness. The indifference of their administrators to the underlying causes of Indian behavior also discouraged teachers from developing a sympathetic attitude. As one state Indian superintendent wrote, the teachers "simply mirror the attitudes of those who control their professional destinies and so they can be even more difficult to convert than the community itself."[32] There were many exceptions, however. In Nevada in the mid thirties several communities flatly refused to allow Indian children to attend their public schools. But on the Flathead Reservation in western Montana Indians had begun attending public schools shortly after the turn of the century, and the idea of barring Indian children from these schools ran contrary to several decades of experience.[33]

Many Bureau educators were convinced that most public schools were unsympathetic toward Indian children, and whenever they compared the two systems public education came out a poor second. As Willard Beatty concluded, "school for school, the teachers of the Indian Service are superior in training and character to those found in many small rural public schools. . . . administrative direction of the Federal schools is superior, and the supervision more continuous . . . than is true in any state school system."[34] Beatty was basing his conclusions upon the efforts of his own administration, and there is no question that during his term of office teachers received better training than under any other administrator. The in-service training program was highly successful and the efforts to encourage Progressive Education within the Indian Service were so well known by the late thirties that one state director of public instruction, in the process of negotiating a contract with the Department of the Interior, commented, "With the progressive and practical ideas of education that Willard Beatty has we can get ideas across to our public school people by learning by [sic] what is being done in Indian Education."[35] Beatty's own teachers may not have been as uniformly Progressive-minded as he wished, but unlike many rural schoolteachers, they did have the opportunity to keep abreast of current trends in education and to receive special training for teaching Indian children.

In its efforts to prepare the public schools for programs that would meet Indian student needs, the Education Division attempted to respond to the tremendous variety of conditions within the states and in the individual school districts. In some areas, the greatest needs were physical—transportation, school lunches, even clothing and shoes. It was not unusual for Indian families to send their children to federal schools primarily because these needs were supplied. Transfer of their children to public schools did not lessen the need. Nonetheless, the Bureau was reluctant to extend this aid to children in public schools. When Henry Roe Cloud, Haskell Institute superintendent, requested clothing for a number of Kansas Indian children who were to be transferred to public school, Collier advised that help should be given "only in terms of actual need"; "Wherever feasible," he added, "the principle of work in return for help should be insisted upon." He stressed the importance of having Indian families buy out of their wages the "things they need for their children rather than to have them given to them."[36] Occasionally requests for clothing or shoes were accompanied by explanations from sympathetic education employees who suggested that the children's need was also psychological: They might be clothed, but sometimes they were painfully embarrassed to go to public schools without better clothing.

Most Indian parents could provide clothing, but many were dependent on school lunches, which were often the only nourishing meal of the day for their children. On at least one occasion a sympathetic teacher used this program as a means of educating the children about the values of a balanced diet and how to plan, purchase, and cook meals. In the tiny Bishop Whipple School near Redwood Falls, Minnesota, twenty-nine Sioux children prepared their own lunches under the direction of their teacher, who introduced principles of mathematics into the activity, as well as methods of raising produce from the school garden.[37] In some areas, such as the remote stretches of the larger reservations among the Dakota Sioux or the Navajo, the greatest physical problem was transportation. From these areas the boarding schools had filled their quotas during the assimilation period. They had also been the proving grounds for the community day school experiment of the 1930s, which failed because of transportation difficulties and other problems during World War II. On the perimeters of these reservations, where white towns rubbed shoulders with Indian land, some children could be enrolled in public school if transportation could be provided for them.

The physical needs of the children were important, but sometimes other needs were equally urgent. These were more easily ignored. If children needed busing to school or a free meal or a pair of shoes, it was fairly obvious. If they needed special guidance in order to adjust to a new environment, or to determine vocational training; if the relationship between the family and the school needed the assistance of a social worker; if the children would benefit from courses on Indian history or from bilingual courses —these needs were less easily recognized. One source of this problem was lack of communication. Parents had little idea of what went on in the schools, since many of them had not attended school or had dropped out. As far as Indian parents were concerned, there was little community direction of the school; any "community" direction came from the white community. Nor did the Indian students speak out about their needs; they felt that their teachers and their non-Indian classmates had little sympathy for them. They were taught the culture and history of mainstream, non-Indian America, and from this perspective they learned that they were nonentities, or worse, "savages," as outdated textbooks continued to describe them even in the 1960s.

In the first years of J-O'M contracting Bureau leaders expressed a guarded hope that special programs for Indian students would be implemented through the public-school system. In Oklahoma, George C. Wells, one of the most enthusiastic state directors of Indian education and an Indian Service employee, outlined a number of suggestions which would have been sound advice for most communities involved with Indian education. These included: a system of close supervision and in-service training of rural teachers (in cooperation with the state); use of health workers and social workers in Indian communities; training to properly equip Indians to serve as teachers, physicians, nurses, and so on; a program to make both whites and Indians more conscious of the contributions the Indian has made to civilization; and an increase of the part played by Indians in working out their own problems.[38] The idealism of Wells in formulating this plan, which he appropriately titled "Some Principles and Ultimate Goals," was by no means a uniform characteristic of these liaison employees. A more usual attitude was frustration from daily encounters with state departments of public instruction. But in formal policy statements the Bureau perpetuated an optimism not unlike that of the Oklahoma supervisor. In the same year that J-O'M was enacted, Collier wrote in the *Annual Report* that the Indian Service would not transfer "extensive and important Indian educational work to the States or to their subdivisions except where careful preparations have been made." By this time, the Educaton Division knew that "most of the hoped for gains" from such changes would "eventuate only when adequate replacement arrangements are set up."[39] In the next few years the truth of this statement was proved, but often through the unhappy discovery that "replacement arrangements" simply could not be made.

There are only scattered indications of successful adaptation of Bureau programs. When the Genoa Boarding School in Nebraska was closed, the Bureau tried to help the children by sending social workers to work with the families and providing a physical-education instructor at the Winnebago-Omaha Agency, which supervised the area. At local schools, the Bureau helped to introduce shopwork and to strengthen home economics programs. In the state of Washington, which had transferred all Indian children to public schools before the J-O'M Act was passed, the Superintendent of Indian Education also attempted to adapt Bureau principles to public schools.[40] He planned to employ four visiting teachers paid by the Indian Service to relieve congestion in overcrowded community schools. With public-school cooperation, he was also introducing vocational education in schools that had never before offered these courses. In addition to the standard tuition payment, in some parts of the state the federal government provided funds for books, supplies, and clothing. Reports from other areas indicate that the Bureau's major success in attempting to establish programs for Indian pupils was in vocational education and in meeting the children's physical needs. Interest in courses related to Indian culture was rare.

Thus the Education Division was generally unsuccessful in its effort to influence public-school education. When the states began to administer federal funds, they were no longer directly responsible to the Bureau. The failure of the Bureau to maintain control in the 1930s and early 1940s meant, therefore, that it had lost its opportunity to affect the public schools. The primary weakness in the J-O'M program that prevented the Education Division from implementing its ideas can be summarized as follows: the poor quality of teachers and administrators; the hostile attitudes of communities; the public schools' greater interest in funding than in the Indian students themselves; the diversity of conditions among and within the states; and the difficult relationships between state and federal administrators. All of these led to a type of education ill suited to the needs of the Indian child.

9

WORLD WAR II AND
THE POSTWAR YEARS

Beatty's last years with the Bureau were in many ways an anticlimax to the brief but enthusiastic period before World War II. The momentum of the New Deal years carried over into the first months of the war, but as the conflict continued, its effect on federal Indian education became more severe. The war itself served as the dividing line, for the issues of education in the postwar period were significantly altered from those of the years before the war. Of primary importance was the change effected among the Indian people, who began to demand the education they had long been denied. Beatty molded his postwar programs in terms of the changes that he saw among the Indian people, and in response to the national shifts in employment opportunities. In contrast to the Depression years, when he had discouraged vocational training for nonexistent jobs in the city, he urged postwar students to train for jobs in the growing metropolitan areas.

Thus Beatty shifted the major emphasis in federal Indian education from cross-cultural education, which emphasized both Indian and non-Indian value systems, to education for assimilation, which trained young Indians for urban life where they would be assimilated into mainstream society. Assimilation education assumed that the Indian youth would choose to live in the city rather than return to the reservation. The most significant illustration of this new system was the Navajo Special Education Program, which prepared overage Navajo youths for urban employment.

Beatty's postwar program in the Education Division was also a response to a major policy shift within the Bureau itself. The years immediately after the war saw the beginnings of the termination policy, which reached its height during Dwight D. Eisenhower's administration. To ignore the threat of termination, which encouraged the Indian to assimilate into mainstream America, would have been folly on Beatty's part. Thus despite his stated reasons for a new type of federal Indian education, his response was in part a matter of political expedience.

Beatty rode the crest of these postwar changes until 1950. In this year, however, the appointment of Dillon S. Myer as Commissioner of Indian Affairs brought an end to Beatty's years of successful rapport with commissioners. As Bureau leadership became increasingly attuned to congressional demands for termination, Beatty saw the writing on the wall, and when his own position was stripped of its authority he submitted his resignation.

Beatty was convinced that his postwar program was meeting the needs of the Indian people, yet he failed to include them in the decision-making process. Nonetheless, Indian leaders developed a political awareness in this period that would serve them well later. In response to the need for more education, but particularly in the fight against termination, Indian leaders learned to combat the political power structure. Although they did not at that time test this knowledge on control of education, they would do so in the future; thus this period was an important prelude to the rise of self-determination in education.

The growth of Indian leadership during the 1940s was due, in large part, to the effects of the war. World War II had a tremendous impact on the Indian people. Given the comparatively short time span of the conflict, it affected some tribes more than any other major event in the four centuries of Indian-white relations.[1] The demands made by the war cut across Indian tribal society, and there were few who escaped its influence. The most obvious demand, of course, was actual enlistment. More than 24,000 Indians served in the U.S. armed forces during the war, and many of them gave their lives for their country. Equally significant were the thousands of Indians who participated in war work. Seeking jobs in other areas, approximately 40,000 Indians left their reservations for new employment. Among those reservations most affected were ones far removed from centers of population.[2] For many it is likely that the Indian CCC of the Depression years had provided the preparatory training. However, war employment was more diversified than CCC jobs had been, and tended to concentrate in urban areas. Factory work of all kinds, shipbuilding, aircraft production, mining, railroad work, and even farming drew the Indians away from reservation life and into new environments. Families and homes were uprooted; perspectives were broadened and changed.

A temporarily altered economic pattern was perhaps the most obvious change on the reservations. The sudden input of both civilian and servicemen's earnings increased the cash income. The pull of off-reservation employment also discouraged the development of reservation resources initiated during the New Deal through the Revolving Loan Fund and the Indian CCC.

Social changes were more subtle, but they also were significant. Abrupt contact with white America had effects on the Indian people that continued to reverberate long after the war was over. Some became so accustomed to the conveniences of urban life that they chose not to return to the reservation when the war ended. Those who did return brought with them some of the trappings of urban culture. Of those who left, the servicemen were probably the most deeply affected. During their enlistment they were almost completly separated from the communal link of family and tribal association. Thrown in with all elements of society, they were forced to deal with it as individuals, and in turn they were treated not as Indians but as servicemen. Consequently, when they returned to civilian status and were forced to contend once again with familiar types of discrimination, their bitterness was no longer passive.

One of the convictions that the servicemen brought back with them was a recognition of the value of education. The importance of understanding and speaking English was illustrated to them time and again during their wartime experiences. They also became aware of the advantages of vocational training. They gained a new respect for the training necessary to establish a foothold in the white man's system of economy. It was not by mere coincidence, therefore, that Indian concern for education was more clearly articulated in the postwar period.

Indians who remained on the reservations during the war also developed an increasing awareness of the need for education. Since Indian schools were generally caught in the backwash of federal government spending during the war, many reservation parents were faced with the immediate task of how to maintain schools without adequate funds.[3] Indians in two of the major problem areas for Indian Service education, the Sioux reservations in North and South Dakota and the Navajo Reservation, watched anxiously as the belated progress of the education programs of the 1930s was eaten away by war budgeting and personnel demands. As the conflict dragged on, the community day schools became more and more dependent upon equipment purchased during the last years of the prewar budgets. Without facilities for repair, crucial items such as buses or kitchen equipment, and finally even the buildings themselves, deteriorated until they were beyond repair.

Under these conditions, many schools were eventually forced to close. On the Navajo Reservation almost twenty day schools had ceased operation by 1944.[4] At least one of the older boarding schools had shut down by the end of the war; others were partially or completely abandoned shortly thereafter. Day school closure was postponed as long as possible, in part because of the efforts of many parents to keep the schools running. The irony of this situation did not escape some of the Indian Service employees who had been instrumental in developing the community day-school program in the thirties. Their primary goal had been to encourage both parents and children to participate in these schools, but just when their efforts had begun to bear fruit, the war budget forced them to go back on their word. Simultaneous with the appearance of more and more children each fall came the reductions in personnel and construction programs, which meant that expansion was impossible and staff unavailable. Dedicated employees squeezed as many children as they could into already overcrowded facilities, but in many cases eventual closure was inevitable.[5]

At this time, closure of community schools received special support from Congress. The report of the House Select Committee to Investigate Indian Affairs and Conditions, issued in 1944, deplored the trend toward community day schools. It suggested that children who attended these schools suffered from the "handicap of having to spend their out of school hours in tepees, in shacks with dirt floors and no windows, in tents, in wickiups, in hogans where English is never spoken . . . and where there is sometimes an active antagonism or an abysmal indifference to the virtues of education." If these young children were going to "progress" toward acceptance and appreciation of the "white man's way of life," the report continued, they should attend off-reservation boarding schools.[6]

This point of view was significant in that it separated the approach of Indian New Deal education from that of post–World War II. While the report was probably the most vehement attack on the community day-school program since its inception a decade earlier, it was also a precursor of the coming trend toward urban-oriented education. As Lehman Brightman, director of the Indian Studies Program at the University of California, Berkeley, observed in 1971, the report served as an official notice that " 'De-Indianizing the Indian' was back in fashion."[7] Finally, by dismissing the merits of the day schools, the report denounced the only type of federal schooling in which the Indians themselves had expressed any degree of interest and approval.

On the Navajo Reservation, however, Indian parents were so determined to have their children educated they managed to maintain some schools during the war by converting them into temporary boarding schools, which they staffed with volunteers who took turns staying with the children. While Indian Service employees were being stymied by federal policy changes, these Indians demonstrated a tenacity greater than that of the bureaucracy created to serve them. But despite these individual efforts, the overall enrollment of children in federal schools was increasingly lowered by the war. Reservation day schools showed the greatest decline, losing almost two thousand students or 25 percent of their enrollment between 1942 and 1945. The total enrollment decline for all types of schools was about three thousand or 12 percent.[8]

Boarding schools began losing pupils even before the attack on Pearl Harbor. In the spring of 1941, G. Warren Spaulding, superintendent at Haskell Institute, complained that the school had already lost "many boys to the war."[9] In the following year Don C. Foster, superintendent at Carson, reported that the students "really have war fever and, week after week, since war was declared, our boys have been joining the armed forces, particularly the marines."[10] Many pupils were attracted to the employment boom as well. Boarding schools themselves participated in defense preparation by offering training courses for war industry. Courses in welding, machine shop work, aircraft assembly, and manufacturing were developed to meet immediate demand. Even those pupils who remained were subject to conditions imposed by the war. General shortages made raising, canning, and preserving crops imperative. In the first months of the war a number of schools switched to a six-day work week; thus the training born of necessity during the Depression came to fruition in the following decade.

During this period the Education Division limped along on a limited budget and a reduced staff.[11] In one location after another, from the Pacific Northwest to Oklahoma, key employees turned in their resignations to report for military duty, and those who were left had to get along. In Alaska, in a six-month period in 1942–43, one hundred teachers from the 120 schools in the territory resigned and had to be replaced. An Eskimo cook who was being paid $100 per month by the Education Division was hired by the Civil Aeronautics Authority for $200 and then by a mining concern for $250—all within the space of two months.[12] On the Cheyenne River Reservation, an acting superintendent reported in the summer of 1944 that during the previous seven months, the position of reservation principal had been vacated twice by individuals who had joined the armed forces. "I wish to be put on record as stating that the situation here is a 'mess,' " he wrote.[13] By the end of the war approximately one out of every eight Indian Service employees had served in the armed forces.[14]

The innovative programs of New Deal years were increasingly curtailed as the war continued. This was the fate not only of the community schools; it also affected the cross-cultural program. Although most of the bilingual books were published during the war, interest in them soon declined. By the late forties the cross-cultural education ideas that Ryan and Beatty had struggled with in the thirties were no longer a viable feature of Bureau education. Even the in-service training program felt the effects of the war economy. Both the 1942 and 1946 summer sessions were canceled for budgetary reasons.[15]

If most of the programs of the Education Division were curtailed by the war, those of the Bureau itself were also subject to drastic revision. All of the major sources of funding that had contributed to the unique shape of the Indian New Deal were cut sharply or dropped during the war years,[16] and the Bureau budget suffered wartime cuts. The total budget for 1944, including both federal and tribal funds, was $28,843,902—even less than the 1932 budget of $30,445,092.[17] One of Collier's chief sources of pride in his administration was his success in procuring financial support. When it ebbed he forecast grave consequences. Shortly before his resignation he observed that the "crucial" funding for adult, economic, community, and social needs had "continued to shrink," whereas the "institutional" funding had come to be interpreted in the narrow sense of the word. As a result, he said, schools "are being expected to carry nearly the whole load of the work of Indian betterment, while the medical system is coerced in the direction of costly institutional work as distinct from public health work, health education. . . ."[18] In other words, insofar as education was concerned, congressional funding had limited the programs to the pre—Meriam Report interpretation of education.

In spite of his concern for the future of the Indian people, Collier retained his faith in their way of life. From this perspective, he viewed the war as yet another disaster for Western civilization. Almost a decade after he had concluded that the white race was shattered, Collier wrote a long essay that expressed his concern over the war and probed for an explanation to the disastrous condition of the Western spirit. Drawing on the philosophy of Henri Bergson, he suggested that the solution lay in bringing the "means of technology under the control of the ends of the soul, of the conscience and of the heart."[19] Collier still pinned his hopes on the spiritual outlook of the Indian for the salvation of Western man. A number of factors led him to conclude, however, that he could no longer administer effectively, and on January 19, 1945, he submitted his letter of resignation to President Roosevelt.

Collier's departure from the Bureau marked the end of an era. Although he attempted to guarantee the continuation of his policies by handpicking his successor, William A. Brophy, an attorney for the Pueblo Indians, the ensuing decade and a half made it impossible for any person, no matter how well intentioned, to halt the trend toward termination. The journal of the American Association on Indian Affairs warned that Brophy would need the "constant support of every agency committed to Indian welfare," but the postwar mood of the nation's legislators was not to be overcome. A Congress that was determined to reduce government expenses listened only to those who supported its position.

In the last month of the war an article by O. K. Armstrong entitled "Set the American Indians Free" appeared in *Reader's Digest.*[20] An emotional plea for separating the Indians from their tribal ties and their excessive land acreage, this article anticipated termination arguments of the next decade and a half and set the style and tone used by its advocates. Based on the appealing rationale that American Indian soldiers who had fought for their country should therein be given the opportunity to become totally assimilated in the mainstream culture, the article was a fairly accurate barometer of the shift in attitudes that would develop in postwar America. The nation's treatment of the Indian had come full circle. From the early twenties to the early forties the pendulum had swung toward recognition and encouragement of Indian culture; as the war ended, it began to swing toward assimilation. Thus Armstrong's article relied on arguments used during the reform movement that led to the Allotment Act of 1887.[21]

There were, however, a number of features of this decade and a half of assimilation that were radically different from the period of the Allotment Act. In the first place, the Bureau itself hesitated to support all of the radical schemes of termination proponents—although it did little to discourage the initiation of the policy. The major impetus for termination came from Congress, while the reform groups of this period, unlike their counterparts in the late nineteenth century, were vehemently opposed to the concept. In addition to the somewhat altered roles of these three groups, another factor made a singular difference in this termination period. In post—World War II America these traditonal sources of power —the Indian Bureau, Congress, and the reform groups—were joined by a new force, that of organized Indian leadership.

During the most challenging years of the termination fight, the group most responsible for stemming the tide of legislative action was the National Congress of American Indians. Founded in Denver on November 15, 1944, the National Congress had scarcely had time to organize when it was confronted with a Congress bent on termination.[22] In Eisenhower's administration, Congress passed several measures that encouraged general termination of Bureau services, and others that established termination timetables for individual tribes.[23]

That Congress was not more successful was largely due to the leaders of the National Congress and, in particular, to Joseph R. Garry (Coeur d'Alene), who was president during these crucial years. Garry's antitermination campaigning typified the committed leadership of a growing number of national Indian leaders. The job of convincing Congress that it was opposing the wishes of the Indian people was all consuming, yet most of its demands, including extensive travel, testimony before congressional committees, all-night sessions, and overlapping committee meetings, were to become standard routine. The fight against termination served as a unifying force and propelled Indians into an increasingly responsible role in controlling their future.

This assumption of leadership presented an awkward situation to those who had always considered themselves spokesmen for the Indian people. The American Association on Indian Affairs initiated its campaign against termination with the same gusto that had characterized the reform movement of the twenties.[24] Indian leadership then represented a threat to the reformers, who were not eager to share the limelight. While some Indian leaders were willing to accept the reformers' aid, this was contingent on their willingness to work. Friction developed between the two groups as the Indians began to assume control, and gradually the philanthropists retreated.[25]

The termination fight, therefore, witnessed the awakening of Indian leaders to the need for close contact with the political centers of power in Washington, D.C. Later experiments in self-determination in education were guided, in part, by the lessons learned on the battlegrounds of termination. The first examples of educational control, such as Rough Rock Demonstration School (1966) and Navajo Community College (1969), could therefore be seen as the culmination of two previous steps: the growth of interest in education, which developed during the war, and the knowledge of how to achieve control of education, which was gained in large part in the termination period.

A significant number of tribes emerged from the war with a new outlook on the priority of their needs and a new awareness of how the federal government could assist them in filling those needs. Within a number of tribes education had leaped to the forefront. In widely scattered areas, from the Plateau country to the central Plains and thence south, Indian leaders and parents, Indian elders, and returning Indian veterans faced the postwar period with a deep conviction that education for their children was imperative. A number of tribal councils passed compulsory education ordinances even before the war was over and others began to enforce similar regulations that they had neglected. One of the most promising developments was tribal support of higher education. Many tribes began to encourage their high school graduates to go on to college by setting aside tribal funds for scholarships.[26] In addition, some tribes requested that the federal government improve their existing school facilities.

Since the need for education was perhaps greater among the Navajos than almost any other tribe, it was not surprising that one of the most outspoken demands for improved education developed among the Navajo people. Several unusual circumstances on this reservation made the Navajo problem unique. In the first place, the Navajos were the largest tribe and through sheer numbers could make an impact on the national conscience. Secondly, few other tribes were as profoundly affected by the war. Despite their numbers, before the effects of the war reached into their reservation the Navajos had managed to keep pretty much to themselves. Their attitude toward education typified their approach to white culture. Whereas some tribes had been sending their children to public schools since the turn of the century, and in a few cases since the late nineteenth century, the Navajos had had little use for white education. For many of these people, the significance of the war lay in the birth of the concept that education should become an immediate goal. Suddenly they believed that the initial step toward the solution of their problems was adequate schooling for their young people. The fact that this tremendous shift had occurred in such a short time period gave their new attitude an even greater authority.

It was this conviction that led a delegation of Navajos to Washington, D.C., in the spring of 1946. In presenting their demands, which sought, primarily, a fulfillment of the promises of the Treaty of 1868, they pointed out that their first need was education. "First and foremost," wrote Alice Henderson Rossin in *The American Indian*, "they asked for adequate educational facilities for the entire tribe."[27] There was no need for the Navajos to exaggerate the inadequacies of their educational facilities. In that year alone, of 20,000 to 22,000 children, some 12,000 to 14,000 were not in school. Despite the prodigious efforts of the Education Division to build community schools in the 1930s, the disastrous effects of the war coupled with the population boom on the reservation meant that there were more children out of school in 1946 than there had been when the Meriam Report was published in 1928.

The circumstances that led to this situation also contributed to the awkward age level of most of these children. At least five-sixths or

10,000 of them had reached the age of twelve or thirteen without receiving any formal education. Any program developed for them would have to be tailored to their unique needs. With all of these considerations in mind, Beatty instituted the Navajo Special Education Program in the fall of 1946.[28] From 1946 until the early 1960s this program was responsible for educating about 4,300 Navajo overage students. As far as Bureau educators were concerned, the Special Program was an overwhelming success. Most of the students achieved the two aims of the course, which were general learning about white culture, including a knowledge of English and an understanding of social customs and attitudes, and specific vocational training to enable them to find jobs.

Job training was geared primarily for urban living, for one of the raisons d'être of the program was to offer a partial solution to the population problem that plagued the Navajo Reservation. By 1946 it had become apparent that the reservation simply could not support its burgeoning populace. The land set aside in 1868 was intended to sustain 7,500 people; even with reservation additions and the livestock reduction efforts that had been completed in the intervening years, the 1946 population of 59,000 was already too great.

Response to the Special Education Program indicated that Navajos not only recognized the problem but also were willing to take action. Whereas the pre–World War II educators had to beg or steal children to get them to school, the Indian Service directors of this program had more volunteers than they knew what to do with. When the first group was selected for the pilot program at Sherman Institute, California, the maximum number of enrollees was set at 200. Scores of additional children appeared at the departure point, anxious to be included. Their disappointment was so great that the directors relented and somehow found room at the school for another group of 127, who arrived a month late, in October 1946.[29]

It soon became obvious that the facilities of Sherman Institute alone would not fill the need. Within the next few years a number of other boarding schools made room for these students.[30] In 1950, Intermountain Indian School, Brigham City, Utah, enrolled its first class of Navajo pupils. A converted U.S. Army hospital, this huge complex of buildings accommodated about 2,000 pupils. During the fifties it educated so many overage Navajo students that its name became synonymous with the Navajo Special Education Program and the urban education approach of the Bureau. It was no coincidence that Intermountain was the stepchild of Senator Arthur V. Watkins (Republican, Utah), the most outspoken congressional advocate of termination.

The Navajo program was the reflection of intensive preparation on the part of Bureau administrators. Under the guidance of Willard Beatty, the director was Hildegard Thompson, who later succeeded Beatty on his retirement. Thompson had had broad experience as an educator, in the Philippines and in the Indian Service itself, where she had served in Oklahoma and as Director of Education on the Navajo Reservation. She had, as one Bureau administrator described it, "a real empathy for kids." Despite the tremendous responsibilities of her positions, she never lost sight of the fact that children are individuals who need someone to represent them. This was the approach she followed in preparing and administering the Navajo Special Education Program, and the results clearly reflected her influence.

The goal of the intensive program was to provide in five years the same education that the students would have received in ten to twelve years if they had started school at the usual age. The directors assumed that the primary learning period for these students would not stretch much beyond their eighteenth year. They had a lot of catching up to do, but on the other hand they were much more highly motivated. It was obvious that the material—first readers, for example—would have to be geared to their age level. Special books were written in Navajo, using a beginner's vocabulary for young adults. The first three years of the program concentrated on general skills, the last two on a selection of marketable vocational skills from which the students could choose.[31] Thompson attempted to secure the best teachers in the Service, teachers who were not only experienced but also respecters of children. Some years later one staff member wrote in retrospect, "I considered each student with whom I worked as I would my own brother or sister [and] I tried to prevent any student from having an 'unwanted feeling.' "[32]

The successes of this program were not easily duplicated. It roused a growing envy on the part of teachers at the regular boarding schools, who found it much more difficult to change their own programs. In the area of job placement, the results of the Navajo program were so impressive that education workers in the regular program tried to revise their own job placement service.[33]

A singular side effect of the Navajo Special Education Program was that it tended to reveal the built-in weaknesses of traditional boarding schools. In the first place, these schools were at a disadvantage because they lacked the stimulus of immediate, foreseeable goals. Secondly, they were not staffed by a hand-picked group of experts. Even though the quality of the educational staff had been improved by revision of civil service exams and Beatty's in-service training, once instructors were hired they had little reason to fear being fired—and consequently the quality of the staff was at best uneven. The war years had also taken their toll, and the mood of the late forties was far removed from the optimism of Beatty's earlier administration.

The war itself had both immediate and long-term effects upon the traditional boarding schools. Largely responsible for a decline in enrollment from 1941 to 1946, it was also partly responsible for the increase in enrollment in the late forties and early fifties. The swelling of numbers in the boarding schools was reminiscent of the early Depression, when economic factors forced many families to turn to these schools as a last resort. In the postwar years both economic and social reasons provided the incentive. War industry and the armed forces uprooted many families, increasing mobility and, at the same time, instability. Many jobs readily available during the fighting ceased to exist after 1945. All of these factors led to family stress and broken homes, and in such cases, boarding school appeared to be the only solution for the children.[34]

School superintendents during these years were distressed with the growing number of problem children being admitted to their schools. While Bureau schools had always had to deal with children who suffered from severe emotional difficulties, never before had they appeared as such a threat.[35] In the two decades after the war the percentage of problem children rose to alarming proportions. Bureau education leaders were unable to cope with the ramifications of the situation. These students needed either special counseling or a special school, but neither was forthcoming.

Other aspects of the traditional boarding schools, however, were extensively revised in the late forties. During his last years in office, Beatty remolded the school curriculum to meet the new problems faced by Indian young people in the postwar years. Although he was under pressure from the increasingly powerful termination viewpoint, Beatty himself believed that Indian education should move with the times and that the approach of the 1930s was no longer valid in 1945. As he wrote in 1946, the war brought "tremendous and unexpected changes" in the lives of the American Indians.[36] Beatty observed that after the war many Indians were, in some ways, not the same persons that they had been before. They had new perspectives, and thus new needs. Veterans eligible for the G.I. Bill of Rights (P.L. 346) or the Vocational Rehabilitation Bill (P.L. 16) reentered Indian Service schools for vocational training, which sometimes led to urban jobs. Other students who had grown up in towns and cities during the war hesitated to return to the Indian communities their parents had left when they could find off-reservation jobs. As the influence of these uprooted individuals spread, the spillover affected many lives.

Beatty had all of these changes in mind when he contemplated the directions of postwar educational policy. The clearest illustration of his revised approach was indicated in the methods and aims of the Navajo Special Education Program. Although in theory he maintained the older policy of cross-cultural education, in practice he altered it sufficiently to transfer emphasis from Indian culture to white culture. He promised that the dual program of training for both reservation and off-reservation life would continue, but now he suggested that Bureau schools should be a "vehicle for cultural change."[37] Beatty was convinced that the Indian people endorsed the latter goal. "Without sacrificing racial pride or identification with their Indian past," he wrote, "Indian parents and pupils are determined to gain from education a mastery of the English language and of the manual and intellectual skills of their white brethren." According to Beatty, the Indians had begun to recognize that their "richest future" lay in the "mastery of the material culture of the dominant race."[38]

Beatty's emphasis on mainstream culture foreshadowed forthcoming changes in federal Indian policy. As Ryan pointed out in 1928 and as Hildegard Thompson would repeat in the 1950s, education was the primary role of the Bureau, and there was no better forecast of the direction in which the Bureau was moving than policy changes in the Education Division itself.

When Beatty became convinced that the new policy was justified, he adopted it with his usual vigor and enthusiasm. If Indian children were to master the way of life that they would follow when they graduated, they should learn about it when they were in school. If they were going to find a job, they would have to know how to apply; if they were going to live in the city, they would need to be acquainted with the ways of the city. Thus, Bureau schools began to include course material that stressed "elements on white cultural behavior." Pioneering this approach was the Navajo Special Education Program, which developed the first comprehensive curriculum intended to transform a reservation youth into an urban adult. Basic elements of white culture taught in these courses included a strong emphasis on how to handle money (how to budget, how to save, and how to live on a limited income); how to care for clothing, as well as how to buy it; how to maintain good health; the importance of good grooming; and the need for proper manners, including correct eating habits.

Most of the children who attended boarding school were unacquainted with these customs. As Beatty pointed out, the "home from which the child comes does not practice any of them." Beatty still believed that the child should attend school near home for his early education, but his new attitude in terms of the boarding-school curriculum harked back to the assimilation rhetoric of the late nineteenth century. His assertion that "whatever the child learns within the home is contrary to the thing he needs to know rather than helpful"[39] might have been taken from the pages of an agent's report in the post–Civil War years. The fundamental difference between the two approaches was that Beatty believed he was responding to the wishes of the Indians.

Beatty's assessment of the postwar milieu was basically accurate. Indians had changed and they had developed a greater concern for education. Still, his position regarding the new direction of this education lacked one important element, because it failed to allow for Indian participation. While the concept of the Navajo program was subject to the approval of tribal leaders, implementation of the program lay in the hands of Indian Service educators. The Navajos themselves were not the directors of Sherman Institute or Intermountain School, nor had they any control over the traditional boarding schools. They had now made it quite clear that they wanted education for their children; in order to get it, they would have to accept federal education programs. Implicit in this acceptance was their tacit agreement to the nature and location of these programs.[40]

This arrangement was not limited to the Navajos. At Haskell Institute administrators clashed with tribal leaders on interpretation of school policy in the 1940s. Administrators later rejected any suggestion that during the prewar years the school encouraged graduates to return to their reservations. Even though Indian tribes had, from time to time, "exerted pressure" on the Education Division to pursue this policy—in order that young educated Indians might assist in the "development and operation of various tribal activities"—Haskell directors denied that they had ever responded to this pressure, saying that to have done so would have been to encourage a "limited economic future."[41]

Nor was this an isolated example. Within the Bureau school system, tribal leadership and control in the 1940s were almost nonexistent. Although Indian leaders were invited to participate in occasional policy discussions, they were seldom included in policy direction, which remained the prerogative of Bureau educators.

In terms of Education Division goals, however, Beatty's last years in office witnessed significant accomplishments. First, through the Navajo Special Education Program and the beginnings of school construction to replace buildings that had deteriorated during the war, Beatty attacked one of the chronic problems of Indian Service schooling—the high percentage of children not in school. Second, by shifting the boarding-school curriculum to an emphasis on training for off-reservation living, he had begun to support the increasingly positive Bureau attitude toward assimilation.

For these reasons, Beatty should have received the support of Indian Commissioner Dillon S. Myer (1950–1953), an avowed proponent of assimilation. The fact that he was eased out indicates that his position was as dependent on politics as that of any other Bureau leader. To Myer, Beatty was a holdover from the Collier administration—anathema to the new commissioner. Former director of the War Relocation Authority, Myer had been in charge of dismantling these camps and returning the Japanese to their homes. His approach to the Indian Service may have been influenced by this experience, for during his term of office he not only tightened up the administration of the Bureau but also did everything within his power to accelerate the process of assimilation. As he commented in 1952, the ultimate objective of Indian education is "complete integration in the American way of life." Beatty may have been moving in this direction, but Myer did not give him a chance to prove himself.

In 1950 Commissioner Myer reorganized the Indian Bureau along lines intended to modernize the administration. He transferred the authority of field offices, which numbered more than a hundred, to the newly formed area offices, which would number only eleven.[42] The line authority that division directors—including the Director of Education—had held was effectively canceled by making the area offices independent islands of power responsible to the commissioner. At this time the Education Division became the Branch of Education. Whereas the Education Director had formerly given orders to the field offices, he was not permitted to give orders to the area offices. This meant, in effect, that the authority that had sustained Beatty's policies for fourteen years was removed. In 1952, therefore, just two years after Myer became commissioner, Beatty turned in his resignation.[43]

10 | HILDEGARD THOMPSON: EDUCATION FOR AN URBAN, TECHNOLOGICAL SOCIETY

Hildegard Thompson accepted the position of Director of the Branch of Education in 1952, thus beginning another phase of her career with the Indian Bureau. She held this position for thirteen years, until her retirement in 1965, a term that almost equaled the duration of Beatty's. When Thompson viewed her career in retrospect, she saw these two administrations as one long continuum in aim and direction and attributed the strength of the programs from the 1930s to 1965 to this "continuity." "For over a quarter of a century," she concluded, "two directors with similar philosophies and objectives served. . . . In other words, there was a minimum of lost motion."[1]

Critics of Thompson's administration fail to agree with this interpretation. A number of long-term Bureau employees (including some in leadership positions) have concurred that Indian Service education began to decline with Beatty's resignation. If this assessment is to be fair, however, it must take into consideration the fact that Thompson began her job with two strikes against her. First, she accepted a position that had only a fraction of its former authority —the reality that had forced Beatty himself to resign. Second, at the time she was hired and during the first years of her administration, the threat of termination was most serious, and any efforts toward innovative education that ran counter to the push for assimilation stood little chance of success.

Few leaders would have accepted a position with these built-in handicaps. The fact that Hildegard Thompson did is, in itself, an indication of the kind of leadership she gave to the Bureau. Beatty's selection of her for the job demonstrates that he had no reservations about her ability to cope with the confining characteristics of the position itself or the restrictive milieu of federal Indian policy at this time. Thompson had the patience to persevere through compromise, and often compromise was the only means by which limited goals were reached; Beatty himself is reported to have said of his successor that she could "bend farther without breaking than anyone I have ever seen."[2]

This ability enabled Thompson to establish workable goals. One of her primary aims was to increase enrollment, which she accomplished through extensive construction and a complex shifting of pupils from one area to another. As enrollment improved, she began to attack the high dropout rate, using as one of her major weapons a broad range of summer programs for Indian children. Not even a terminationist like Commissioner Glenn L. Emmons (1953–1960) chose to argue with this goal. In turn, she cooperated with the terminationists by attempting to coordinate vocational training programs for terminating tribes and for individual Indians under the relocation program and by transferring Indian children from federal to public schools.

Within the federal boarding schools, Thompson sought to alter curriculum in order to prepare Indian young people for an urban, technological society. Growing national concern for education geared to meet the new demands of technology led her to deemphasize vocational training in the boarding schools. She hoped thereby to encourage post–high school training, either in vocational school or college. Convinced that teachers and staff were at the heart of any success in boarding-school programs, she initiated a new salary grade level for master teachers and experimented with in-service training workshops for administrators, education specialists, and supervisory personnel.

Despite her efforts in these areas, Thompson did little to introduce Indian culture or to guide her program toward Indian self-determination. Nor did she move in this direction under the administration of Philleo Nash (1961–66). A John F. Kennedy appointee, Nash was an anthropologist who developed a close rapport with the Indian people during his term as commissioner. Under the more favorable conditions of Nash's administration, Thompson might have shifted emphasis, but the administrative restrictions on her position meant that she still could not move with freedom.

If these constraints on her job, which might easily have defeated another type of person, caused Thompson some frustration, she seldom showed it. In this respect her practicality stood her in good stead. Rather than strive for the impossible, she worked tirelessly toward realistic goals. What she lacked in imagination she made up in perseverence. In an address to a group of graduating seniors at an Indian Service school, she advised the students, "It still takes hard work, dependability, loyalty, and courage to get along well in this world. But when we do the very best we can, the satisfactions and success that come to us are greater than we would have supposed possible."[3] This was her personal approach, and she adhered to it through her years as Education Director.

When Hildegard Thompson took office there was one very obvious failure of Indian education that could be corrected only by increased funds and concerted effort. This was the large percentage of children not in school. In 1953, about 19,000 or 15 percent of the total number of Indian children were not enrolled in school. In some areas the number of children not in school equaled that of children in school. With the approval of newly appointed Commissioner Emmons, the Branch of Education initiated its attack on this "backlog" of children.

One of the areas of greatest need continued to be the Navajo Reservation. The Navajo Special Education Program, which had been in effect for seven years, was producing results, but it had not affected a vast number of children who had no school facilities. In 1953, out of 19,000 children not in school, 14,000 or about three-fourths were Navajo. For this reason Navajo education was given first priority. Between 1953 and 1955, the Branch of Education carried out the Emergency Navajo Program with the aid of congressional funding, expanding facilities to make room for an additional 13,000 children. This required some intricate juggling. Children were squeezed into already overcrowded facilities, or were transferred to public schools near the edge of the reservation. In some cases it was possible to expand boarding schools on the reservation. Finally, the one new concept, the bordertown program, completed the expansion to accommodate these children.

The bordertown program, which was initiated to solve unique

problems of Navajo education, was a compromise between the traditional Bureau boarding school and the assimilative public school. By the postwar years the Bureau had abandoned as almost futile the earlier efforts to establish community schools on this reservation. Despite the favorable reactions of the Navajos themselves, the Bureau concluded that community schooling was too expensive. The bordertown program thus was the Bureau's partial substitute for the community school. The two concepts had little in common, however. There was no connection between a bordertown school and the home communities of the children who were enrolled, and consequently there was no parental involvement. The justification for the program was that it offered the child the advantage of attending public school while at the same time receiving room and board at an off-reservation boarding school. These schools were necessary to the Navajo Emergency Program, for by 1959 they were providing facilities for 3,169 students.[4]

The Branch of Education also attacked the out-of-school problem for the Choctaws in Mississippi. The Alaskan Natives, however, were at the bottom of the priority list. By 1956, when the Navajo program had reached its goal, about 10 percent or 1,000 of the Native children in Alaska were still out of school.

By the spring of 1961 there was still a backlog of about 9,000 Indian children not in school. This year marked the beginning of a four-year accelerated program of construction to catch up with the backlog, to replace worn-out facilities, and to keep pace with population increase. During this period construction costs accounted for a large proportion of the education budget. In one year alone, forty-three construction projects were completed at a cost of more than $30 million—only $5 million below the total Indian Bureau budget for 1945. Commissioner Philleo Nash pointed out that during his administration education accounted for almost three out of every five dollars spent in the Bureau. The building program added thousands of new spaces for children. Between 1962 and 1967 the Bureau was budgeted for construction of about 20,000 student spaces and in 1963 alone more than 5,000 spaces were added. Nonetheless, in 1965 there were still 8,600 children not in school. During Thompson's term of office the percentage of children not in school had declined from about 15 percent to less than 10 percent, and in this she had come close to achieving one of her personal goals.

A large portion of the construction program was geared to meet the continuing need on the Navajo Reservation, where the Bureau continued to depend on boarding schools. By the late 1960s the ratio of Navajo children who attended boarding school to those who attended day school was about twenty-three to one. During the late 1930s the ratio had been only about three to one in favor of the boarding school. By the 1960s, therefore, the Indian Bureau had found space for most Navajo children, but it had done so at the expense of the community-school concept.[5]

In Alaska, the second major problem area, boarding schools also served as a partial solution. Although more than half of the Alaskan Native children were enrolled in public schools by the late 1960s, a significant number of them continued to attend federal schools. As opposed to the situation on the Navajo Reservation, however, federal enrollment among Alaskan Natives was weighted heavily toward elementary day schools. In 1968 there were almost three times as many Alaskan Native children in day school as in boarding school. When these children reached the eighth grade they presented a real problem for the enrollment-conscious Branch of Education. Despite Thompson's efforts, in the fall after she retired there were 400 eighth-grade graduates for whom there was no space available in existing boarding-school facilities.[6] At the urging of Senator E. L. Bartlett of Alaska, the Branch of Education determined to use the space available at Chilocco (Oklahoma). "While recognizing the potential criticism of moving Alaskan students to Oklahoma to attend school," the Bureau wrote, "it was considered to be preferable to having them out of school entirely."[7]

In some respects these students were like those enrolled in the Navajo Special Education Program developed by Beatty after World War II. They fit into the category described by the Bureau as "overage" and "underachieving."[8] Consequently, the Branch of Education believed that it was imperative to continue their schooling without a break. The Bureau enrolled 204 Alaskan Natives in the Chilocco program. Response of the students was varied; a small percentage of them chose to return even before Christmas, but most of them stayed through the first year—perhaps in part because Bureau leaders made it difficult if not impossible for students to leave. "Each student," the Juneau Area Director advised, "must be encouraged, persuaded, and even discreetly forced to remain at Chilocco."[9] The Bureau attitude was based on the premise that if the student failed at Chilocco there was no other "educational avenue" open to him. However, Bureau leaders neglected to recall that their own policy had compelled the student to attend Chilocco and thus they themselves shared the responsibility if he failed.

Without question, the decision to use the space at Chilocco was attuned to Bureau goals rather than to the needs of the students. Restricted by budgetary limitations and anxious to increase the percentage of pupils in school, the Branch of Education juggled students to fit spaces, regardless of the effect on the students themselves. Hildegard Thompson and her successors reaped the harvest of previous Bureau policy, which had disregarded the education of many young people; thus, when they did act, they had very few choices to offer, and the student was often caught without any alternative. If he was unable to resolve his problems at Chilocco or another boarding school, he had reached a dead end. But despite the unhappy circumstances of many boarding-school students, Thompson continued to push for increased enrollment. She maintained her stand that Indian young people must be educated in order to find a place in the technological society, and if some of the conditions of their schooling were not the best, it was still better for them to be in school.

Although Thompson's primary goal was improvement of Bureau education, she was also committed to public schooling. Wherever possible, she transferred federal responsibility for Indian education to the public schools. Increased public-school enrollment attested the success of her efforts. In 1952, about 53,000 Indian children attended public school. By 1964, this figure had jumped to about 80,000. This meant that of the total number of Indian children in school, the proportion of those enrolled in public school had increased from 52 percent in 1952 to 60 percent in 1964.

In Thompson's view, enrollment served as the key for the long-term impact of education. Like Willard Beatty, she believed that education made itself felt through an accelerating effect, with each generation advancing in its schooling a little farther than the previous one. One generation might attend grade school, the next might graduate from high school, and the third might finish college. Consequently, the initiation of the cycle was crucial. In the case of the Navajos, Choctaws, and Alaskan Natives, failure to enroll significant numbers of children meant that illiteracy might have been extended another fifty to seventy-five years.[10] To Thompson the question of whether these children could adapt to the twentieth century was not even relevant until they were in school.

Finding places for children in the schools was no guarantee that they would receive an education. Bureau educators in the fifties and sixties were plagued by the high dropout rate for Indian children in both federal and public schools. During these decades boarding-school superintendents became increasingly aware of the growing number of public-school dropouts who applied to Bureau schools for admission. Like the problem of the runaway, which had declined but never quite died out, the problem of the dropout revealed that the young Indian was rejecting the education made available to him. While the high dropout rate had been a chronic feature of federal Indian education since its inception, it became a focus of Bureau criticism when statistics revealed that most Indian children finally were enrolled in school.

When the Branch of Education was grappling with this problem in the late fifties, summer-school programs were proposed as a possible aid in raising the educational achievement level of Indian children. Achievement level in itself was one of the major causes of the dropout problem. The children fell behind their normal class levels from about third grade on, and by sixth grade it was common for them to be two or more grades behind. Of those who did start high school, 60 percent did not finish. This continuing failure not only was damaging to the ego; it also meant that when the pupil quit school he was ill equipped to find a job, either in an urban area or on his reservation. George Boyce, a prominent Bureau educator, suggested that summer programs might "arrest" the failures before the children fell too far behind to recover. This "chain of maladjustment" should be studied "link by link," he pointed out, in order to avoid the "ultimate loss" of a contributing member of society.[11] Boyce argued that if these children could be given a variety of remedial programs during successive summer vacations, they might eventually make the adjustment necessary to complete their schooling.

With this theoretical backdrop, the Branch of Education initiated the first summer programs in 1960. The experiment was begun on a trial basis with an enrollment of 2,200, but the Branch of Education was so pleased with the response that it expanded the program in 1961. In the second summer the enrollment tripled, and by the third year 20,000 students were participating in a variety of activities.

"Summer school" was interpreted broadly, and many of the activities were not directly connected with a formal education structure. Though Thompson herself quite frankly preferred academic and work projects and gave them priority, they were but two of the four main types of programs, which also included recreation and field trips.

Most of these activities were developed as unique responses to local conditions. In many cases they were dependent on cooperation with a tribal council or tribal parents; in other cases the tribe itself assumed responsibility (see Chapter 12). On the San Carlos Apache Reservation the Tribal Council developed a number of programs with the aid of a grant from the Bureau, including a youth summer camp and a singular project for a group of twenty teen-age girls. The girls spent half the day in class learning sewing, cooking, basket making, and so on; then they worked for half the day renovating two reservation homes owned by widows with large families. The girls, who were paid two dollars a day, were so enthusiastic that all of them completed the projects and in the process gained a new feeling for the community.[12]

In 1961 Stewart Indian School (formerly Carson) took a group of Nevada children twelve to fourteen years old on a trip to Southern California, where they saw, among other things, Disneyland, the San Diego Zoo, and the Pacific Ocean. Stewart, like other boarding schools, also developed work programs. These had a twofold purpose: to enable teenagers to earn some money and to give them practice in a vocation, varying from masonry to agriculture. The Portland Area began a work-camp session reminiscent of the Indian CCC, involving building of fire towers and other construction projects in forest areas. On many reservations tribal councils and parents hoped that the programs would also fill the emptiness of summer time, a period that often witnessed an increase in delinquency of one form or another. Thus, while the San Carlos Tribal Council planned a summer youth camp in part to provide employment for "needy boys," it also expected to provide "recreational and educational facilities . . . in order to combat juvenile delinquency."[13] Many reservations reported a decline in juvenile problems while summer programs were in operation.

Academic schooling at all levels was another aspect of the program. From pre–first-grade to brushup training for college, students were given the opportunity to enroll in courses that anticipated problems that might arise during the school year. Although the Bureau did not budget money for kindergartens until 1967, brief introductory preschool sessions were offered in the summer school program as early as 1962. The college preparatory course offered at Haskell Institute was a response to the sudden upswing in college enrollment. The first session in 1963 was attended by seventy-seven students who wanted to go to college and who were already aware of difficulties they might encounter, ranging from inability to cope with a particular subject like history or math to simply not knowing how to study. In an effort to determine the effectiveness of this program, the Education Branch kept track of some of the students who had attended. Generally, the results were discouraging. About a third of the students dropped out of college within one or two years after enrolling in a summer session, and of those who remained in school fewer than half maintained a C or passing average. As one assistant area director pointed out, the Haskell course should have placed more stress on "independence in homework and self-discipline." He added that the students also needed more help simply in becoming acquainted with the structure of a college campus. Not knowing where to turn for assistance made a crucial difference in the decision of whether to stay or drop out.[14]

Despite these difficulties, Thompson strongly encouraged college education. She foresaw that all forms of post–high school training should be developed as a necessary response to the new age of technology, and believed that the Indian child must be trained to adapt with ease to twentieth-century America. In part, her conviction was molded by the abrupt changes that were taking place. This was the period when television came into its own, bringing with it an even more pervasive form of media control. Development of the transistor and other crucial breakthroughs in electronics also dominated these years and, in turn, led to the success of Sputnik, an event that contributed to one of the most frantic about-faces in the history of American education. The combination of these factors led America to the threshold of a new age. The technological revolution had begun, and its implications were not lost on Hildegard Thompson. She geared her education program to its demands and encouraged all of her students to equip themselves for it. Thompson was firmly convinced that America was entering a new era and this time, for once, she wanted the Indians to have a slice of the economic pie. The summer programs were one means of improving the child's ability to stay in school and thus to cope eventually with the changing world. Thompson ranked teachers and supervisory personnel a close second.

Ryan and Beatty had devoted themselves to improving the quality of teaching through professionalization and in-service training of Indian Service teachers. Hildegard Thompson altered the character of in-service training by switching from one or two large sessions each summer to local summer workshops for each area. Except for a recommended session in the first year with the Indian Service, she preferred to have teachers enroll in college courses during their educational leave. Self-improvement was the guideline she drew for Indian Service teachers. In the early sixties, however, she introduced the G.S.-9 civil service rating for teachers—a more practical incentive for individual improvement.

The decades of the fifties and sixties witnessed a lively national debate among teachers and their representative groups over the advantages and disadvantages of the "merit system." Briefly, the system suggested that certain teachers of outstanding ability and service should be paid salaries above the normal scale or should be advanced more rapidly. Seldom far removed from current educational trends, Indian Service educators began to discuss the possibility of adapting the merit system to teachers in federal schools. In the late fifties the Branch of Education introduced a proposal that would establish a Grade 9 Master Teacher level for outstanding Indian Service Teachers. Up to this time the highest level a teacher could reach was Grade 7. Those who sought the Grade 9 salary level had to move to administrative or supervisory positions, which were not always suited to their talents. This was such a revolutionary concept for the Indian Bureau that it required no less than three years of discussion, special sessions, and even a survey of Indian Service teachers before the Branch of Education determined that the proposal should be accepted. The outcome was heavily weighted by the fact that the Grade 9 level was supported not only by the majority of teachers[15] but by Hildegard Thompson herself. In 1962 she predicted that if the Branch of Education failed to build a corps of teachers whose performance was at a "level of excellence beyond the ordinary," it would mean that the present "generation of Indians will find themselves undereducated in terms of the demands the rapidly changing world will make of them."[16]

While Thompson was concerned with the quality of teaching, she also devoted a great deal of time to finding ways to improve the administrative and supervisory staff in federal schools. One of the early shifts in her administration was to transfer the emphasis in summer training sessions from teachers to administrators and supervisory personnel. The purpose of these two-week workshops was to enable groups of education personnel to explore and seek solutions to common problems. In 1957, 1958, and 1959, summer sessions were held for administrators and educational specialists.[17] Typical of the problems they discussed were how to improve reading instruction, realign vocational instruction, and upgrade dormitory living. In the early 1960s workshops were held for guidance personnel, including principals of large boarding schools and dormitory supervisors. These workshops were clearly a response to a pressing need. Child guidance for the many disturbed youngsters in boarding schools had not improved very much in the decade since the National Congress of American Indians in its 1951 convention had called for a "comprehensive child guidance program in all Bureau schools."[18]

Thompson believed that there were inherent dangers in educating Indian young people in the complex milieu of mid-twentieth-century America, an era described by her assistant Almira D. Franchville as "critical, complicated, and sometimes frightening." Thompson suggested that too rapid inculcation of new ideas could push a child to the dangerous point of "losing his sense of direction and balance." She urged instructors to move with caution in order to help the child maintain his sense of direction "by building the new into the solid values of his own way of life."[19]

This position was very similar to Beatty's educational philosophy of the postwar years. Neither approach attempted to reinforce those values that belonged to the Indian child by right of his own heritage. As a result, far too many young Indian people succumbed to the ills Thompson feared. When the person does not know what he believes, she counseled, "and tensions are great, as they certainly are today, it can result in fanaticism, frustration, rebellion, and delinquency."[20] In this crucial aspect of education—culture reinforcement—guidance programs during Thompson's administration waged an uphill battle.

Thompson regarded successful job placement as another vital link in the adjustment of Indian youth to the urban world, and accordingly she introduced concrete alterations in the Bureau high school curriculum. "Opportunities increasingly are shifting toward professions and technical occupations," she wrote in the early 1960s.[21] Continued stress on vocational training throughout high school, therefore, would ignore the growing national emphasis on post–high school training.[22] Thompson believed that academic training should be stressed in order to give high school graduates the option to choose college. The Sputnik scare had generated a widespread interest in the sciences and mathematics, and educators generally believed that these would be the disciplines of the future. A number of Bureau educators therefore wanted to adapt Indian education to meet the demands of these disciplines. Failure to give Indian young people the "training necessary to meet the new age" would mean that "others will be picking off the plums," wrote one Bureau administrator; "our mathematics and science teaching must meet every test—it must be second to none."[23]

The high school program was restructured to prepare students for post–high school training, replacing most vocational training by a more academically oriented curriculum. By restricting vocational courses to the last two years of high school, Thompson limited the student's possibilities for finding a job and encouraged him to continue his schooling. Two major avenues were open for post–high school training: The student could specialize in a vocational skill, or he could go on to college.[24]

The new emphasis on an academic curriculum in high school assumed that an increasing number of high school graduates would attend college. Thompson predicted that Indian enrollment in college would take a big jump in the 1960s. In 1961 sixty-six Indians graduated from four-year institutions; by 1968 this figure had almost tripled.[25] One of the primary reasons for the increase was the new funding made available to Indian college students. By this time college aid came from many sources: private groups; colleges and universities themselves; tribes; and the federal government, including newer sources like the Office of Economic Opportunity.

Assistance for Indian students to attend college began in the colonial period. Dartmouth College, founded in 1769, was established for the express purpose of providing higher education for Indians. However, the amount of aid available remained very limited until after World War II. Federal assistance extended during the Indian New Deal was in the form of loans. The Indian

Reorganization Act of 1934 provided for a $250,000 loan fund for higher education. When this is contrasted with the $3 million the Bureau allocated for scholarship aid in 1969, federal assistance of the New Deal period appears rather meager. Nonetheless, it was a beginning, and it did encourage the Education Division to provide for the position of Guidance Officer, who was in charge of the loan fund and who also served as counselor for the students.

During Collier's administration Ruth Muskrat Bronson (Cherokee) held this position for twelve years. Bronson's "Advanced Education Survey" of 1932 was conducted to determine "where best a selected Indian leadership might be trained." She concluded that the U.S. government had done very little to encourage the "development of an adequately trained native leadership." She pointed out that there were only 385 Indian students enrolled in college in 1932; that she could locate definite records for only 52 Indian college graduates; and that Indian scholarships were being offered at only five colleges and universities.[26] According to Bronson, these statistics reflected the traditionally negative attitude of the Indian Bureau toward advanced education, as well as the "poor training" that the Bureau offered in its elementary and secondary schools. Futhermore, in at least one university (Brown), Indian students tested significantly lower than other college freshmen. According to the report, this was the direct result of "shoddy teaching methods," which forced students to learn how to study after they entered college.[27]

The conclusions that Bronson reached in 1932 were still valid some thirty years later. The postwar period witnessed a growing enrollment of Indian students in college, but their attrition rate was still high.[28] As the Haskell Institute summer program demonstrated, Indian college students of this period suffered from many of the same problems experienced by students before World War II. Increased enrollment did not necessarily mean greater success, for Indian high school graduates continued to be ill prepared for college.[29] Despite the financial boost given to higher education, it appeared that it would be a long time before these college students could overcome the poor education they had received.[30] Nor could they easily dismiss the cultural barrier maintained by persistent discrimination and the difficulty of adjusting to the life style of non-Indian America. Ironically, the increased enrollment of Indian students in college thus served to demonstrate the weaknesses of

Bureau education in the lower grades, and to reiterate the sharp cultural distinctions that separated these students from their counterparts in non-Indian America. Increasingly, Indian students rebelled against the structure of colleges because they represented the mainstream society.

Many boarding-school graduates chose vocational training rather than college. Some students were able to begin this training before graduation by attending one of the schools that continued to emphasize this type of curriculum, for one of the immediate effects of the new program was to transfer the burden of vocational education to a few selected boarding schools. In the early 1960s these included Haskell Institute, Chilocco, and the Institute of American Indian Arts. Haskell Institute had long been known for its courses in commercial training and had been a traditional source of secretaries and office workers for the Bureau itself. In accordance with the new policy, however, it began to phase out its high school curriculum. By the fall of 1965 the last high school class had graduated, and the school became known as Haskell Indian Junior College. Although it continued to emphasize business training, it added courses in electronics, the building trades, and service occupations. The transformation at Chilocco was less extensive, since it provided needed space for Navajo and Alaskan Native students. However, its major emphasis was on vocational training and it did offer post–high school courses in some distributive and service occupations.[31] The Institute of American Indian Arts replaced the Santa Fe Boarding School. Opening in October 1962, it offered high school courses and two post–high school years of work in various media, including painting, sculpture, jewelry, ceramics, design and printing of textiles, and creative writing. Like Chilocco and Haskell, the Institute attracted pupils from all over the country, including Alaska.[32]

The emphasis on post–high school education, a major policy shift, was criticized within the Bureau and the Indian community. Some critics attacked Thompson for reacting too swiftly to the job market opened by the technological age. By deemphasizing vocational education, they asserted, she forced the students into making a more limited career choice. Her supporters were firmly convinced that changes in the job market were significant enough to demand a revamping of federal Indian education. One Bureau educator recalled that "equal pressure" was put on Thompson "from the

Indian people, to restore the old vocational programs, and from educational theorists, to make them college preparatory." The debate notwithstanding, the decade of the sixties witnessed a significant jump in post–high school enrollment as more Indian students entered college or enrolled in vocational training. The results in terms of individual fulfillment, however, remained to be seen.

The shift to post–high school vocational training meant that the Branch of Education had become, in large part, a job training agency. During Thompson's administration this concept was interpreted broadly to include vocational training for adults who had received little schooling. This was the direct result of pressures by the terminationists, who advocated any action that would assimilate the Indian into urban society. Assimilation was pushed through two concrete measures: individual relocation, or direct urging of Indians to move to the cities, in a twentieth-century version of removal; and termination of federal services for a tribe. Most adult education was geared to one of these two programs and, in the long run, was aimed toward individual economic improvement.

In 1955 the Branch of Education introduced a pilot program of adult education designed to improve adult English literacy on five reservations: Papago, Fort Hall, Turtle Mountain, Seminole, and Rosebud. In the same year the Bureau supported legislation to introduce aid for adult vocational training. This was achieved in 1956 with the passage of P.L. 959, an adult vocational training act (August 3, 1956, 70 *Stat.*, 986), which provided financial assistance for any Indian between the ages of eighteen and thirty-five who sought vocational training. Other sources of federal funding also became available during this period.[33] Most of these programs sought to teach or improve upon a marketable skill for urban employment. The only exception was a program that assisted Indians in finding jobs on or near reservations. In the ten-year span between 1956 and 1966, the Bureau submitted that it had helped 45,400 Indians find jobs both on and off reservations.[34]

Although many Indians had already been drawn to the cities, federal legislation provided a new incentive and swelled the Indian ghettos in metropolitan areas such as Los Angeles, Seattle, Minneapolis, and Chicago.[35] At best, however, vocational training for relocation was sporadic, and in many cases the parents of a relocated family had received no preparation for the new environment.[36] Adjustment to city living was often difficult for the rural Indian. Long established habits made the confines of routine work and urban slums much less desirable than the conditions, however poor, on reservations. These frustrations were not eased by the high incidence of alcoholism.[37] Unfortunately, most of those who sought to return to their reservations were unable to do so. They had made the move with the understanding that when they arrived in the city the government would take care of them. They had no funds for the trip home.[38]

The services of the Branch of Education were in demand for both programs of assimilation—relocation and tribal termination—because of the congressional afterthought that these uprooted people might need some special training in order to earn a living under vastly altered conditions. The need for special educational programs for terminating tribes was thrust on the Branch of Education in such an abrupt manner that it upset the usually even-tempered director. Procedures for tribes and bands being terminated were pushed through with a general disregard for the long-term planning and organization preferred by Hildegard Thompson. When the Branch of Education was notified of the need for educational aid to the Paiutes, she responded with an uncharacteristic vehemence: "We all recognize," she wrote, that this legislation (P.L. 762, Termination of the Paiute Bands of Southern Utah) "was enacted without too much preplanning with the Tribe," and the "long years of experience of the Bureau" were not "fully utilized. . . . In the future," she added, the Bureau should "spell out, in specifications the educational programs it wants. . . . such programs and contracts should come during the preparation stage with the Tribe instead of at the termination time."[39]

Comments by individual Indians, particularly among the Klamath and Paiutes, indicated that they had little if any comprehension of the extent or the nature of termination. In all of the cases, however, it was clear that the groups were not prepared for the drastic effects of the measure. In Thompson's report on the Paiutes, she suggested that in the future the Bureau should be more prepared to deal effectively with the tribe concerned, basing its plans on an understanding of the background and needs of the tribe and establishing "more rapid lines of communication" between tribe, Area Office, and the Washington Office.[40] Yet just eight months later, when several Paiutes wrote letters of complaint to Senator Arthur Watkins, Commissioner Emmons asserted that these were the first complaints that the Bureau had heard.[41] Direct communication between individual Indians and the Bureau was apparently more an ideal than a reality.

That the Indians failed to sympathize with the concept of termination was revealed by their indifference to the education programs the Bureau established for their benefit. The Branch of Education, attempting to persuade members of terminating groups to enroll in vocational training classes, found the response disappointing. Even the Bureau's assurance that these courses would enable them "to assume their responsibilities as citizens without special services . . . and to conduct their own affairs" had little effect.[42] The superintendent at the Uintah and Ouray Agency in Utah was so desperate to find enrollees that he wrote in his final plea, "You are being given ONE LAST CHANCE to take advantage of relocating on the VOCATIONAL TRAINING PROGRAM."[43] A month later a Bureau official wrote that he was "disappointed that there is not more response from the people who need education the most."[44] This situation was repeated among other terminating groups.[45] Each of these groups was given the opportunity for job training; their refusal to respond, in itself, served to censure the hasty and ill-planned congressional termination measures.

The Branch of Education was not responsible for these ineffectual programs, but its participation in them was another sign of the role of compromise in Hildegard Thompson's administration. Restricted by an overanxious Congress and hampered by the administrative organization of the Bureau, by her perseverence Thompson demonstrated her faith in the long-range goals of Bureau education.

To the extent that she had to work within the context of an almost frantic eagerness for termination, the fifties proved to be her most difficult years. However, Hildegard Thompson remained as Director of Education until November 1965, serving throughout the administration of Commissioner Nash, whose appointment marked the decline of termination. Under the Nash administration Thompson should have been able to encourage measures such as the introduction of Indian culture in federal schools. That she failed to shift her goals to allow for the change in Bureau leadership was in part because she still lacked administrative authority; the Branch of Education and its director remained at the same ineffective level assigned in 1950. Thompson continued to make progress toward her limited goals, but she did not make any major changes under the Nash administration.

As long as Hildegard Thompson was in office, proponents of self-determination had to postpone their plans, for Bureau education was not prepared to adjust to them. Perhaps she failed to sense the current of change that was to come shortly after her retirement. Perhaps, as one education leader of the period concluded, she "lacked the authority to swim against the tide . . . and when it came to the showdown of getting change, getting money, she wasn't able to succeed."[46] It appears more likely, however, that Hildegard Thompson was proud of the education goals she had established under termination, and saw no reason to make any drastic changes in them in her last years before retirement.

1. Will Carson Ryan, Director of Education, Bureau of Indian Affairs, 1930–35. Courtesy of Carson V. Ryan.

Willard Walcott Beatty, Director of Education, Bureau Indian Affairs, 1936–52. Courtesy of Walcott Hersey tty.

3. John Collier, Commissioner of Indian Affairs, 1933–45. Bureau of Indian Affairs photo in the National Archives.

4. "Best girls squad for the year," Chilocco Indian School (Oklahoma), 1928. National Archives.

5. "Best boys company," Chilocco Indian School (Oklahoma), 1928. National Archives.

6. "Dairying at the Albuquerque Indian School," 1930s. Courtesy of the Albuquerque Indian School.

7. Instruction in auto mechanics, Haskell Institute (Lawrence, Kansas), 1931. National Archives.

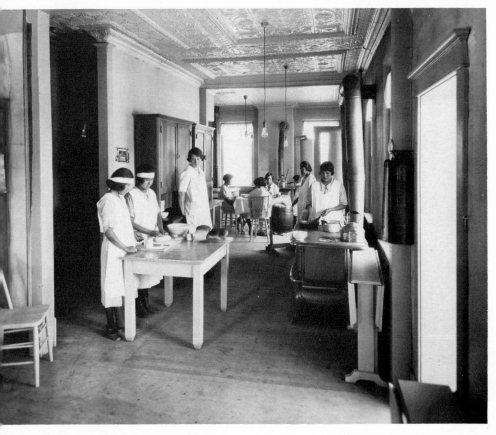

8. "Domestic science at the Albuquerque Indian School," 1930s. Courtesy of the Albuquerque Indian School.

9. "Bridger 4-H Potato Club meeting," Cheyenne River Agency (South Dakota), 1931. National Archives.

10. "Kewonga Public School, Potawatomi Indian Reservation, grades 1-8." National Archives.

11. "Navajo rug weavers at the Albuquerque Indian School," 1930s. Courtesy of the Albuquerque Indian School.

12. "Football team in action," Chilocco Indian School (Oklahoma), 1928. National Archives.

14. Parade, Haskell Institute (Lawrence, Kansas), 1920s. Courtesy of Haskell Indian Junior College. Photo by Moore, Lawrence, Kansas.

15. "Afternoon tea given during Christmas holiday" (Social Skills training), Navajo Special Program, Intermountain Indian School (Brigham City, Utah), 1951. Courtesy of George Boyce.

16. "Girls leaving for jobs." Left foreground, George Boyce, Director, Intermountain Indian School (Brigham City, Utah), Navajo Special Program, 1950s. Courtesy of George Boyce.

17. Hildegard Thompson, Director of Education, Bureau of Indian Affairs, 1952–65. Courtesy of George Boyce.

18. Student government, Haskell Indian Junior College (Lawrence, Kansas), 1972–73. Courtesy of Haskell Indian Junior College.

19. Physical Education building, Southwestern Indian Polytechnic Institute (Albuquerque, New Mexico). Courtesy of the Southwestern Indian Polytechnic Institute.

20. High school graduating class, Institute of American Indian Art (Santa Fe, New Mexico), 1974. Background, gallery-museum on campus; foreground, concrete waterfall designed by Douglas Crowder (Choctaw) and Leo Proctor (Cherokee), students of Ottelie Loloma. Photo by Kay Wiest (IAIA).

21. Graphics class, Institute of American Indian Art (Santa Fe, New Mexico). Piece shown is by Benny Martinez, studying with Seymour Tubis. Photo by Kay Wiest (IAIA).

22. Administration building, Institute of American Indian Art (Santa Fe, New Mexico), Christmas Day, 1965. Photo by Leo Downwind (Chippewa), photography student of Kay Wiest (IAIA).

23. Camp Chaparral summer school, directed by the Yakima Indian Nation, Yakima Reservation (Washington State). Courtesy of the Yakima Nation.

24. Children at Rough Rock Demonstration School (Chinle, Arizona), late 1960s. Courtesy of Rough Rock Demonstration School.

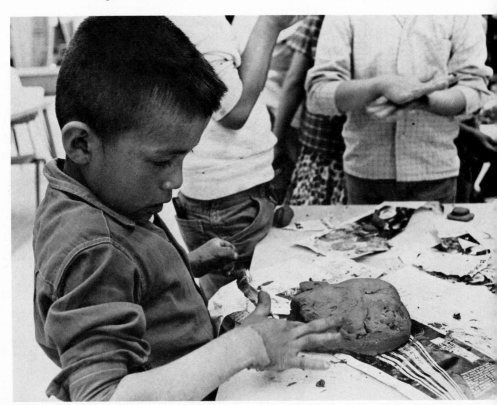

25. "Making Navajo fried bread," Rough Rock Demonstration School (Chinle, Arizona), late 1960s. Courtesy of Rough Rock Demonstration School.

26. High school students, Rough Rock Demonstration School (Chinle, Arizona), early 1970s. Courtesy of Rough Rock Demonstration School. Photo by Arlene Bowman.

27. Cafeteria, Navajo Community College. Courtesy of Navajo Community College.

28. Dormitories, Navajo Community College. Courtesy of Navajo Community College.

11

NEW DIRECTIONS IN FEDERAL CONTROL

In April 1966, Lyndon B. Johnson appointed the first Indian to serve as Commissioner of Indian Affairs since Ely S. Parker (Seneca, 1869–71). Robert Lafollette Bennett (1966–69) was an Oneida who had earned the respect of Indians and federal administrators during his thirty-two years with the Indian Bureau. A 1932 graduate of Haskell Institute, Bennett had been serving as Area Director for Alaska when his nomination was announced.

Bennett's appointment was a milestone in federal Indian policy. The fact that he was followed by Louis R. Bruce (Mohawk-Sioux, 1969–72), who was then succeeded by Morris Thompson (Athabaskan, Alaska, 1973–76), established a clear precedent. Henceforth the Commissioner of Indian Affairs would be an Indian.

During the six months preceding Bennett's nomination, Bureau leadership was the target of Secretary of the Interior Stewart L. Udall (1961–69). Under heavy attack from the Interior committees of both houses of Congress, Udall's personal dissatisfaction with the Indian Bureau was strengthened by political pressures.

By the spring of 1966 it was evident that the Indian Bureau was in the beginning stages of another about-face. Thompson had retired in November; Philleo Nash announced his resignation in March.[1] Early in April, just before Bennett's nomination, Secretary Udall scheduled a mid-month Area Directors' conference in Santa Fe. The mood that evolved from this conference forecast the climate of coming administrations. With the support of Secretary Udall, the Area Directors expressed a new optimism concerning the achievement of quality education. Secretary Udall had already stipulated that education would be given high priority, and he had personally appeared at congressional hearings on the Bureau budget to urge increased funding for Bureau education. At the conference, as Madison Coombs wrote, the "air was electric with portents of change." Indeed, those who were present anticipated revisions that would have the "most beneficial effects on Indian education" and would "make the Bureau's educational enterprise a much more exciting one in which to work."[2]

In July 1966 the Bureau announced the appointment of Dr. Carl Marburger, Secretary Udall's personal choice for Assistant Commissioner for Education. Marburger was well qualified for the job in terms of professional background. He had received his Ed.D. at Wayne State University and had worked with disadvantaged children under the U.S. Office of Education before coming to the Bureau.

Marburger joined the Bureau with some enthusiasm, but he was soon disillusioned. Although he encouraged changes, within a few months he became convinced that it was impossible to cut through the red tape of the bureaucratic system. One of the chief difficulties that he encountered, and the one that may well have led him to resign, was the peculiar arrangement of duplicate authority. Although his position had been granted line authority, each of the ten Area Directors held the same type of authority. Marburger could issue a directive, but it could be countermanded by an Area Director. This meant, in effect, that he could not implement any of his policies. He soon made it known that he wanted direct line authority to his educational administrators in the field, but by this action he alienated nearly all of the Area Directors, thus defeating his own purpose. Some time later he recalled that his "greatest difficulty" in office was the fact that he "had little line control" over the educators "under his jurisdiction."[3]

Just a year after he was appointed, Marburger resigned. He had attempted to fight the system but had failed. This news was distressing to many educators, who had confidence in his ability to make the Education Division more responsive to the wishes of the Indian people. As Robert Roessel, a prominent figure in Navajo education and director of Rough Rock at this time, wrote on learning of Marburger's resignation, "While you were in Washington, leading and directing Indian education, we at Rough Rock felt that there was a bright light in Washington. . . . Now, . . . the bright light . . . has gone out."[4]

Thus, within a period of twelve months, Bureau education was without a permanent director for the second time. The next appointment was not long in coming. Charles N. Zellers, like Marburger, came to the Bureau from the U.S. Office of Education. Both men were outsiders—a sign that Secretary Udall believed the Education Division itself could produce no leaders capable of implementing his ideas for change. Zellers's appointment broke the tradition, established with Ryan, of hiring an educator for the position. Zellers had been trained in business administration and had taught that subject at Youngstown University. He had also worked as a business administrator for the public school system of the District of Columbia before joining the U.S. Office of Education. By avoiding Marburger's tactics of confrontation, Zellers maintained a more amiable relationship with the Area Directors, but his administrative plans were increasingly frustrated. In 1969, his last year in office, two major events brought Bureau education under attack from the press as a system fraught with inexcusable failures. The first of these was a widely publicized exposé of physical abuse of Chilocco students. The second was the Kennedy Report. When Zellers's position as Assistant Commissioner for Education was abolished by incoming President Richard M. Nixon, he resigned. Thus, by January 1970, the Education Division was again without a permanent director.

From 1966 to 1970 two men had served as Assistant Commissioner for Education. From 1970 to 1976 three more men served as Director of Education Programs. Within one decade, therefore, it took five persons to fill the role that Beatty and Thompson had successively covered for almost thirty years. This rapid turnover gives an indication of the turmoil that characterized the Indian Bureau in the late sixties and early seventies.

The first of the Nixon appointees was James Hawkins. An experienced administrator, both in the Indian Bureau as Area Director for Alaska and Minneapolis, and in other capacities, Hawkins took on his new position as Director of Education Programs during a difficult period for the Bureau. In these years Indian activism led to two major upsets: the takeover of the Bureau's Central Office in November 1972, and the thirty-seven-day siege of Wounded Knee, South Dakota, in March and April 1973. The immediate effects on the Bureau were the resignation of Commissioner Bruce and the appointment of Marvin L. Franklin (Iowa) as Acting Assistant to the Secretary for Indian Affairs.[5] The unstable condition of Bureau leadership prevailed until the Senate's approval of Morris Thompson as new Indian Commissioner in November 1973.

During Hawkins's administration the Indian Education Act of 1972, which affected several programs administered by the U.S. Office of Education (USOE), became law (see Epilogue), but it was not until January 1975 that legislation affecting J-O'M programs administered by the Indian Bureau was passed. In the interim, Clennon E. Sockeye succeeded Hawkins and served as Education Director for a little over a year. Sockeye's resignation occurred before the new legislation went into effect. Thus William G. Demmert, Jr. (Tlingit, Alaska), who was appointed in March 1976, became the first Education Director to deal with the new contract methods authorized by the Indian Self-Determination and Education Assistance Act of 1975 (see Epilogue). Demmert transferred to the Indian Bureau from USOE, where he had served as the first Deputy Commissioner of Indian Education.

The early reforms of this post-Beatty-Thompson decade were as radical for the late sixties as were Demmert's ideas for the mid seventies. Under Marburger and Zellers, the Bureau began to respond to the need for cross-cultural education. It also agreed to contract for the first Indian-controlled schools, and encouraged further Indian participation and direction. Through other curriculum changes, such as the addition of kindergartens to federal schools, the Bureau became a part of new educational trends.[6] In the early seventies the momentum of these changes accelerated when Indian groups became involved in educational decision making and control.[7]

During this period there were some Bureau leaders who welcomed the new ideas, but the primary impetus for reform came from several forces outside the Bureau. One of the most significant of these influences was Indian leadership. The Indian Bureau had always reflected the national mood, and the late 1960s were no exception. Since one of the dominant trends of this decade was the emergence of ethnic minorities, the Bureau was eventually forced to modify its Indian policy to serve the growing self-determination of Indian people. While there were other reasons for the rise of Indian leadership, the national milieu served as a stimulant and thus provided part of the impetus for change.

Congress was also responsible for giving Bureau education a push toward greater Indian participation. Despite the fact that the Indian Bureau was accustomed to carrying on a steady battle over appropriations and policy direction with both Congress and the Bureau of the Budget, this particular congressional attack proved extremely annoying. Centered among a small group of congressmen, including members of the Senate Subcommittee on Indian Education, the criticism was a combination of political opportunism and honest concern for the Indian cause. Thus it sought to dilute Bureau control of Indian education by encouraging an educational structure that would be responsive to the needs and under the direction of Indians themselves.

A third influence on Bureau education was the leadership demonstrated by other federal agencies. By the mid sixties federal Indian policy had become a shared responsibility. Although the Indian Bureau still shouldered the major burden, significant portions were carried by Health, Education and Welfare (U.S. Public Health Service and U.S. Office of Education) and the newly created Office of Economic Opportunity (OEO). The programs pioneered by these agencies, such as Head Start and the Community Action Program, demonstrated concepts that might well have been developed by the Indian Bureau itself.

The mood for change within the federal power structure, which was reciprocated by Indian leaders, led to a number of reappraisals of the Indian Bureau. Each of the U.S. presidents of the 1960s established a presidential task force to analyze the role of the Bureau. In addition, studies were made by private foundations,[8] government agencies, Congress, and Indian groups such as the National Congress of American Indians. The studies recommended numerous alternatives, including new locations for the Bureau within the federal government and revamping its administrative organization. In the early seventies the Bureau was still the responsibility of the Secretary of the Interior and the administrative structure was only slightly altered. By the mid seventies, however, structural alterations in the Bureau indicated that self-determination might become a reality. The potential for Indian leadership and control was more promising than at any other time in the history of U.S. Indian policy.

In this context, therefore, it is necessary to explore the means by which these outside forces—the national milieu and its encouragement of Indian self-determination; congressional criticism; and the input of federal agencies—influenced the Bureau.

The burgeoning quantity of writing on Indian education affected the Bureau's educational policy by providing an impact on public opinion. In the sixties, interest in Indian culture and self-determination was spurred by the increasing attention given to minority groups. This publicity, combined with the struggle for civil rights and the Kennedy-Johnson administrations' war on poverty, led the nation to realize that the traditional melting-pot theme, long a substantive basis for the national ethos, had arrived at its moment of truth. No group had a more historical claim to the refutation of this concept than the American Indian. For centuries Indians had been engaged in a struggle to retain their cultures and to direct their own affairs. Their involvement in the renaissance of ethnic minority cultures was thus the culmination of a long-term commitment.

Prominent among those who wrote on Indian education were a number of scholars, primarily non-Indian, who were trained in education and the social sciences.[9] These writers were students of diversified Indian cultures, and they approached these cultures from the different perspectives of their sometimes narrow disciplines, but their variations developed around a common theme. This was that at the heart of Indian failure in school were two major weaknesses in the education systems of both federal and public schools: the disregard for Indian cultural heritage and the singular lack of encouragement for Indian participation.

The direct relationship between culture and student interest was summarized by Edward P. Dozier, who concluded that the "high drop out rates of Indian students, as we go up the scale of grade levels, is largely the result of the negative rating given the Indian's background as compared to the positive rating attributed to Euro-American culture."[10] By teaching Indian children the values of urban middle-class culture, these writers observed, the schools have ignored the concepts by which they were raised, "their own hierarchy of values . . . their implicit premises about their world."[11] This interpretation of conflicting value systems was reminiscent of the approach suggested by anthropologists and Progressive Bureau educators. Scudder Mekeel had written in 1936, "it is unwise to educate an individual too far from the standards set by his community. Such a person . . . must either throw off his education to reestablish rapport with the group or leave the reservation. . . ."[12] These ideas had been ignored for at least two decades, and one of the most important contributions of the scholars of the late sixties and early seventies was to reintroduce them as suggested guidelines for the Bureau.

Although the concept of Indian participation in education had fewer historical antecedents, these writers concluded that Indian self-determination was equally important to the success of Indian education. Murray Wax and Rosalie Wax suggested that the Ogalala Sioux "feel that the schools are instrumentalities of the Whites, designed to inculcate Indian children with alien values and to transform them into 'whites.' "[13] Edward Parmee pointed out that this attitude was also prevalent among the San Carlos Apache. Certainly it was true in parts of the Navajo Reservation, and it also became a battle cry for California Indians who were dissatisfied with both school control and materials. If Indian criticism of school systems was as widespread as these writers indicated, then the solution, as John F. Bryde suggested, was obvious: "Indian parents should control the education of their children and should set their own educational goals for them consonant with their cultural needs. . . ."[14]

This critique of Indian education was generally supported by government and private studies of the Bureau. President Kennedy's Task Force Report recommended that the Branch of Education place greater stress on the bilingual training program. "One of the major problems in educating Indian youngsters," it observed, "stems from the fact that English is often not their home language." Therefore, the Bureau not only must keep "abreast of the latest developments in language training"; it should introduce an in-service training program in this area. The Task Force also criticized the Bureau for suggesting that the formation of tribal education committees would suffice for Indian involvement in education. Of utmost importance, the report asserted, was participation of parents. "If our goal is the ultimate transfer of educational responsibility to local school districts," it observed, "then the Bureau must do everything it can now to help Indian parents learn of their rights and duties with respect to schools."[15]

Shortly thereafter, the Brophy, Aberle study pointed out that the Indian child "must understand his own heritage" in order "to assess his place in modern society." For this reason, the report went on to say, "he needs books or other materials that stress tribal values, history and culture . . . to demonstrate the Indians' rich inheritance."[16] Alvin M. Josephy's report on the Indian Bureau for President Nixon, written early in 1969, suggested that "training programs, and adequate orientation seminars in Indian (and tribal) history and cultures" be established for "every level" of Bureau personnel.[17] Josephy's report predated any extensive Indian leadership within Bureau education programs, with the exception of a few schools. On the other hand, by 1969 stress on Indian cultural heritage (including language) had become an established Bureau policy. Thus, Josephy's recommendation that Bureau employees should be educated in the area of Indian cultures was the logical step toward implementation of this policy—yet another reminder of the unusual foresight of Beatty's in-service training programs.

In 1967 the U.S. Office of Education (USOE) offered to fund one of the most significant critiques of this period, *The National Study of American Indian Education: The Education of Indian Children and Youth* (n.p., 1970). A five-year project, this exhaustive evaluation of contemporary Indian schooling was directed by Robert J. Havighurst of the University of Chicago and included a sizable proportion of Indian participants. In 1972, Havighurst and Estelle Fuchs, an associate director of the study, coauthored *To Live on This Earth*, a comprehensive synthesis of the findings of the USOE study. In their analysis of the major problems confronting current Indian education, they suggested that there was a "need to re-evaluate goals in terms defined by Indian people themselves."[18]

The Education Division, deluged by all this advice, found it necessary to defend its policies against three powerful forces: the Congress, OEO, and a politically acute Indian leadership. Congress was one of the oldest sparring partners of the Bureau. Time and again it had demonstrated its power to determine the direction of federal Indian policy. In the 1960s, despite the fact that ethnic self-determination dominated the national milieu, Congress itself was dominated by those who had encouraged termination. Congressional committee chairmen who controlled the committees that determined Indian policy—Senate and House Committees on Interior and Insular Affairs, and the Committees on Appropriations —had no inclination to relinquish any of their authority. The seniority system almost invariably guaranteed that these chairmen would be older men who were often unwilling to change long-established policy positions.

Wayne Norvell Aspinall (Democrat, Colorado) typified these leaders. Sixty-three years old when he was appointed chairman of the House Interior and Insular Affairs Committee, he ran the committee according to his own dictates throughout this decade. Indian leaders who knew where the source of power lay were careful to treat Aspinall with the necessary respect. His counterpart in the Senate was Senator Clinton P. Anderson (Democrat, New Mexico), chairman of the Senate committee from 1961 to 1963. Long known as an "out and out assimilationist," Anderson was another veteran of Congress, having served in the Senate since 1949. Anderson's successor, Henry M. Jackson (Democrat, Washington), was a modest exception to the longevity norm. Only fifty-one when he became chairman of the Senate Interior and Insular Affairs Committee, he was one of the younger chairmen. An aspiring politician, Jackson was willing to produce favors for tribes in his own state in return for their support, but his general attitude toward federal Indian policy was akin to that of his predecessor.[19] The combined leadership of Aspinall, Anderson, and Jackson was seemingly invincible.[20]

As a result, congressmen who sought to reform federal Indian policy and in particular Indian education resorted to circumvention of the traditional sources of power. Representative Lloyd Meeds (Democrat, Washington), who later sponsored one of the several Indian education bills considered by Congress in the early 1970s, summarized the attitude of reform-minded congressmen. "The major thrust in the House of Representatives for Indian education reform will not come from the Interior Committee," he observed. "There is not the present impetus there to take the leadership in reform that should be there."[21] Congressional reformers believed that it was impossible for existing leadership on Interior committees to consider a new approach. The status quo, they reasoned, would not change until these chairmen ceased to think in terms of the Department of the Interior, the parent organization of the Bureau of Indian Affairs. As Senator Walter F. Mondale (Democrat, Minnesota), coauthor of the Kennedy-Mondale bill on Indian education (S. 2482), put it succinctly, "[Congress] continually places a higher priority on land and resource policies than it does on the human need programs of Indians."[22]

This was the major thrust of those who wanted to reform Indian policy—to transfer emphasis from natural resources, which was the only link between Indian policy and the rest of the Department of the Interior, to human needs. Some of those who began to think in these terms were Senator Paul J. Fannin (Republican, Arizona),[23] Senator George McGovern (Democrat, South Dakota), Senator Robert F. Kennedy (Democrat, New York), and Senator Mondale. In terms of numbers, these congressmen were not impressive; in terms of concrete results within the system of Indian education, their efforts must await judgment, since many of their recommendations had not been acted upon in the early 1970s. But in terms of influence in remolding the national conscience and perhaps that of the Bureau as well, the effect of their commitment may have been as significant as that of the Meriam Report.

The procedure used by these congressional reformers was to initiate an investigation of Indian education through a newly formed subcommittee. In July 1967, Senator Fannin wrote to Senator Wayne Morse (Democrat, Oregon), chairman of the Senate Committee on Labor and Public Welfare, to suggest that a Special Subcommittee on Indian Education be established.[24] The subcommittee was authorized on August 31, 1967 (S. Res. 165), with Senator Robert Kennedy as its chairman. The purpose of the subcommittee was summarized as an effort to "examine, investigate, and make a complete study of any and all matters pertaining to the education of Indian children."[25] This was a broad challenge, and the investigation stretched out over a period of two years. Its leadership passed from the capable hands of Robert Kennedy following the assassination of June 1968, to the direction of Senator Morse, who remained chairman until his election loss in November of that year. The final chairman was Senator Edward Kennedy, who directed the last months of research and writing, from January to November 1969.

The Kennedy Report was as grave a censure of federal Indian policy as the nation had ever witnessed. Perhaps the fact that many of its recommendations had been made in the Meriam Report some forty years earlier guided the extraordinarily negative conclusions that it drew. It concluded that the "dominant policy of the Federal Government towards the American Indian has been one of coercive assimilation," and that this policy "has had disastrous effects on the education of Indian children." It said the primary results of federal Indian policy have been the following: Schools attended by Indian children have become a "kind of battleground where the Indian child attempts to protect his integrity and identity as an individual by defeating the purposes of the school"; these schools have failed to "understand or adapt to, and in fact often denigrate, cultural differences"; the schools have blamed "their own failures on the Indian student," which reinforces his "defensiveness"; the schools have failed "to recognize the importance and validity of the Indian community"; and the community and child have retaliated "by treating the school as an alien institution." The effect of this type of schooling on Indian children, the report concluded, has been a "dismal record of absenteeism, dropouts, negative self-image, low achievement, and, ultimately, academic failure for many Indian children." For these reasons, the report stated, there has been a "perpetuation of the cycle of poverty which undermines the success of all other Federal programs."[26]

The conclusions were the result of extensive research. The subcommittee reviewed both the history and the literature of Indian education in the United States.[27] It conducted on-site investigations of federal boarding schools, field investigations in representative parts of the country, and field hearings. It held hearings in Washington, D.C. Finally, it made use of professional consultants who investigated organizational failures of the Indian Bureau education program as well as mental health problems of federal boarding schools. The negative findings of the subcommittee were reinforced by sixty separate recommendations. Prominent among these were the inclusion of Indian culture, history, and language as part of the curriculum, and involvement of Indian parents in the education of their children. It is significant that these were the same conclusions drawn by individual writers and studies made of the Bureau during this decade. The Kennedy Report also recommended increased funding, the expansion of some specific programs, most of which were already in existence,[28] and a number of immediate steps, including: a White House conference on American Indian affairs; establishment of a Senate committee on human needs of the American Indian (a direct slap in the face to the Interior and Insular Affairs Committee); upgrading of the position of Commissioner of Indian Affairs to the concurrent position of Assistant Secretary of Indian Affairs; establishment of a graduate institute of Indian languages, history, and culture; and creation of a national board of Indian education. The report made several policy statements on

Indian affairs, including one on termination to the effect that the federal government shall not terminate any services to Indians without consent "by those Indians affected by such termination."[29]

Not surprisingly, the Kennedy Report was ill received by the Bureau of Indian Affairs. Within a few months, an important rebuttal to the report was published by Madison Coombs, a retired Bureau administrator who had been one of the most able leaders in the Education Division. The title of Coombs's rebuttal, "The Indian Student Is *Not* Low Man on the Totem Pole," summarized his thesis. Although he questioned many of the statistics gathered by the subcommittee, his major criticism was with the negativism of the report. "My complaint," he wrote, "is not that I disagree . . . with [the report] basically but that [it is] overstated, slanted, and in some cases downright inaccurate." It was this method, Coombs asserted, that enabled the subcommittee to render an "unbelievably negative" judgment, which in itself was harmful to the progress of Indian education. "In the end," he concluded, "the Senate Subcommittee may have accomplished by indirection what it did not do directly —by painting such a black picture of ineptitude, rigidity, and unconcern on the part of the BIA that that agency's ability to function effectively is no longer credible. . . ."[30]

Coombs's suggestion that the subcommittee might have threatened the Bureau's credibility was in the nature of an anticlimax, since anyone who had studied, even summarily, the history of federal Indian policy was aware that the credibility of the Bureau and the federal government had been questioned by the Indian people since the nation was formed. The right of the subcommittee to render a negative judgment was not the important question. The significance of the Kennedy Report was whether or not its recommendations would improve Indian education. Nonetheless, the Senate Subcommittee on Indian Education, the Office of Economic Opportunity, and the National Council on Indian Opportunity (appointed by President Johnson in 1968) served as a threat to the Education Division. The fact that other groups were tackling the issues that had traditionally been the sole prerogative of the Indian Bureau meant that the divisions within the Bureau, and particularly the Education Division, were forced to defend or revise their existing policies.

Typical of this reaction was Bureau response to the Head Start Program of OEO. This program was funded as one of the numerous projects propelled out of this office after the passage of the Economic Opportunity Act in 1964. An effort to give disadvantaged children the opportunity of preschool learning, it predated the kindergarten program of the Bureau's Education Division, which was unable to begin classes until the fall of 1967. The Education Division's sensitivity to the successes of OEO was betrayed by a comment made by a panel of Bureau educators: While the programs under the Economic Opportunity Act had been of "great value" to Indian children, they observed, "they should be viewed, however, as supplements to, not replacements of, on-going education programs."[31] However, when the Bureau opened its first thirty-four kindergartens, it graciously admitted that they would "complement the Head Start program of the OEO that has operated successfully for several years. . . ."[32]

The financial aid made available through OEO was a significant contribution. The establishment of Rough Rock Demonstration School on the Navajo Reservation was just one example of innovative ventures made possible through OEO funds. By the end of the sixties this office was spending between $60 and $65 million a year on "educational activities that directly or indirectly affected Indians."[33] This was a little more than half of what the Bureau itself had budgeted for education.[34] The combination of funds from OEO and USOE (through federal aid programs to Indian children in public school) provided the first extensive financial commitment to Indian education since the 1930s.

The introduction of innovative ideas in the Education Division owed its origins to the impact of these agencies, as well as to the Senate Subcommittee on Education, and the growing demand by Indians themselves. The combination of these forces led the Bureau to encourage both Indian culture and Indian participation in federal schools. During Zellers's administration the Education Division announced that cross-cultural education would forthwith be considered as an official policy. In order to implement this decision, it began to develop a new curriculum "designed to bring to Indian children a fuller appreciation of their origins and an understanding of their own importance in the history of their country."[35] Although this change was still in the introductory stage, at least one of the programs had already been started. In 1967–68 the Bureau contracted with Bryde, who had worked with the Sioux at Pine Ridge for some twenty-two years, to develop a course that would encourage

Indian heritage. The tentative name of the course was announced as "Acculturational Psychology," or "How to Be a Modern Indian."

One of the most important aspects of cross-cultural education was language. In 1967 bilingual education in the United States received a significant psychological boost in the passage of the Bilingual Education Act, which amended Title VII of the Elementary and Secondary Education Act of 1965. While funding for Indian programs under this act was comparatively small, it was a beginning, and it also stimulated the Bureau to revise its own programs. At this time the Education Division contracted with the Center for Applied Linguistics (founded in 1959) to analyze the difficulties involved in teaching English to Indians. The Center's report, *The Study of the Problems of Teaching English to American Indians* (University of Kansas, 1967) by Sirarpi Ohannessian, made several recommendations. It suggested that all teachers of Indian children have some training in the techniques of teaching English to non-English speakers; that instructional aides (who were usually Indian) be trained as teachers in Indian schools; that public school for Indian children be encouraged wherever possible and that the bordertown program be promoted as second choice for seventh- through twelfth-grade pupils when public schools were unavailable; and that the Bureau conduct research on the processes by which Indians learn English and on Indian attitudes toward English.

The Education Division had been offering English as a Second Language (ESL) instruction to Bureau teachers throughout the decade, but this report spurred interest in the need for greater emphasis on teacher training and on the development of ESL programs. During Zellers's administration the division initiated a newsletter to supplement ESL training sessions. The newsletter, *English for American Indians,* was edited by Ohannessian and prepared by the Center for Applied Linguistics.[36]

The Education Division also contracted with Mrs. T. D. Allen to introduce creative writing in a selected number of federal boarding high schools. Allen, who was well known as an author (*Navajos Have Five Fingers,* Norman, Oklahoma, 1963) and teacher, had been instructor of writing at the American Institute of Indian Arts in Santa Fe before accepting this assignment. At the same time the Bureau signed a contract with the Center for Arts of Indian America, in an effort to improve the teaching of Indian music, drama, and art. In the first experiments of this program, widely scattered projects were begun—a scholarship program for Indian graduate students to train to become drama teachers, a traveling exhibition of Indian art on the Navajo Reservation to train Bureau teachers, and a traveling group of Indian musicians to tour elementary schools on the Navajo Reservation. Finally, Bureau educators were revamping the social science curriculum to make it "relevant to the beliefs and ideals of Indian and Eskimo students."[37]

The decisions to introduce almost all of these projects had been made with little preparation. Few leaders of the sixties remembered or knew about the experiments of the thirties, and those who did recall this period had been forced to disregard it in the intervening years. Thus, Bureau education leaders had to make up for lost time in their efforts to introduce Indian culture into the curriculum.

For Indian participation, however, there was no precedent; even the innovative thirties had failed in this area. The number of breakthroughs in Indian direction that occurred in the late 1960s must be attributed, therefore, to an increasingly articulate Indian leadership, which in turn was aided by the other influences on Bureau education. The results speak for themselves. In the spring of 1966, Rough Rock, the first Indian-directed, locally controlled school, was established. In 1969, Navajo Community College, the first Indian community college, was established. In 1967, Marburger organized the National Indian Education Advisory Commission, a sixteen-member board to advise on policy in Bureau schools. Throughout this brief period the number of Indians on school boards for both public and federal schools increased significantly. In 1969, the National Indian Education Association was founded; it held its first meeting in November of that year.

A decade earlier none of these changes could have taken place; but the events of the sixties had opened up a new role for the Indian people. Widespread federal commitments reinforced by a favorable milieu had led Indian leaders to accept a growing responsibility for determining the nature of their children's education.

12

INDIAN ORGANIZATION
AND LEADERSHIP

The late 1960s witnessed the beginning of self-determination in Indian education. Educational experiments went on almost simultaneously in widely scattered areas and in diverse types of schools. Events from 1966 to 1970 included the development of Indian education organizations; the establishment of individual schools under tribal or community control; increasingly vocal concern with the nature of Bureau schooling; a growing Indian participation in public-school direction and in federal aid programs; and a renewed interest in the study of Indian culture. But there was no parallel revolution in the Bureau itself. Changes in Indian Bureau education, slow in coming, did not begin to appear until the decade came to a close. As Alvin Josephy observed, until 1970 the federal bureaucracy that controlled Indian affairs was still "accountable" to Congress and the Bureau of the Budget rather than to the Indian people.[1]

An incident that occurred in 1966 illustrated the Bureau's attitude toward Indian participation. In April of that year, after easing Philleo Nash out of the commissionership, Secretary of the Interior Udall met with some fifty Bureau administrators to discuss proposed organizational changes. Gathering in Santa Fe in well-publicized but secret sessions, Udall and his select group began to plan the future of the Bureau. When Indian leaders heard of the proposed sessions, they called an emergency meeting in Santa Fe of the National Congress of American Indians. Convinced of their right to be present, they requested that they be included in the Bureau sessions. The request was denied. Vine Deloria, Jr., Executive Director of the

National Congress, commented that "it seemed ironic that the people 'whose future they're planning' were excluded from the talks."[2] Undaunted the Indians continued to meet nearby. Within two days' time—perhaps because of the media coverage Udall's policy of exclusion received—they were invited into the Bureau sessions.[3] The Indians had made their point: They were no longer willing to accept the traditional paternalism of the Bureau. For several years more, however, such victories remained the exception rather than the rule.

What encouragement Indians did receive from the federal government came primarily from Congress and the Office of Economic Opportunity (OEO). Despite new Indian leadership for the Indian Bureau in the late sixties, Commissioner Bennett and his successors continued to be caught in the crossfire between the Department of the Interior, Congress, and the Bureau of the Budget, and the move toward self-determination was painfully slow. Further down the scale, Indian Bureau education directors chafed under restricted authority. Unfortunately, none of the education directors of the late sixties and early seventies stayed in office long enough to be effective.

For these reasons, growth of Indian self-determination in education depended on forces outside of the Bureau. The well-publicized hearings of the Senate Subcommittee on Indian Education permeated the national conscience as well as Congress itself, but their effect on Indian leaders was even greater. When Indian witnesses testified that their children "were being destroyed by the white man's school system"[4] they were not saying anything new, but as these opinions became newsworthy they acquired more force. To read in the *New York Times* a corroboration of what one has known to be true all of his life is a strong form of encouragement. This type of influence appeared to have a spin-off effect on Indian education leaders. In the late sixties and early seventies, when the committee was in the news, a number of education and education-related organizations sprang into being.

The new policy of the Office of Economic Opportunity, which sought to directly involve the recipients of its aid, provided further impetus for self-determination in education. The notion of actually involving the poor was anathema to conservatives, but its effectiveness, at least in the eyes of the Indians, was like a bolt of lightning. The success of the OEO Head Start preschool program was attributed primarily to the fact that Indians were "allowed to operate programs." For the first time in history, Deloria commented, "Indian parents have become excited about education for their children. . . . For the last 100 years, the Government has been doing things for us and telling us what is best for Indians . . . of course there has been no progress. . . ."[5]

The drive for Indian self-determination was fueled by these new forces within the federal government, but knowledge of how to achieve this goal grew out of the practical lessons Indian leaders had been learning since the early 1950s. The political awareness developed in the fight against termination became a formidable tool in the hands of these leaders in the 1960s. Not until they had learned who held the reins of power could they begin to deal with the sources of its strength. As one leader recalled, for years Indians thought they should take their problems to the Commissioner of Indian Affairs. When they discovered that the real power lay elsewhere, then they began to bypass the commissioner.[6]

One of the first signs of the new sophistication of Indian leadership was the widespread use of publicity for influencing national opinion. This tactic, which had been used for years by Indian reform groups, was adopted in the 1960s by individual Indians, new organizations, and tribes. To older leaders this was a new phenomenon; although a few had become well known as authors, their books were not best sellers and their articles seldom appeared in popular publications.[7] A younger generation of leaders who came into their own in this decade viewed the popular press as a sounding board for their ideas. No two individuals exemplify this generation more accurately than N. Scott Momaday (Kiowa) and Vine Deloria, Jr. (Standing Rock Sioux). In spite of the vast difference in their choice of genre, each has a great deal to say in terms of an Indian outlook on the world, and both have been well received, although Deloria's polemics have drawn a more hostile response.[8]

In California a group of Indians selected another media outlet. Determined to acquaint Indians—and, rather incidentally, non-Indians—with the history of Indian peoples, this group founded the Indian Historian Press, which printed the first issue of its quarterly, *The Indian Historian,* in December 1964. Rupert Costo (Coahuilla), spokesman for this venture, edited *Textbooks and the American Indian,* the first book to be published by the press. A vitriolic attack on the traditional treatment of the Indian in American history, this book encouraged California Indians in their drive to ban unfair texts in the California public schools.[9] The young press, therefore, could point to direct results of its venture into the publishing world. Other Indian organizations and tribes followed suit. Anxious to learn from each other, they exchanged ideas at regional and national meetings, where those who had launched into new fields were questioned by representatives from distant tribes. Thus the use of publicity came to be recognized as a valuable asset.[10]

Another manifestation of the new political awareness was the organization of special-interest groups. The first of these was created at the urging of the federal government. The National Indian Education Advisory Commission was one of the few efforts by the Indian Bureau to encourage Indian participation and direction. The organization was not without critics. Because of its direct relationship to the Bureau, people like Rupert Costo assumed that it was doomed from the start. When the group met with Bureau educators for a well-publicized conference in the spring of 1969, Costo claimed that the "workable program" submitted by the Indian educators was "scuttled by the Bureau officialdom in the education division." While Indian scholars continued to play the role of "consultants," Costo concluded the "whites hold the reins of power."[11] But although the Advisory Commission may not have achieved the independence idealized by Costo, it was a positive measure. On the other hand, Costo's criticism, like that of young Indian radicals of this decade, served as a useful goad to federal paternalism. The Education Division may have been at least five years behind where Costo wanted it to be, but it was beginning to change its way of thinking. As Zellers commented in 1969, what is needed is "Indian involvement," "Indian supervision," and "local Indian control."

The National Council on Indian Opportunity, which was created by President Johnson in 1968, also encouraged Indian self-determination through federal sponsorship. Like the National Indian Education Advisory Commission, this organization came under fire from critics, including LaDonna Harris, the Comanche wife of Senator Fred M. Harris of Oklahoma. Mrs. Harris, a member of the National Council, became so disgusted with its lack of activity under the direction of Vice President Spiro Agnew that she resigned her position and formed her own group, which she called Americans for Indian Opportunity. Criticism notwithstanding, the National Council stood behind the Senate Subcommittee on Indian Education when its report was published in 1969. About two months later the Indian members of the National Council formulated their own recommendations for Indian education. In many respects, these were a carbon copy of the subcommittee report. The support of these prominent leaders was further indication of general Indian agreement with the Kennedy Report.[12] While the National Council was not an education-oriented organization, its concern with education was symptomatic of an increasingly common theme among Indian leaders, many of whom believed that education was both the source of their problems and the hope for their solution.

That these federally sponsored organizations were sharply criticized by Indian leaders was indicative of the mood of the late sixties. The new perspective dictated that independent groups be created as an alternative, and Indian educators therefore met to form their own organization. Spurred by the strong education leadership in the state of Minnesota, the National Indian Education Association held its first meeting in Minneapolis on November 20–21, 1969. The Minnesota Indians were taking a bold step in assuming that there would be a nucleus of educators to make the conference worthwhile; ten years earlier the success of such a gathering would have been dubious, as indicated by the youth of the leaders in Indian education. In 1969, however, the timing was right, and the success of the meeting guaranteed that it would be an annual gathering. For one more year the association met in Minneapolis, but in 1972, it moved to Albuquerque, where the host and cosponsor was Diné Bi'Olta, the Navajo Education Association, formed in 1970. At the third meeting, it was observed that the success of the two previous conferences meant "that the American Indian people stand firmly behind an effort to attack the problems of Indian Education on a national level." Reaffirming the importance of self-determination, the directors of the conference added, "Because a major concern is the development and maintenance of forceful leadership from within, the National Education Conference is again being planned *by* Indian people *for* Indian people."[13]

Between national conferences, one of the aims of the association was to provide the federal government with Indian response to legislation and administrative measures affecting Indian education. Between 1970 and 1972 the most compelling project was working with legislators who were writing Indian education bills for Congress. William G. Demmert, Jr., treasurer of the association, served as a go-between for legislators and Indian educators.[14] Demmert, who later became Director of Indian Education Programs for the Indian Bureau, was responsible for surveying Native Americans to determine their reaction to proposed legislation. The response of association members to questionnaires was disappointing, for it indicated that the interest level was much lower than expected.[15] Unfortunately, it also exemplified the legacy of paternalism, which had spun its tight web under decades of federal control. In countering this legacy, education activists like Demmert realized that turning self-determination into reality required more than a tacit agreement with the concept itself. Thus, while the national conferences provided a unique opportunity for educators to exchange ideas and revealed that experiments were widespread and diversified, at the same time they demonstrated that Indian participation and direction were just beginning.

The National Indian Education Association was the educators' equivalent of the National Congress of American Indians. Like other groups that began to form during this period, it represented not a threat to the National Congress, but one of a number of vehicles for more specialized interests. The National Indian Leadership Training Program was founded primarily to solve economic problems within tribes. The National Tribal Chairman's Association (April 25, 1971) was intended to respond promptly to measures taken by the federal government; its size alone gave it a maneuverability that the oftentimes unwieldy National Congress lacked.[16] A short-lived group that also formed during this period was the staff of Indian consultants who conducted the survey "Project Outreach." This survey, which assisted the National Council on Indian Opportunity, sought to assess "tribal attitudes" and to appraise the "extent of tribal council experience in administering Federal assistance programs." The survey, completed in about two months, managed to present a representative cross-section of Indian attitudes.[17]

In December 1971, a group of representatives from several Indian schools formed the Coalition of Indian Controlled School Boards (CICSB), a group of Indian-controlled schools and organizations concerned with educational reform. Dissatisfied with the Indian Bureau's "strong resistance" to tribal control,[18] and convinced that "if American Indians are to survive as a people, they must develop and control their own schools," these educators determined to create an alternative solution.[19] In its first year, the coalition provided technical assistance in all aspects of education for Indian school boards, communities, and organizations, and served as a clearing house for information on legislation and other matters pertaining to Indian education. Less than two years after it was formed, CICSB was serving eighty-seven schools and organizations.

The significant feature of almost all of these new organizations was that they were concerned with Indian control of education. Project Outreach emphasized that tribes were generally dissatisfied with education and said that both Indian Bureau and public schools were "seriously deficient in terms of the education of the Indian students they serve." In conclusion, it recommended that "greater Indian control of the schools that served Indians was necessary in order that these schools be relevant to the needs of Indian children."[20] These conclusions were supported by the National Indian Leadership Training Program. Myron Jones (Tuscarora), director of the education work of this program,[21] implemented the recommendations of Project Outreach through his unique plan for teaching Indian parents about federal programs for their children. Jones reasoned that if parents understood the complexities of these programs they would feel better qualified to participate in their direction.[22]

Many of the early successes in Indian self-determination appear to have been centered in the Southwest. Actually, however, the movement was spread across the country. At the end of the 1960s there was more talk than action. This was due, in part, to the fact that many Indians had been trapped by non-Indian culture for upwards of two hundred years and relearning traditions was not easy. The reawakening of cultural awareness was often a slow process. In some places—the deep woods of northern Maine, for example—the strength of these traditions, including language, was surprisingly strong. In others, like the perimeters of Puget Sound in western Washington, where languages themselves were almost gone, "tradition" might be limited to a different value system. Those who had to pull the remnants of their culture together were not as fortunate as the Southwest Indians, nor could they use the same means as these tribes. In an area where children were enrolled in public school, like the Yakima Reservation in central Washington, it was not practical even to consider establishing a separate school. However, efforts could be made toward introducing Indian history, culture, and sometimes even language into the public-school system. In order to make this possible, Indians of a given area had to participate actively in the operation of the school, seeking positions on the school board and encouraging young people to become teachers and return to the area after their schooling.

The Yakima education programs exemplified the initial steps being taken by these more acculturated tribes. Stanley Smartlowit, who had been chairman of Yakima education since 1963, was a practical person who felt that what was needed was more action. "It's time . . . we [the American Indian] started doing something about education instead of just talking about our problems," he observed in 1970.[23] In his first seven years in office, Yakima school enrollment climbed from 1,000 to 1,600. It was his aim to encourage more and more of these children to complete high school and go on for post–high school work.[24]

Smartlowit established a number of projects aimed at achieving this goal. The first of these was a remedial summer program held at Camp Chaparral, a remote site at the base of Mount Adams. In order to be eligible for this program, children had to be at least two years behind in at least one course in school. At the camp the children were not confronted by the cultural barrier of public school, and in the familiar environment of their own people they made noteworthy progress. The second project, with the cooperation of Central Washington State University, was a summer program begun on the campus in 1969. Students who attended this session had one of three reasons for enrolling: They were high school dropouts; they needed the credits for graduation; or they sought preparation for college. This course resembled the one offered at Haskell, except that Yakimas who attended this session paid their own tuition and were perhaps more highly motivated. Out of forty-one who were enrolled, thirty-eight finished the course.

The third project initiated by Smartlowit was a summer-school program at one of the local public-schools. Concentrating on course work in Yakima history and culture, the program attracted sixty-five students who came from all over the reservation to learn about their own traditions. This program owed its success to Smartlowit's practical philosophy. For several years he had worked to develop a rapport between the tribe and the local school boards. Toward this end he had established an annual conservation program for public-school children. Each May, the children were taken in groups of eighty for a three-day excursion to Camp Chaparral, where they were taught the rudiments of the tribe's conservation methods. By 1969 the public school system began to repay these efforts, and tribal use of public-school facilities was a concrete illustration of the new cooperation.

In other areas, progress came more slowly. Very few Yakimas were members of local school boards. The tribal education fund, which had jumped from $10,000 in 1953 to $100,000 in 1969 (plus a trust fund that provided $300,000 annually for selected young people), was increasingly pressed to meet the growing need. Another difficulty was the lack of returning college graduates. Those who were most likely to return, Smartlowit pointed out, were students from vocational schools. In spite of continuing problems, however, the educational program of the Yakimas had progressed remarkably in this decade of change.

Successful programs of other tribes were scattered and, at best, uneven. In California, one of the chief accomplishments of the many small groups of Indians was the textbook battle, which had finally given legal support to the minority case. In southern Idaho, the Shoshone-Bannocks secured the addition of Indian arts and crafts at Blackfoot High School. They were also writing their own version of state history, which they planned to submit to the school board. In the Browning High School in Montana, the Blackfeet were successful in having Indian history added to the curriculum. In Maine, the Algonquins were very active during the last part of the decade. In 1966 the state of Maine had, somewhat belatedly, established a department of Indian education. In this instance the state, rather than the Indian Bureau, was responsible for Indians living within its boundaries. By 1970 these Indians had obtained autonomy of educational control. In Bar Harbor, Maine, they established Independent International Indian High School, which drew its student body from thirty-five reservations with a total population of 20,000. With a 90-percent school dropout rate to overcome, the Maine Indians had a challenge ahead of them, but their eagerness was infectious and they were optimistic about gains.[25]

In western Washington, on the slopes of the Olympic Mountains, the Quinault Indians were learning Indian culture, including arts and crafts, from Clarence Pickernell, a Quinault artist and teacher. "A decade ago," Pickernell observed at the end of the sixties, "I would have said the culture and traditions were gone, dead. But when I came back from overseas . . . a change had taken place. There was a spontanteous re-awakening." Pickernell added that he saw the relocation program as perhaps the chief cause for the change. The negative effect of this program caused a whiplash reaction among Indians, who then realized "how much they needed depth and strength to their cultural roots." In the city they were unable to "melt" into the non-Indian culture, yet they had also "lost touch" with their own culture.[26] Although this was not the main cause for the reawakening, it may have contributed to a renewed search for indentity, which was expressed according to the needs and circumstances of individual groups of Indians.

At the end of the decade Indian Bureau boarding schools began to feel the pressure of Indian self-determination. The Education Division responded by introducing a number of curriculum changes and by instituting all-Indian school boards for each of the boarding schools. These boards represented the major tribes that made up the student body for each school. In addition, the Education Division initiated a series of program reviews for some of the schools with the tentative idea of turning over the operation of at least one of them to a private firm. However, during the first review, which was of Chilocco, Bureau education leaders stumbled into a hornets' nest. The review of this school coincided roughly with a national exposé of brutality and harsh treatment of the Chilocco students. The uproar that followed involved Congress, the press, Indian groups, and the students themselves, who rose to the defense of their school. As a result, rather than introducing what it had hoped would be a quiet change, the Education Division was forced to reshuffle its own staff at the school and drop its plans. At the same time, the Department of the Interior issued a statement to concerned Indian leaders that it would not make any change opposed by the "will of the Indian people" themselves.[27] The Education Division was again reminded that major policy shifts were no longer feasible without Indian approval.

In other parts of the country tribes began to pressure the Bureau to make boarding schools responsible to Indians who lived in the immediate area. This was the first indication of Indian response to the Navajo and Alaskan Native programs, which involved extensive transportation and were achieved at the expense of Indians who had depended upon the facilities used by these programs. In the 1960s, the tribal groups of Nevada began a campaign to restore Stewart, the only boarding school in the area, to Nevada Indians and other citizens of the state. Since this school was "originally organized to serve Nevada interests," wrote one of the groups, it should "once again fill the need of Nevadans for vocational training."[28] The tribes of the Pacific Northwest had suffered a similar setback at Chemawa, the only boarding school remaining in the area. By the mid 1960s the entire student body of Chemawa was either Navajo or Alaskan Native. At the end of the decade, after a persistent struggle, Northwest tribes were once again permitted to send students to the school. These demands showed that Indians were not necessarily opposed to boarding schools; in many cases they preferred to send their children to a school attended only by Indians. However, they did want more control over these schools and were beginning to see some progress toward this goal.

The national media were quick to expand upon the changes taking place among the Indian people. In the late sixties and early seventies, almost every popular national magazine ran at least one article on Indians.[29] At the same time colleges and universities were beset with requests to establish Indian Studies programs, to increase their scholarship aid to Indian students, and to consider developing a major in American Indian Studies.[30] Quick to respond to the potential for federal grants, many schools planned programs that could be supported by federal money. Although this idea was boosted by an increasingly active Indian youth, part of the reason for its rapid spread was the increased national interest in minority groups. Programs in Black Studies, Chicano Studies, and Indian Studies were often established simultaneously.

This was a sudden change, for as late as the mid 1960s the idea of Indian Studies programs was not even under consideration. Even in the traditional areas of Indian interest like Arizona and New Mexico, the only school that had expressed a concern for Indian education was Arizona State University, the first school in the nation to offer courses on Indian education. The Arizona State Indian Education Center was founded in 1954 and provided both graduate and undergraduate courses.[31] By the early 1970s, however, Indian Studies programs had sprung up on numerous campuses, and several major institutions were already revising their programs in terms of establishing a major in this subject.[32] At the same time, Utah State University received funding to initiate a program, scheduled to begin in 1970, to train administrators and guidance counselors who wanted to work with Indian youth in Bureau or public schools.[33] The program directors expressed the hope that most of the applicants would be Indian. Another innovative idea was the American Indian Law Center at the University of New Mexico. This center, begun in 1967, was developed in answer to the tremendous demand for Indian lawyers. In 1966 there were only twelve Indian attorneys in the country; in 1971, under the direction of this center, seventy-six Indians were enrolled in law schools. Thus, by the early 1970s, the few schools that had aided Indian students since their inception, such as Bacone College, Oklahoma, and Fort Lewis College, Durango, Colorado, suddenly found their numbers swelling as higher institutions jumped on the bandwagon of ethnic studies.[34]

Private foundations also responded to the growing interest in ethnic groups by increasing financial aid. Whereas OEO was the new benefactor in the federal government, in private aid the crucial source of support was the foundation. In its second year of operation Navajo Community College (NCC) received more than a half-million dollars from three private foundations. The National Indian Leadership Training Program was totally dependent on private funding. The American Scholarship Grants program received part of its funds from the federal government but could not have existed without private funding. The Rocky Boy School District (Montana) had to turn to private funding to stay afloat. Foundations, however, were not the only source of aid. As Roessel discovered in his fund-raising trips for NCC, private corporations were often willing to help. "Some people realize," he observed, "that this is the sort of thing that industry and people who have money . . . need to do . . . to help people to help themselves."[35] Standard Oil planned to construct a gas station at the new NCC campus at a cost of $1 million and to teach standard mechanics and gas-station operation. Other companies donated large gifts to the general operation of the school. In order to survive, it had become necessary for Indian leaders, whether tribal education directors, project chairmen, or board members of Indian-controlled schools, to tap this reservoir of private money.[36] This potential assistance had been available for generations, but it failed to serve Indian people until the late 1960s.

The decade of the sixties, therefore, could be seen as the testing ground for the first steps in Indian self-determination in education. Indian leaders began to apply their political knowledge toward educational goals. They had become aware of the sources of financial aid, both federal and private, and they knew how to construct a convincing case for the needs of their people. They had learned where the sources of political power lay, and they began to go directly to these sources. Finally, they began to clarify in their own minds the nature of their most pressing educational problems. They saw the need of establishing primary educational goals, and of determining the procedure they should follow to reach these goals.

The challenge that lay before them was awesome, but because they had been powerless even to attempt to meet it for so many generations, they now revealed a courage and a determination that few peoples have demonstrated. Throughout the struggle, they managed to cling to their traditional view of education as a means of perpetuating their cultural heritage. In this perspective, their early successes in educational control, while few in number, were great symbolic victories.

13

INDIAN-CONTROLLED SCHOOLS

In the decade of the 1950s it did not seem that within a few years self-determination would become a potent force. Indian leadership was pressed by more immediate challenges and community education remained in the background as long as termination loomed in every session of Congress. Nor was there any indication that funding would have been available. Economy in federal government spending was still the order of the day. But during this decade there was a singular experiment with community schooling on the Navajo Reservation. While this experiment was noteworthy chiefly because it was the exception rather than the norm, it also was a forerunner for the late 1960s.

Robert A. Roessel, Jr., one of the leading figures in Indian education, tackled his first educational challenges in the hostile environment of the 1950s. An Indian Service employee and an Anglo-American, Roessel began his first community school experiment in the Navajo community of Round Rock. Tremendously enthusiastic, he encouraged involvement of everyone in the area. Gradually, as he recalled later, the whole community developed an interest and, "through its own actions and activities, achieved its pre-determined goals."[1] In Round Rock the community accepted the responsibility for creating its own education program, including adult education.

Shortly thereafter Roessel took on a new educational challenge in the community of Low Mountain. In this experiment he had the valuable assistance of his wife, Ruth, a Navajo whom he had met at

Round Rock. Low Mountain had a number of inherent disadvantages, chief of which was its impassable roads. The community volunteered "thousands of hours" to improve the roads and facilitate school transportation, but in spite of the fact that the bad roads were one of the chief barriers to community schools on this reservation, the Bureau refused to help, maintaining that the expense of improving them was prohibitive.[2] A second impediment to success at Low Mountain was Roessel's own willful, independent personality. His direction of the project irritated the Bureau administrators who read the Low Mountain reports. Thus, in spite of an apparently honest commitment by the community, the Low Mountain experiment died for lack of Bureau support. As Roessel described it, the "community withdrew from the school . . . and reverted to 'let the government do it.' "[3] Nonetheless, within the next decade further experiments on the Navajo Reservation demonstrated that a more congenial milieu could lead to a greater degree of success.

In the early 1960s, however, Bureau educators still offered little concrete support to the community-school idea. This was illustrated by the wide gap between declaration and implementation of policy. On more than one occasion, Hildegard Thompson professed a belief in this concept. Bemoaning the Bureau's lack of community education, which would lead to an "intimacy between parents and school," she asked, might it not be "far more economical in social costs to take the school to the community than it is to take the children out of the community?"[4] But her administration did little to encourage community schools. From 1950 to 1965 one of the top priorities of the Branch of Education was increased enrollment. Consequently, during this time it opened Intermountain Indian School, which housed about 2,000 students, began the bordertown program, shifted Alaskan Native Americans thousands of miles from home to attend boarding school, and encouraged public school for Indian children. None of these remotely resembled the concept of the community school.

By the mid 1960s conditions had altered, and experiments with community schools appeared to be more feasible. Bureau education leadership was changing, and new attitudes seemed probable; the Office of Economic Opportunity (OEO) had developed as a new source of funds; and Indians themselves had begun to take an active interest in community education. Although community schools were needed on many reservations, Alaskan Natives and Navajos had the most pressing need simply because so many of their children were sent long distances from home. On the Navajo Reservation near Chinle, Arizona, circumstances were particularly favorable for an experimental community school. A newly constructed $3-million Bureau boarding school had not yet been put into operation and was available. Financial support appeared likely, since at the urging of Allen D. Yazzie, chairman of the Navajo Tribal Education Committee, and Roessel, among others, OEO had agreed that it should fund an experimental school run by the Navajos themselves.[5] In the spring of 1966, the Bureau of Indian Affairs and the Office of Economic Opportunity signed a contract with a group of Navajo leaders who incorporated under the name of DINE, and Rough Rock Demonstration School was born.[6]

By 1973 eleven additional schools had contracted with the Bureau to become locally directed community enterprises (see the list following Map 2), but none of these was as well known or widely publicized as Rough Rock, and most of them did not sign their first contracts before 1970. For several years, therefore, Rough Rock stood as a solitary example of an active experiment in Indian self-determination in education. This made it difficult for the school to proceed under normal conditions. The first two directors, Roessel and his successor, Dillon Platero (Navajo), were deluged with visitors.[7] The directors were also very much aware of the distant yet pervasive presence of the Bureau: Even though the Indian Bureau had no direct control over the administration, the amount of Bureau funding gave it the right to disapprove contract renewal.[8]

As one of the partners to the contract, OEO was also concerned about the school. In 1968 it contracted with Donald A. Erickson, education professor at the University of Chicago, for an official survey. Erickson had been a proponent of Rough Rock and a critic of the Indian Bureau, but his findings in the survey led him to change his mind on both counts. When the study compared Rough Rock with Rocky Point, an Indian Bureau school on the reservation, Rough Rock came out a poor second. Erickson pointed out that Rough Rock's Navajo school board virtually ignored the academic program. Its primary concern was development of the school as a means for economic improvement in the community. While the final report recommended re-funding, Erickson's reservations led several members of the academic community to launch a severe attack on the study. Liberal proponents of self-determination were afraid that Rough Rock would not be touted as an exemplary model for Indian-directed schools.[9]

As a community enterprise, Rough Rock gave an economic boost to local families. The community itself had voted in favor of its establishment and found that it brought many advantages, including employment, laundry facilities, and some improvement in homes and diet. The school board was made up of local residents and the dorm attendents were parents who worked one of two shifts, from September to December or from January to June. Parents were invited to visit the school at any time, and they were also encouraged to participate in a summer adult-education program.[10] Perhaps the most significant demonstration of the meaning of Rough Rock for the Navajo people was the name they gave to it. In Navajo, Bureau schools were called "Washington bi 'olta," or "school of the federal government." Public schools were called "Bilagaana Yazhi bi 'olta," or "white children's school." Mission schools were called "ee'neeshoodii bi 'olta," or "the long coats' school." Rough Rock was the only school called "Diné bi 'olta"—"the Navajos' school."[11]

The Navajo Curriculum Center, funded early in 1967 by a grant from Title I of the Elementary and Secondary Education Act, was an innovative program within the school. This project was undertaken to fill the need for materials in teaching Navajo history and culture, an essential part of the daily curriculum. When the directors, supported by the community, determined to add Navajo history and culture to the curriculum, they discovered that what they had to work with was still basically an oral tradition. The Curriculum Center was an attempt to transform the oral tradition into the written word. Although its initial works were published in English, they were based on Navajo stories and were enlivened by illustrations by Navajo artists.[12]

During its first four years Rough Rock remained a unique school and it appeared as though its unusual position might not be duplicated. There were several reasons why other schools of its type did not develop quickly. In the first place, the thread of its existence was dependent on the financial good will of the federal government, and it was doubtful if another school would be equally fortunate in terms of lavish funding. The initial budget, with the combined funding of the two federal agencies, came to a total of $636,000—almost twice the budget for a boarding school the size of Rough Rock.[13] Secondly, the impetus for the school was largely due to the persistent effort of several people who were committed to self-determination. Roessel summarized this attitude shortly after he was appointed director. "To me it is a significant step in the right direction," he wrote, for it "places the responsibility and decision-making in the hands of the Indian people and this is something that I feel is so extremely important."[14] This was especially important for the Navajos because of the size of their reservation and the life style of the people. In areas where children attended public schools, community control had to be achieved through other means, such as membership on school boards and in parent-teacher organizations. The third reason for Rough Rock's uniqueness was, therefore, its unusually close relationship with the community.

Even though Bureau educators were skeptical of this experiment, perhaps the most important evaluation for the Navajos themselves was made by four Navajo leaders invited by the Rough Rock Board of Education to analyze the school. Their report, published in 1969, concluded that the involvement of parents and community in the school led to a "feeling of great pride in the people—pride in what they are doing for their community, pride in what they are doing for their school, and pride in what they are doing for their children." The report had a number of critical comments but hastened to point out that the parents themselves understood there had not been "total achievement"; still, their children were getting "better education" because it was community education and tribal education. "Community education," the evaluators observed, "is what Navajos as well as other tribes are working to get. . . . It is a system that binds people together—much stronger. It is an ideal most looked for but mostly rarely achieved. . . . But at Rough Rock," they added, "it is being achieved."[15]

In their general conclusions, the evaluators stressed that Rough Rock should continue its operation because it served as a model for other Navajo community schools and also as an example to other schools.[16] In 1970, four years after Rough Rock opened, a small Navajo community in western New Mexico took these words to heart and opened its own high school. The village of Ramah is situated among the low hills that skirt the edge of the Zuni Reservation. Basically a Navajo community, geographically it is some distance from the main Navajo Reservation and must make some decisions for itself. In 1968, when the local high school was closed because of deteriorating facilities, parents were forced to send their children to distant boarding schools. The nearest facilities—more than twenty miles away—were unavailable because the school district could not provide adequate transportation.[17] Unhappy with this situation and anxious to have their children home, parents determined to form their own school board through a local election and to apply to the Indian Bureau for a grant. In 1970, a contract was negotiated between the Ramah school board and the Indian Bureau, which agreed to provide financial aid equivalent to what it would cost to support a comparable boarding school.[18] In addition, OEO provided a grant of $65,000 to renovate the deteriorated school structure.

In the fall of 1970 it appeared that the Ramah community had won a significant victory. Its success drew national attention and the *Washington Post* carried an article heralding the importance of the achievement.[19] But the battle was not over, and in some respects it had just begun. One of the first opponents of Ramah's struggle for self-determination was the New Mexico State Department of Public Instruction. In a bitter dispute waged over a five-month period from September 1970 to January 1971, Leonard DeLayo, State School Superintendent, sought to impose state curriculum and teacher standards upon the school. DeLayo demanded that Ramah High School submit an "approvable plan of operation" to the State Board of Education. Ramah School Board members submitted that their plan would not conform to state regulations because their conditions and their aims were not the same as those in other parts of the state. They wanted to gear their curriculum to include Navajo culture and history and, as a result, employed teacher aides who did not meet the state requirement of a high school diploma. After DeLayo threatened to close the school on the grounds that parents were violating the state compulsory attendance law by sending their children to an unaccredited school, community leaders took their case to Senator Joseph M. Montoya (Democrat, New Mexico). Within a few weeks after Montoya's pledge of assistance, the State Board of Education had granted "conditional approval" to Ramah High School. This victory was vital for the school, for without approval it could not receive any of the federal programs administered through the State Department of Public Instruction.

It was still a struggle for the school to achieve its goals. Its curriculum and teaching, like those of Rough Rock, failed to satisfy educators from the Indian Bureau. Madison Coombs pointed out that the Indian Bureau evaluative visit to Ramah "found the school program a shambles." Lumping Rough Rock and Ramah into one category, Coombs concluded that they "have furnished clear evidence that control and not the quality of education is the significant goal of the sponsors."[20] These communities might have agreed with Coombs's emphasis on control—without question, this was a necessary prerequisite for developing the kind of school they wanted for their children. But the question of quality was debatable, because quality to a Bureau educator was obviously not quality to many Indian parents. Both Ramah and Rough Rock had achieved one of the primary goals of the Navajo people, community control. Whether they would be able to give Navajo children a better education than they would receive in a Bureau school remained to be seen.[21]

The mood for Indian control was spreading across the country. The next successful effort belonged to Chippewa and Cree Indians on the Rocky Boy Reservation in northern Montana. Like the Ramah Navajos, these Indians had lost control of their school, but their experience had a new twist. In the late 1950s the Indian Bureau school on this reservation was transferred to public-school control and became part of the Havre School District. During the following twelve years the Indians grew increasingly dissatisfied with the situation. Control and direction of their children's education was in the hands of a school board and administration located in the primarily non-Indian community of Havre, some thirty miles away. The Indian community tried for several years to establish a separate school district before they gained sufficient political power to do so. In 1970, the same year that Ramah High School came under the control of the Navajo community, an all-Indian board of education assumed control of the Rocky Boy School District. The Rocky Boy directors also found that with the attainment of self-control their problems had just began. Finances were their greatest challenge. Dependent almost entirely upon impacted-area aid, the school was also forced to seek funds from private sources and additional federal sources.[22]

The immense pressures brought to bear on these schools made it clear that education was an established business that did not welcome newcomers. All of the complexities of administration, funding, and budgeting, which were well known to the establishment, had to be mastered by these Indian communities in order for their ventures to survive. Their initial successes, however, indicate that they were beginning to understand the game. Indian political leaders had already proved that it was profitable to emulate procedures used by non-Indian politicians, and Indian education leaders began to use tactics common among non-Indian educators. The appeal by the Ramah community to Senator Montoya suggests that these Navajos had learned one lesson: When threatened by opposition at one level, negotiate with a higher level of power.

Perhaps the most significant example of this new political awareness was the establishment of Navajo Community College (NCC), the first Indian-controlled and Indian-directed college in the country. NCC was founded on July 1, 1968, and classes began on Janury 20, 1969. The school, lacking a physical plant, was forced to share facilities with the Indian Bureau boarding school at Many Farms. This location was separated from the Rough Rock Demonstration School by less than twenty miles of typical Navajo road: hard-packed dirt in cold weather, dust in warm weather, and an almost impassable surface in rain and snow. NCC's proximity to Rough Rock, both geographically and chronologically, was not a coincidence. Several of the people who had promoted Rough Rock were also instrumental in the founding of NCC. In addition, Rough Rock had given the Navajo people confidence in determining their own institutions, and it provided much of the impetus for this second Navajo school.

The initial idea of NCC was in the air long before the school opened, but funds for researching the project were not available until OEO became interested. In 1965 OEO began a Community Action Project that led to a joint research effort by the Navajo Tribe and Arizona State University. Thereafter, actually starting up the school required intensive work by the Tribal Education Committee, Raymond Nakai, tribal chairman, Graham Holmes, Navajo Area Director, and Robert and Ruth Roessel. Their work was made easier by increasingly favorable circumstances. As Roessel recalled, the "climate was ripe" for the establishment of a college. The Navajo people were ready for a second experiment and the "top people" at the Indian Bureau were willing to give their support.[23] With this backing, the nucleus of leaders went "begging" for financial aid, as Roessel termed it. In the first year they secured support from several sources, a pattern of financing followed in the ensuing years. In 1968–69, donations included $450,000 (to be given annually for three years) from OEO; $250,000 from the Navajo Tribe; and $60,000 from the Donner Foundation, with the promise of $100,000 for the following year.[24]

Roessel was rewarded for his efforts by the honor of becoming the first president of the college. He stepped from the position of director of Rough Rock Demonstration School to the presidency of Navajo Community College. He had, indeed, come a long way from the failure at Low Mountain in the 1950s. In retrospect, he attributed the successes of Indian self-determination to the Navajo people and to the changes in the Indian Bureau. The Bureau that he had dealt with in the mid 1950s, he pointed out, was not the same organization that he cooperated with at the end of the 1960s. "The Bureau," he observed in 1970, "has finally learned to listen to Indians."[25] Furthermore, he suggested that the change had evolved since the opening of Rough Rock. Although Bureau leaders supported NCC (with a few exceptions), generally they had been unfavorable toward Rough Rock. It appeared, therefore, that NCC was riding the crest of the wave of Indian self-determination and that the timing of its entrance into the education world was well gauged.

In spite of Roessel's tremendous contributions to Navajo education, his leadership was often criticized. A dynamic, assertive individual, he did not have a compromising nature, and some suggested that his role in these Navajo experiments was too dominant. Despite his obvious support of Indian leadership, he was an Anglo, and there was some irony in the fact that one of the most vocal supporters of Indian self-determination was not an Indian. This may have led Roessel to modify his position when self-determination turned against Anglos in the operational procedures of NCC. When the college decided that non-Indian faculty members should have no voice in the decision-making process of the school, Roessel was distressed, saying that the Board of Regents should try to tear walls down rather than to build them up.[26]

Perhaps even Roessel had not anticipated the zeal of Indian control when given full rein. As if in response to Roessel's criticism, Ned Hatathli, Navajo president of NCC who succeeded Roessel after one year, stated the position of the college vis-à-vis self determination: "This is an Indian owned and an Indian operated institution," Hatathli said, "and we certainly don't want any people other than

Indian to dictate to us what is good for us."[27] The college sought to solidify this position through direction by two all-Navajo governing bodies. The lesser of these was the All Indian Council, a board composed equally of faculty, students, and administration, which established the day-to-day policy of the school but in reality was only a recommending body. Final policy decisions were made by the Board of Regents, made up of five at-large members representing the five reservation agencies, the tribal chairman, and the student body president. The college gave no encouragement to non-Indians except for their financial contributions and their willingness to be on the faculty. In 1970, the faculty was only one-third Navajo and forty percent Indian. However, as Hatathli pointed out, non-Indian faculty members were simply "working themselves out of a job."[28] While they could teach as long as there was a need, there was no guarantee that they would be rehired if an Indian applied to take their place.

The curriculum at NCC was consistent with this attitude. One of the major areas of emphasis was the Navajo Studies program, which offered courses not only in arts and crafts but in areas that had seldom been included in Bureau schools. Navajo history and culture, a three-semester course in which the final semester dealt with current tribal problems, was taught in Navajo with one section offered in English. Also included in the offerings that dealt exclusively with Navajo affairs were courses in Navajo culture change, the Navajo language, and Navajo creative writing. In addition, the curriculum concentrated on a wide variety of materials pertaining to the American Indian. There were courses in the history of Indian affairs and in Anglo-Indian relations. All of these approached their subject matter from an Indian point of view. The Navajos were attempting to make up for lost decades when their cultural heritage was excluded from their children's education.

Other requirements, however, necessitated a broader curriculum. The college attempted to prepare its students for one of two alternatives. For those who would transfer from NCC to a four-year institution, the curriculum included courses to meet the requirements of four-year schools.[29] It was felt that these students were particulary in need of the Navajo Studies program. The aim of this course work was, in essence, to teach them who they were in order that they might not suffer an identity crisis when thrust into Anglo society. For those students who would seek a job on the reservation,

NCC offered courses applicable to reservation job opportunities-nursing, secretarial training, welding, auto mechanics, agriculture, commercial art, drafting, and so on. By attempting to match job training with job opportunity, NCC sought to improve upon the often-criticized vocational training program of the Indian Bureau.

For the founders of Navajo Community College, the thirteenth of April, 1972, was a milestone. On this date, at the site where the school's new campus was to be constructed, the ground was blessed in the Navajo way in a ceremony dedicated to the future. The location was Tsaile Lake, where a tract of land had been purchased by the tribal council at the foot of the Lukachukai Mountains, some forty miles northeast of Window Rock and on the eastern edge of Canyon de Chelly. The event was the result of years of work, culminating in the passage of the Navajo Community College bill by Congress in December 1971. This bill guaranteed the largest single addition to the school's financial sources. It provided that the Indian Bureau would allocate funds to NCC equivalent to Bureau funding for Indian students in Bureau post–high school programs such as Haskell Indian Junior College. Since this amount alone would provide 65 percent of the total budget for NCC, it was essential to assured future growth. With the passage of this legislation, NCC was able to begin the first phase of construction, a $5.3-million project that would provide facilities for the initial stage of 500 students. As more funds were procured, the school eventually planned to expand to a total student body of 1,500.

Thus, after only a brief venture in the complex world of higher education, NCC, as Roessel concluded, had "gone further and faster than anyone had a right to expect." Yet even Roessel, whose enthusiasm had been fed by these recent successes, was pessimistic about the possibility of other Indian community colleges.[30] He had already concluded that the reason for the overwhelming response to NCC's financial need was the unique nature of the school. If there were a dozen like it, he explained, they would all be in trouble. The unusual appeal of this college had evoked such a wide range of funding that Roessel compared it to "God and Motherhood—nobody's against it."[31] Financial success notwithstanding, perhaps the most important feature of NCC, and of other Indian-controlled schools, was that it belonged to the Indian people. Here, all ages of students, from eighteen to thirty-five, regardless of their former education, could come and learn. Here was an institution that 40,000

Navajo children in school in 1969 could look forward to attending. As the 1971 student-body president, Raymond Brown, observed, "NCC is what we have always needed. It . . . teaches our young people to become leaders among our own people . . . it teaches what we, the American Indian want to learn."[32]

14

INDIAN CHILDREN AND
PUBLIC SCHOOLS: 1945–1972

Despite the numerous shortcomings of the Johnson-O'Malley program, Indian enrollment in public schools continued to grow in the postwar years. By 1953 there were 51,000 Indian children in public schools, 31,000 of them in schools that received Johnson-O'Malley (J-O'M) funds. The number of participating states had jumped to fifteen, and individual districts in other states as well as the Territory of Alaska were also in the program. Most states administered the federal funds themselves.

The year 1953, which was the nineteenth year of the J-O'M program, was a dividing line for Indian education in public schools. It marked the end of a single federal program to aid public schools and launched the new sources of aid that would take more and more of the burden away from J-O'M itself. However, the new legislation had no immediate effect on the use of funds established by J-O'M. Although public schools often received additional appropriations through the new programs, they continued to use them in their general school budgets.

In 1950 Congress passed two bills that became known as the "federally impacted area" legislation (P.L. 874, 64 *Stat.*, 1100 and P.L. 815, 64 *Stat.*, 967–78). These laws were intended to provide federal funds to compensate school districts for the financial burdens placed on them by federal activities. P.L. 874 was to provide funds for general operating expenses, in lieu of local taxes; P.L. 815 was to provide funds for school construction in federally impacted areas. When these laws were passed, they were not applied to

Indians; they were intended primarily for areas that supported military installations. In 1953, however, they were amended to include Indians. In the case of P.L. 815, a further section (14) was enacted to enable the federal government to provide funds to school districts where there was a need for additional facilities for Indian enrollment.[1]

In the case of P.L. 874, the legislation took a more complex twist. Before it was amended in 1953, it was the subject of extensive debate between state education administrators and the U.S. Office of Education under the Department of Health, Education and Welfare. Many state officials objected to a mandatory transfer of funding from J-O'M to P.L. 874, in the event that the latter was amended to include Indians, because they preferred the flexibility of the J-O'M program. J-O'M was funded according to school district need, that is, according to the "tax-exempt land and Indian children to educate." P.L. 874 would be funded according to entitlement: "only children whose parents lived on or worked on trust land [would be] considered for Federal aid." In other words, the amount of funds a district would receive would be based on the "specific number of eligible Indian children."[2] There was some question as to whether this numerically based formula was a wise criterion for funding, and whether the Indian child might not suffer in the long run. One other reason for state opposition was that state departments of public instruction were familiar with the J-O'M program. They had come to rely on these funds and, in many cases, administered them independently.

The outcome of this debate was an amendment that tried to please everyone. Although it permitted Indian children to receive funds from P.L. 874, their eligibility would be determined by the state in which they resided. The governor of each state that held a J-O'M contract would decide whether he wanted to transfer to P.L. 874 funding, but transfer meant a cutoff of J-O'M funds. This amendment became known as the "governor's clause" (64 *Stat.*, 536–37).

For the next five years P.L. 874 remained unchanged. Most states remained opposed to the new form of funding, and only two of them transferred.[3] In 1957, at a meeting of state Indian education administrators, with one exception[4] the states voted in favor of the governor's choice clause. Despite this mandate of state opinion, in 1958 Congress passed a second amendment to P.L. 874 requiring all

J-O'M states to transfer to P.L. 874. This was not, however, the mandatory change that state educators had feared in 1953, for it did not terminate the J-O'M Act. In some states, under certain conditions, school districts would be eligible for both types of funding. The new amendment stipulated that states must apply for P.L. 874 funding as their primary source of aid. If this assistance was equal to or greater than the previous J-O'M funding, then the latter contract would be canceled. On the other hand, if the total funding under P.L. 874 did not equal that of the previous contract, then J-O'M funds would make up the difference. P.L. 874 was intended to provide the basic support for these children, hitherto provided by J-O'M; and J-O'M was now to be used only for special needs.[5]

In many cases the passage of this amendment meant additional funds for school districts, but still the measure created a great deal of concern for state education administrators. Their immediate problem was adjusting their budgets for the fiscal year 1958–59. Since Congress did not pass the measure until August 13, it became law after all of the state budgets under the J-O'M program had been approved for the fiscal year. An even tougher problem was complete revision of the state plans. Under the J-O'M program each state submitted an annual state plan that outlined its Indian education program for the coming fiscal year. These plans would have to be completely altered in accordance with the new system of funding. The Bureau also had to revise its program, since it was not responsible for avoiding duplication of aid.

Less than ten years later these state plans had to be revised again. On April 11, 1965, Congress passed the Elementary and Secondary Education Act. In theory, this measure was totally different from either the Johnson-O'Malley Act or the impacted-area legislation. J-O'M and P.L. 874 were intended to meet the financial need of the school districts. The Elementary and Secondary Education Act was intended to meet the "special educational needs of children of low-income families." In other words, the Elementary and Secondary Education Act marked the first official recognition of the special needs of the children to whom it applied. For more than thirty years the federal government had refused to acknowledge that there was any need other than the financial aid it provided to the school districts themselves. Belatedly, this legislation recognized that the children themselves should be considered.

Almost all Indian children were to benefit directly from Title I of

184   CHAPTER 14

this new legislation (79 *Stat.*, 27–36), since the funding was to be allocated according to the number of children in the school district whose families were either receiving Aid to Families with Dependent Children payments or had an income of less than $2,000 per year. If they failed to qualify under these conditions, they would probably be eligible through the stipulation that provided for all students who attended schools with high concentrations of "educationally deprived" pupils from low-income families.[6] There was really no question that Indian students were qualified for aid from Title I. Most of them were from low-income families[7] and most of them displayed the characteristics of the educationally deprived. Not only were they well below average in achievement and well above average in the dropout rate, but also a significant number of them were convinced that they simply could not achieve.

Title I funding, like the impacted-area legislation, fell under the direction of the U.S. Office of Education. Unlike the earlier legislation, however, it was not administered by this office. Rather, the Bureau of Indian Affairs submitted its proposal for projects to the U.S. Office of Education, which usually approved them, and then the Indian Office administered the program. In 1969 the funding was broken down: a little over half of the money was allocated for in-service training, teacher aides, and pupil personnel services; the remainder went to curriculum development, enrichment (field trips and the like), language arts, health and food, kindergarten, and mathematics and science.[8]

By the mid 1960s, the federal government was providing three sources of funding to public school districts for their Indian enrollment. The impacted-area legislation was carrying the brunt of the burden with an appropriation of $505,900,000. By comparison, the other two programs operated on very low budgets. The Johnson-O'Malley program was the second largest, with state contracts for 1969 totaling only $11,552,000. Title I funding of the Elementary and Secondary Education Act totaled $9,000,000. Theoretically, this apportioning of funds was justified by the intent of each program as it was written. Thus the program to assist with basic maintenance and operation expenses, that is, P.L. 874–P.L. 815, should have received the heaviest funding, and the programs to provide supplemental and special assistance, that is, J-O'M and Title I, should have been funded sparingly. However, even if this had been the case, critics of this division of the funds countered that the needs of Indian students required much more extensive spending on supplementary programs.

As had been true for the Johnson-O'Malley legislation, there was a wide gap between the intent of the more recent legislation and its implementation. In theory, the remolded J-O'M program and the innovative Title I program were geared to meet the needs of Indian students; in practice, a large portion of this funding was used for basic operating expenses. Many school districts channeled J-O'M and Title I funds into their annual budgets for the entire school system and used the funds so widely that they were not even sure where they went,[9] and impacted-area funds came to be similarly misused. In other words, these special funds, which totaled about $530 million in 1969 and which Congress intended for Indian students, usually were spent for all of the students in the school districts, and in some cases non-Indian students benefited more from them than Indian students themselves.[10]

By the 1960s, then, it had become apparent that the concern of Bureau leaders in the 1930s over public-school funding for 'Indian education had been justified. Their prediction that state school systems would be more interested in the additional money than in the Indian students themselves had proven correct. This situation continued to exist for so many years largely because those who were directly affected by the aid—Indian pupils, parents, and communities—had never been consulted. Throughout most of this period the question of Indian involvement was not even raised.

In the late 1960s young Indian leaders, eager to change the condition of their people, saw federal funding for public schools as a likely target. Interest in J-O'M programs began to be kindled in widely scattered parts of the country. In at least three states— Nebraska, North Dakota, and South Dakota—the intertribal Indian groups acquired the right to review all J-O'M budgets before they became final. In New Mexico, the newly formed National Indian Leadership Training program launched an active campaign to educate parents of children in public schools. If parents were acquainted with J-O'M procedure, National Indian Leadership Training personnel reasoned, they could begin to take an active part in determining what programs their children needed. In the first year of its operation (1971–72) this effort elicited such enthusiastic response that the project director, Myron Jones, determined to introduce a similar program in Arizona.

The growing interest evinced by these leaders and by Indian parents was encouraged by the appearance of two critical studies of Indian education. The first of these was the 1969 report of the Special Senate Subcommittee, *Indian Education: A National Tragedy —A National Challenge*—the Kennedy Report. The second, *An Even Chance* (1971), was the work of the NAACP Legal Defense and Education Fund, Inc. With the sudden upsurge of interest demonstrated by these widely divergent groups, the late 1960s was beginning to take on the appearance of another reform period.

The two reports, as well as the National Indian Leadership Training project, pointed out similar weaknesses in the federal funding programs. They agreed that, regardless of the beneficent intent of the legislation, the Indian child had been denied the benefits intended for him. The most serious weakness was identified as the failure to encourage Indian participation—if Indian parents had been consulted, they would have had the opportunity to correct the other weaknesses. First among these was the lack of proper accounting for funds. Of the three programs, Title I required the most detailed outline for the annual budget. Both Johnson-O'Malley and P.L. 874 were notorious for the freewheeling atmosphere in which funds were guaranteed each year. The annual state plans required for J-O'M programs did not even provide a standard form. Another problem, at least in New Mexico, was that J-O'M budgets were completed before the general school budgets. This was very convenient for public school administrators because it enabled them to apply J-O'M funds to any part of their budget where there was a need. A J-O'M budget might list four teacher aides, while in practice the school system actually hired only one, who served non-Indian children equally. Before these funds were spent properly, they had to be accounted for.

In 1971 the National Indian Leadership Training project began to work toward this goal by encouraging parents to participate in budget-planning sessions. Parental participation might also encourage the development of special Indian programs, in addition to meeting physical needs, one of the few generally successful aspects of federal aid. The other two major criticisms—continued discrimination against Indian pupils and the low quality of teaching—were more difficult to satisfy, but it was felt that parents should be given the opportunity to attempt to do something about these lingering problems.

The failure of federal aid between 1928 and 1973 is illustrated dramatically by the tragic effect it had on Indian children in public school. Throughout these four decades, one of the most persistent problems was that of poor attendance and high dropout rates. Lack of motivation, general defeatism, and a seminomadic pattern of existence—all of these combined to make the Indian child feel there was no reason for attending or continuing school. Consequently, the Indian level of achievement remained well below the national average.[11] Social integration became more difficult for the child as he went beyond the primary years. Although young children might have close friends among other ethnic groups, this often decreased to the point where they clung to their own ethnic groups by the time they were in junior high school. Most Indian students did not go to college. The Coleman Report, *Equality of Educational Opportunity* (Washington, D.C., 1966), observed that fewer than 50 percent said they intended to complete college and those who did attend college suffered from a shockingly high rate of attrition.

15

CONCLUSION

Between 1928 and the early 1970s, Indian Bureau education failed to develop programs geared to the needs of the Indian people. During much of this period Bureau education leaders moved in directions inconsistent with the culture patterns of Indians themselves. Even when they sought to relate their programs to the Indian life style, their efforts were usually reversed by subsequent shifts in policy.

If an interval of hope existed in these decades, it was during the Indian New Deal, which began with Carson Ryan's administration in 1930 and came to a halt with the outbreak of World War II. These years witnessed a new optimism in Bureau and public-school education for Indians. Within the Bureau, for the first time, education leaders expressed a positive attitude toward Indian culture. With John Collier's encouragement, Ryan and Willard Walcott Beatty expanded community schools and worked to develop a curriculum that included aspects of Indian culture as well as practical vocational training. In short, they attempted to prepare students for both reservation and non reservation life. In the public-school system, negotiations began for the first state contracts under the Johnson-O'Malley program, and Bureau education leaders began their unsuccessful effort to convince state administrators that federal funds should be used to develop unique programs to meet the special needs of Indian students in public schools. Before the end of the thirties, Beatty had discovered the hopelessness of this cause.

Beatty's program of the 1930s was unique in that it sought to acquaint Indian Service teachers with Indian cultures. The antithesis of the fifty preceding years of Bureau education, this was a commendable goal. The methods used, however, were suited only to the milieu of the prewar years, and the unusual ideal of including Progressive educators and anthropologists for in-service training sessions was never used again; by the 1960s anthropologists had fallen into disrepute (at least in the opinion of outspoken Indians) and Progressive educators were passé. In the Indian New Deal, however, the radicalism of this idea lent it a boldness that should not be underrated.

World War II destroyed the Bureau education programs of the 1930s. The war itself had disastrous effects upon the Education Division in terms of budget and manpower limitations. Even more serious was the resultant change in attitude. From the termination measures of Congress to the assimilation thrust of the Education Division, the postwar period saw a new approach in federal Indian policy. Beatty himself felt that the goals he had established before the war were no longer appropriate in the late 1940s. As a result, the concepts of community schooling, cross-cultural education, and vocational training for rural living fell before the new program, which pushed education for urban living within the mainstream society. Under Beatty's direction and with the support of the national termination mood, the hard-won achievements of the 1930s were set aside.

Between 1952 and 1965 the postwar pattern established by Beatty was continued under Hildegard Thompson's direction. She fought for increased enrollment, developed a summer-school program, and encouraged post–high school education to equip Indians to compete in the job market, but she gave little or no consideration to including Indian cultural subjects in Bureau schools and she seemed oblivious to the growing movement for Indian self-determination. Although the external pressures for termination were lifted during her last five years in office, she made no significant changes in the pattern she had already established. She never received the authority to implement a dynamic program, and, consequently, Bureau education did not begin to respond to Indian concern until after her retirement.

During these years federal funding for Indian pupils in public schools was extensively increased through the passage of the impacted-area legislation and the Elementary and Secondary Education Act. The Bureau itself pushed public school enrollment wherever possible. Increased enrollment, however, only meant that a greater number of Indian pupils were thrust into schools that were unprepared to deal with them as a unique cultural group. There was little change from the period when Johnson-O'Malley was the only source of funding, and under the new programs most of the funds continued to be absorbed by public schools. By 1965 the federal government had been contributing to the support of Indian pupils in public schools for about seventy-five years, and the primary recipient was still the state education systems.

After 1965, however, Indian education felt the impact of a new element, which had been absent from all previous administrations. For the first time, in both Bureau and public school systems, Indian leadership gave signs of becoming a potent force. This phenomenon brought a new set of conditions and thus led to a period of instability within the Bureau. Education leaders found it impossible to ignore Indian self-determination, but they did not adjust easily to the concept and their reactions were mixed. Conservatives fought the change, while others supported it.

New leadership encouraged experimentation, and within these few years several revolutionary changes were effected. Although the Education Division had never considered the possibility of permitting Indians to run their own schools, in 1966 it signed the contract for Rough Rock Demonstration School, the first Indian-directed educational experiment. The following year, another totally new concept was realized with the formation of the National Indian Education Advisory Commission. While this board was established under the auspices of the Education Division, like the newly created Indian board of directors for each boarding school, it offered direct encouragement of Indian leadership. Finally, the old ideas of cross-cultural education were refurbished and new courses based on specific aspects of Indian culture were introduced.

The battle over federal funds in public schools was not joined until the end of the 1960s, so that it had little effect on state education administrations until the early seventies. In its initial stages the struggle was carried on by small groups working in narrow geographical areas with varying degrees of success. In some states there was no organization to direct the fight; in others, by the end of the sixties, groups were beginning to teach Indian parents about their responsibilities and opportunities in controlling federal funds, and how to acquire that control.

Thus, between 1928 and 1973, for only two brief intervals was Bureau education policy oriented to Indians themselves—1930–41 and 1965–73—and until the last few years of the second period, funding for public-school education consistently ignored benefits for the Indian pupils themselves.

The Bureau education directors shared the burden of guilt for this bleak record with a number of other forces in each period. If the Education Division had operated in a power vacuum, its programs might have taken different directions, but this was not the case. Education policy was molded by many pressures, from within and from outside of the Bureau. Outside pressures included federal Indian policy and national education policy. The education director himself was forced to administer according to the will of the Commissioner of Indian Affairs, the Secretary of the Interior, and the President. He was also restricted by the administrative structure of the Bureau and by other parts of the federal government, including Congress and the Bureau of the Budget.

These pressures were largely responsible for shaping a program that failed to meet Indian needs. Federal Indian policy itself was one of the strongest influences. When Congress urged that federal protection of all Indian tribes be terminated, the Branch of Education pushed vocational training for off-reservation jobs. If the Education Director believed that Indians wanted this type of training, the program reflected these convictions, but in terms of influence the director himself was at the bottom of the ladder, and his convictions were generally overridden unless they were in accord with Congress, the Secretary of the Interior, and all of the other sources of power that encircled the Indian Bureau.

During most of this period Indian education policy conformed to these outside influences. The director's own effectiveness was largely determined by the administrative organization of the Bureau. This was graphically demonstrated during Hildegard Thompson's term of office. No director was more constrained than Thompson. Two years before she took office, Education was demoted from division to branch level, and it remained a branch throughout her administration. Even though division status was restored on Thompson's retirement, the wide-reaching authority that Ryan and Beatty had enjoyed from 1930 to 1950 was never restored. After

1950, Area Directors maintained separate islands of power that served as barriers between the Education Director and the field. Since they had the authority to veto any order issued by an Assistant Commissioner, such as the Education Director, Area Directors could prevent implementation of any policy that displeased them. From 1950 to 1973, or during the last half of this period, the Education Directors were crippled by the administrative structure of the Indian Bureau. It has been suggested that Marburger, the director who followed Thompson, asked to resign after less than a year in office because of the frustrations imposed by this limitation.

In this perspective, the circumstances of the Indian New Deal appear even more remarkable. At this time, the Education Division was supported by influences outside of the Bureau and its administrative structure within the Bureau was sound. When Ryan and Beatty issued a policy directive, it went directly to the field without the intervention of Area Directors, who came later. The chief threat to policy implementation during the New Deal was the lingering power of the Old Guard educators, who were emphatically opposed to the general thrust of Collier's administration. These were the people who balked at the use of Progressive educators in the in-service training sessions. In spite of the Old Guard, however, in the 1930s Ryan and Beatty had greater control over Bureau education than post–1950 directors. It was fortunate that this effective administrative authority coincided with a program that sought to orient Bureau schooling toward Indian cultural needs. The progressiveness of this period lent an even sharper contrast between its short-lived successes and the reversals brought by World War II. The Indian New Deal remained an unparalleled experiment, for the circumstances that molded its policies did not occur again.

In the years after World War II Indian parents and leaders began to make known their responses to these programs of the federal government and to indicate the kind of education they wanted for their children. As the postwar policy turned to termination, they were forced to postpone many of their educational plans, but after the threat of termination became less imminent they found time to develop their ideas. Not until the 1960s did Indian response to Bureau and public-school education become widely known. Increased press coverage, the Senate subcommittee hearings, and individual and group studies made during this decade suddenly revealed that Indians were very unhappy with the education that they had received.

These people had grown weary of government excuses and government promises. They were not concerned with *why* the government had failed in its education programs. Their concern was *that* the government had failed. For almost a century the education offered to them in federal and public schools had failed to recognize their cultures and had disregarded the right of parents and leaders to have a voice in policy formation and administration. Their goal was to revise this education to respond to their needs and be shaped and directed by their own people.

Until the end of the 1960s the federal government had never considered that Indians might determine the shape of their own education. Those who molded federal Indian policy had always measured it against their own standards of effectiveness. The fact that these standards were generally unrelated to the wishes of the Indian people was not considered an important issue. If some controversy arose, selected Indian allies were usually available to lend the policy an appearance of credence.

Even though Bureau policy was divorced from the Indians themselves, Bureau educators maintained that they were working in the best interests of the Indian people. This was Beatty's justification for the radical changes he initiated in the postwar period. Bureau education, he asserted, must revise its programs in accordance with the transformation that had occurred among the Indians themselves. Using the same logic, Hildegard Thompson defended her policy of deemphasizing vocational training in boarding schools in order to push post–high school training. Indians, she reasoned, must recognize that in order to compete in the new job market they need more advanced training. In this same manner, Indian self-determination was rationalized into existence and became the self-serving myth of Bureau education leaders.

When the Education Division analyzed Indian education, naturally, it always found its progress praiseworthy—but the Bureau perspective was not noted for its objectivity. Coombs's rebuttal to the Kennedy Report exemplified the defensive attitude of Bureau educators. Education Division evaluations were usually at odds with studies by outside groups, since critics of Bureau education, with no burden of guilt to bear, could afford to draw negative conclusions. In

1927–28, when Carson Ryan wrote the education section of the Meriam Report, he offered sharp criticism because he bore no responsibility for the inferior quality of Bureau Education. In 1967–68, when the Senate subcommittee wrote the Kennedy Report, it destroyed the image of both Bureau and public-school education.

The effectiveness of these two studies should not be underestimated. The Meriam Report of 1928 caused a major Bureau shakeup and was the dividing line between Bureau policy of the previous fifty years and the Indian New Deal. In the late 1960s, later studies notwithstanding, the Meriam Report was still considered a definitive guideline for the Indian Bureau, and the new policy that began to take shape at this time harked back to its recommendations.

The importance of the Meriam Report was also recognized by members of the Senate subcommittee, who sought in part to match its prestigious reputation. Basing their argument on the thesis that Indian education had not improved since 1928, the subcommittee used the Meriam Report as a point of departure and concluded that, in the main, the intervening years had seen the antithesis of its recommendations.

The Kennedy Report will probably never achieve the stature of the Meriam Report because its objectives were more limited. It did complete an in-depth study of Bureau and public-school education, but it did not address other aspects of Indian affairs. Nonetheless, the growing strength of self-determination meant that the Kennedy Report had a better chance of affecting Indians than the Meriam Report. Indians of the 1960s were very different from their predecessors of the late 1920s. During the interim years they had become increasingly dissatisfied with their schooling, and by the late 1960s they knew that if they were ever to acquire the kind of education they wanted they would have to bear the major responsibility themselves. Given this trend, it is likely that the Kennedy Report will have a continuing effect on Indians for some time to come.

The movement for self-determination, therefore, implied that the most legitimate critics of Indian education were the Indian people. While others might attack Bureau schools and federal funding programs from an administrative point of view, Indians could criticize from experience. Through testimony, speeches, and writings, their responses began to crystallize at this time. Bureau education emerged as an archaic system of paternalism, while public-school education appeared as a force of persistent discrimination.

The fact that both of these systems were hostile to Indian self-determination came as no surprise to the Indians. They already knew that these administrators had to believe in their own indispensability. Bureau reaction to Rough Rock Demonstration School confirmed this. Unfortunately, the school was beset by a number of problems in its first years of operation. Given its unusual conditions, this was not surprising, but as far as the Education Division was concerned, it bordered on disaster. Criticism of Rough Rock was so severe that Indian leaders were forced to conclude that Bureau educators demanded perfection even in the trial years of an experiment in Indian control. The Education Division was judging Indian Schools by a set of standards very different from those applied to Bureau schools. Thus, although there was some cooperation between Bureau and Indian education leaders, strained relations generally characterized this experimental period of Indian control.

One aspect of the new experiments that disturbed Bureau educators was the growth of something akin to nationalism. Even Robert Roessel, who had gone to dramatic extremes to defend self-determination, found the anti-Anglo attitude at Navajo Community College too chauvinistic. When Coombs criticized these experiments for seeking independence for the sake of control rather than from a desire to achieve quality education, he was perhaps partly right. Indian education experiments did need independence from traditional white paternalism. While the type of education they sought might not have met Bureau standards, it appeared to satisfy the standards of parents and community leaders.

Indian-controlled schools placed a high priority on the teaching of tribal culture. When this emphasis was achieved at the expense of other subjects, Bureau educators criticized the schools for developing an unbalanced curriculum. By attacking this action, however, Bureau leaders revealed their failure to comprehend the situation. The tendency to stress Indian culture was only natural at this time. Since mainstream culture had been imposed on Indian pupils for the entire period of Indian education and since federal education itself had been thrust on Indians who had no say in the matter, an opposite reaction was only to be expected.

Federal policy contributed in large part, therefore, to the development of nationalism in Indian education. Indian-controlled schools were a sudden release from the heritage of non-Indian domination. When an Indian community achieved the opportunity to form its own school, it could not be expected to imitate the education it had fought in order to reach this new freedom. The inability of Bureau educators to understand this turn of events was one more symptom of the ills Indian communities were trying to cure in seeking control.

The freedom that Indians achieved in the 1960s was the first sign that the old policy would be lifted. Whether the Bureau would continue to change would depend on the traditional forces that had influenced it in the past. While Indian initiative provided the entrée into the events of the late 1960s, the alliance between Indian education leaders and congressmen who supported self-determination was a new and effective weapon. Conceivably, this combination of forces could lead to a system of Bureau education responsive to Indian needs and amenable to Indian control—a development counter to a century of tradition. During that century, however, Indian education policy was never forced to contend with a movement for self-determination.

Self-determination has always been a difficult concept for the Indian Bureau to grasp, for in essence it implies that the Bureau itself is unnecessary. Ironically, this is the one catastrophe that the Bureau should not fear from the Indians. Indian leaders have consistently defended the Indian Bureau and have opposed any effort to transfer all or part of the Bureau, including the Education Division, to other federal agencies. In recent years this had been due, in part, to post-termination anxiety, which interpreted any alteration of traditional Bureau responsibility as potential termination of federal services. Therefore, Bureau education leaders should be encouraged to understand that self-determination implies internal structural change rather than immediate destruction of the Education Division. The fact that all Indian-controlled schools in 1970 were dependent on the Bureau for at least part of their financial support indicated that it would be a long time before Indian education could dispense with assistance from the Indian Bureau.

Even though the new schools continued to be tied to the old institution, the existence of these and other experiments in Indian control meant that by the early 1970s Indian education was on the threshold of a new direction, a direction that could reverse the trend from 1928 to 1970 as well as that of the preceding fifty years. This would be a remarkable achievement. It would mean not only that the recommendations of the Meriam Report were finally carried out, and that the goal of the Kennedy Report was attained; more important, it would mean that the Indian people, after so many years of denial, had finally achieved the right to determine the education of their own children.

EPILOGUE

Between the Meriam Report of 1928 and the Kennedy Report of 1969 the federal government failed to pass any major legislation affecting Indian self-determination in education. These four decades, however, were not a radical departure from the past. Indian participation in federal education had always been negligible. This was true from the earliest years of federal involvement, when the government made provisions for education in Indian treaties, to the expansion of the manual labor schools in the late nineteenth century. From 1783 to 1971 the government had run the show.

Then, from 1972 to 1975, three major bills affecting Indian education and self-determination were enacted by Congress and signed into law. Since two of these three precedent-shattering laws were passed after this study was first published, the writer found it necessary to revise the epilogue from the 1974 edition.

In a July 1970 message to Congress, President Nixon called for a new Indian policy of "self-determination without termination." The message encouraged contracting for Johnson-O'Malley programs with Indian groups and community control of Indian schools.[1] Within the next two years Congress witnessed a proliferation of Indian education bills. In 1971 Senators Jackson and Montoya sponsored separate measures, but it was Senators Kennedy and Mondale who put together a bill supported by the two elements necessary for its passage—members of Congress and the Indian people.

The Indian Education Act, Title IV of P.L. 92-318 (86 *Stat.,*

334-345), signed into law by President Nixon on June 23, 1972, was the first legislative victory for the Indians, but its successes were limited. It dealt only with public schooling and even here it did not touch on J-O'M, oldest of the federal laws for public schools.

The major thrust of the Indian Education Act was well received by the Indian people.[2] The reasons for this were twofold. In the first place, Title IV set a precedent for Indian control. Under Part A, which amended P.L. 874, parental and community participation in the establishment and direction of impact-aid programs was made mandatory. Furthermore, by allotting a maximum of 10 percent of entitlement payments (as amended in 1975) to schools that were *not* local educational agencies, the act encouraged the establishment of community-run schools. Part B, which amended Title VIII, ESEA, authorized a series of grant programs to stress culturally relevant and bilingual curriculum materials. While grant recipients could be state and local education agencies, institutions of higher education, and Indian tribes or organizations, Indian-controlled agencies and institutions were to be given preference.

Part C, which amended the Adult Education Act, provided grants for adult-education projects, with preference to be given to Indian tribes, institutions, and organizations. Part D established an Office of Indian Education within the U.S. Office of Education, to administer the provisions of Title IV. This office was to be directed by a Deputy Commissioner for Indian Education, to be selected by the U.S. Commissioner of Education from a list of nominees submitted by the newly created National Advisory Council on Indian Education. The Advisory Council was to be a fifteen-member body, all Indian, appointed by the President and serving in an advisory capacity on matters pertaining to Indian education programs. It was to review all applications for grants under the new act. Senator Kennedy pointed out that the Indian Education Sub-committee had intended that the Council would "strengthen and expand Indian participation and influence educational government at the local level," thereby reducing the "over-riding paternalism" of federal policy.[3] Part E provided funds for training teachers for Indian Bureau schools, with preference to be given to Indians.

Indian control, therefore, was the major feature that distinguished Title IV from earlier legislation. Herschel Sahmaunt (Kiowa), president of the National Indian Education Association, wrote in the spring following its passage, "In effect, it is the first piece of legislation enacted into law that gives Indian people on reservations, in rural settings, and in the cities, control over their own education."[4]

Sahmaunt's reference to urban Indians explains, in part, the second reason for Indian support of the act. Indians in urban areas traditionally had been ignored by the Indian Bureau. Under Title IV, urban, state-recognized, and terminated Indians would begin to have a voice in their children's education. This included eastern Indians who had been virtually excluded from federal programs. Thus, Title IV added a broad range of Indians who had been "historically left out in the cold."[5]

The struggle to fund the act exemplified the determination of the Indian people. After the bill became law, they refused to watch it stagnate for lack of funds. The funding battle was fought in two major engagements. In Congress, action was delayed until Indian testimony and pressures led a joint Senate-House committee to authorize $18 million for the 1973 fiscal year.[6] Authorization came in October 1972, four months after the bill became law. Then the administration balked. By January 1973, a number of Indian groups and their attorneys had filed suits against the federal government for release of the money.[7] In May, less than two months before the close of the fiscal year, the District of Columbia federal court ordered the release of the funds. In the next few weeks the funds were allocated to local educational agencies throughout the country.[8]

For Indian leaders, the passage and implementation of Title IV was a proving ground in political expediency. It demonstrated that they could deal with the complex and unique processes by which legislation becomes law and laws are implemented. The legislative process would have been impossible without the cooperation of congressmen such as Senators Kennedy and Mondale. The Indian community, however, furnished the requisite reciprocal leadership. Indian education leaders served as a liaison between Congress and the Indian people. Indian politicians exerted pressure on Congress. Finally, Indian attorneys instituted the necessary legal action.

The skills demonstrated in the Title IV battle were soon tested. Within eighteen months, Indian education leaders had begun to develop proposals that would eventually lead to further legislation. Late in 1973 several of these leaders determined to tackle the most serious gap of Title IV public school measures—J-O'M. In January

1974, representatives of almost forty Indian groups met in Albuquerque to draft a new set of J-O'M regulations. The two major proposals were: (1) to shift control of J-O'M programs from public school districts to Indians, by direct contracting with Indian groups; (2) to assure accountability by providing for a full review of J-O'M programs by the Indian Bureau.[9] Through political pressure this group secured Indian Bureau approval of their measures, labeled the "Red Regs" (regulations), and by September 1974, they had become official policy.

This procedure was but one side of the coin. While Indians were taking direct action at one level, members of Congress were considering legislation at another. Of the several self-determination bills before Congress, one of them, S. 1017, introduced by Senators Jackson and James Abourezk (Democrat, South Dakota, and chairman of the Senate Subcommittee on Indian Affairs), also dealt with J-O'M. Again, through political pressure, including timely action by Senator Kennedy, Indian education leaders achieved most of their goals for this bill. Title I provided for maximum Indian participation in government programs for Indian people; Title II provided for a set of regulations that were almost identical to the "Red Regs." On January 5, 1975, President Gerald R. Ford signed the Indian Self-Determination and Education Assistance Act (P.L. 93-638, 88 *Stat.*, 2203-2217).

Three days earlier, on January 2, 1975, the President signed a law providing for the American Indian Policy Review Commission (P.L. 93-580, 88 *Stat.*, 1910-1914). The AIPRC was touted by Senator Abourezk as "the first of its kind since the Meriam Report," but it differed significantly from the 1928 study, for it was based on the premise that Indians themselves should review government programs and policies involving Native Americans.[10] While the Meriam Report was largely carried out by non-Indian experts, the AIPRC was to be directed by a joint team of congressmen and Indian leaders.

The Indian Education Act of 1972, the Indian Self-Determination and Education Assistance Act, and the AIPRC were milestones for the Indian people. They meant that the web of government control had been loosened. Henceforth, direction and leadership in Indian education should come increasingly from Indians themselves.

NOTES

ABBREVIATIONS

American Indian Law Newsletter: AILN
Annual Report of the Commissioner of Indian Affairs: Report of the Commissioner
Code of Federal Regulations: CFR
Congressional Record: CR
General Service: GS
Indian Reorganization Act: IRA
Interviews conducted for the American Indian History Research Project: Indian History Project
Mississippi Valley Historical Review: MVHR
The National Archives of the United States: NA
A Progress Report from the Commissioner of Indian Affairs: Progress Report
Records of the Bureau of Indian Affairs: Indian Bureau
Survey of Conditions of the Indians of the United States, U.S. Senate Hearings before a
   subcommittee of the Committee on Indian Affairs: *Survey of Conditions of the Indians*
Washington National Record Center, Suitland, Maryland: WNRC

CHAPTER 2
Assimilation and Federal Indian Education, 1870–1926

1. U.S., *Statutes at Large,* vol. 24, pp. 388–91 (hereafter cited as U.S. *Stat.*).

2. In 1819, the first year in which Congress voted a fund for "civilization" of the Indian, it settled upon the figure of $10,000. As Loring B. Priest points out in *Uncle Sam's Stepchildren* (New York: Octagon Books, 1969), before 1880 congressional appropriations for Indian schools had not exceeded $130,000 a year. This figure was to take a tremendous jump within the next decade.

3. The treaty period of U.S.–Indian relations closed officially in 1871 when Congress declared that no Indian nation or tribe within the territory of the United States should thereafter be recognized as an independent power with whom the government might contract by treaty (U.S. *Stat.*, vol. 16, p. 566).

4. The education systems of both the Cherokees and the Choctaws, which were destroyed in 1898 by the Curtis Act, antedated the self-determination education programs of tribes in the 1960s by well over a century. The Creeks, Chickasaws, and Seminoles also had schools in the nineteenth century.

5. Carlisle made use of a deserted army barracks in Carlisle, Pennsylvania. Since then the Bureau has more than once resorted to this type of quarters. Inadequate funding and the need for more facilities have made this a convenient measure, but the use of this type of quarters has encouraged critics to equate boarding-school life with that of the army.

6. The theme of Ruth M. Underhill's novel, *Hawk Over Whirlpools* (New York, 1940), suggests the tragic effect this choice might have on the life of an Indian youth. It was not until the administration of John Collier (1933–45) that the either/or concept was challenged. Collier suggested that *"assimilation and preservation and intensification of heritage"* need not be "hostile choices." Collier, editorial, *Indians at Work* 3 (February 1, 1936):5. In the 1960s, Robert A. Roessel, Jr., a prominent figure in Navajo education, reiterated this idea. Roessel suggested that an "alternative" to the either/or approach would be a *"both/and* concept of Indian education wherein the Indian child is made aware of the positive contributions both of his Indian heritage *and* his American background." Roessel, "Observations on Indian Education within the BIA," February 9, 1966, Navajo Area Office, Records of the Bureau of Indian Affairs, Washington, D.C. These records are in the Bureau office itself (hereafter cited as Indian Bureau).

7. Priest points out that "Congress welcomed the opportunity to economize by reducing transportation costs. . . ." *Uncle Sam's Stepchildren*, p. 151.

8. Priest suggests that even though the idea of compulsory education was viewed with "alarm" by members of Congress, the chief critics of compulsory education were army officers. Ibid., pp. 153, 284. The compulsory attendance law that Congress enacted in the 1890s (act of March 3, 1893, U.S. *Stat.*, vol. 27, p. 635) was intended for reservation schooling. However, the severity of the reaction to this law led Congress to state that compulsory attendance laws were not intended for nonreservation boarding schools. Complaints of enforced off-reservation schooling continued through the 1920s. For a discussion of compulsory attendance legislation, see Theodore Fischbacher, "A Study of the Role of the Federal Government in the Education of the American Indian," Ed.D. diss., Arizona State University. For the period of the 1920s see *Survey of Conditions of the Indians in the United States*, U.S. Senate Hearings before a subcommittee of the Committee on Indian Affairs (hereafter cited as *Survey of Conditions of the Indians*).

9. Robert M. Utley, *The Last Days of the Sioux Nation*, p. 37.

10. In 1909 there were some 900 Indian children in public schools. By 1930, however, over half of all Indian children in school attended public schools. *Annual Report of the Secretary of the Interior*, 1930, p. 27.

11. *Annual Report of the Commissioner of Indian Affairs*, 1902, pp. 368–69 (hereafter cited as *Report of the Commissioner*).

12. Ibid.

13. In 1930, out of a total of approximately 72,000 Indian children in school, 6,000, or about 8.3 percent attended mission schools. *Annual Report of the Secretary of the Interior*, 1930, p. 27. In 1969, out of a total of approximately 178,000 Indian children in school, about 10,500 or 6 percent attended "mission and other schools." *Fiscal Year 1969 Statistics Concerning Indian Education*, p. 7.

14. William M. Chapman, *Remember the Wind*, p. 173.

15. In 1955 the Catholic Sioux Indian Congress wrote to a congressional committee hearing in Rosebud, South Dakota, "we Indians are more and more convinced of the absolute necessity of educating our children well in these difficult times of transition for our people. We believe that the Mission schools have in the past and are today doing an invaluable service in helping our people." Washington National Record Center, Suitland, Maryland (hereafter

cited as WNRC). All records from the National Archives, Washington, D.C., and from WNRC are from Record Group 75.

The 1960s, however, witnessed an increasing level of Indian disenchantment with the mainstream culture of America and a growing interest in Native American traditions. Since religion has always been an integral part of Indian cultures, an increasing rejection of Christianity has become part of the wave of disenchantment. For a vehement expression of Indian reaction to Christianity, see Vine Deloria, Jr., *We Talk, You Listen* (New York, 1970) and *God Is Red* (New York, 1973). For impressions by a white writer of changes taking place in one tribe, see Edmund Wilson, *Apologies to the Iroquois*. Quoting one Mohawk, Wilson wrote (p. 115), "The Catholic Church . . . has always done its best to prevent the Indians from learning anything about their traditions. . . ."

16. Between November 1922 and June 1924, *Sunset* published only six issues without at least one leading article denouncing the Indian Bureau. Randolph C. Downes, "A Crusade for Indian Reform," *Mississippi Valley Historical Review* 32 (December 1945):337 (hereafter cited as *MVHR*).

17. When Collier became commissioner, Wohlke followed him into the Service and held a number of responsible positions over a period of eighteen years. His willingness to work for the Bureau exemplified the type of commitment that such individuals gave to the cause as well as to its chief spokesman, John Collier.

18. *Sunset* 51 (October 1923):87.

19. No complete high school courses were offered in Bureau schools until 1921 and as late as 1928 only six Bureau schools offered a high school education. *Annual Report of the Secretary of the Interior*, 1928, p. 3.

CHAPTER 3
W. Carson Ryan: From the Meriam Report to the Indian New Deal

1. The report was published under the title *The Problem of Indian Administration*.

2. *Survey Graphic* 61 (January 1, 1929):425.

3. Lewis Meriam, "Indian Education Moves Ahead," *Survey Graphic* 66 (June 1, 1931):254.

4. *The Problem of Indian Administration*, p. 11.

5. *Annual Report of the Secretary of the Interior*, 1928, pp. 57, 274.

6. *The Problem of Indian Administration*, p. 11.

7. Cramton, described by John Collier as "the most famous enemy of Indian rights outside the Bureau" (Collier, "The Indian Bureau's Record," *The Nation* 85 [November 1932]:305) was a target for the reformers in the 1920s. Their wrath against him increased when, after he was defeated for reelection in 1930, he was appointed by Secretary Wilbur to the Interior Department, in a job that was to include "important Indian assignments." Secretary Ickes, who followed Wilbur in the Interior Department post, later wrote in a thinly veiled reference to Cramton, "It gave me great joy, as one of my first official acts after I came to Washington, to fire him." Harold Ickes, *The First Thousand Days: The Secret Diary of Harold L. Ickes*, p. 51.

8. Lawrence C. Kelly, *The Navajo Indians and Federal Indian Policy*, p. 145. Kelly discusses the difficulties of the budget and the Bureau in the 1920s (pp. 142–45), as well as how it affected Navajo Indian education (pp. 173–79). He points out that by 1931 the Bureau appropriation for education was larger than the entire Bureau budget ten years earlier. *Annual Report of the Secretary of the Interior*, 1931, p. 1, as quoted by Kelly, p. 180, where he also cited Ray Lyman Wilbur and William A. DuPuy, *Conservation in the Department of the Interior*, (Washington, D.C., 1931), p. 126.

9. *The Problem of Indian Administration*, p. 12.

10. Walter W. Woehlke, "Starving the Nation's Wards," *Sunset* 61 (November 1928):14.

11. *Survey of Conditions of the Indians,* February 23, 1927, p. 716.

12. The first successful experiments in curing trachoma were made in the late 1930s. By 1941 the Indian Service had a staff of twelve special physicians and nineteen nurses who traveled from reservation to reservation prescribing treatment. *Indian Service Trachoma Control,* pp. 2, 3.

13. *Survey of Conditions of the Indians,* February 3, 1927, pp. 5, 217.

14. *The Problem of Indian Administration,* p. 13.

15. Ibid.

16. Ibid.

17. Interview with Pablita Velarde (Santa Clara), February 9, 1972, Albuquerque. This interview was conducted under the auspices of the American Indian History Research Project, sponsored by the Doris Duke Foundation under the direction of the Departments of History and Anthropology, University of New Mexico. The interviews are located as a single collection in the University of New Mexico library (hereafter cited as Indian History Project).

18. Interview with Jerry Suazo (Taos), April 27, 1972, Albuquerque, ibid.

19. Narrative Report, 1922, Haskell Institute, the National Archives of the United States (hereafter cited as NA).

20. *The Problem of Indian Administration,* p. 13.

21. After suspending seven teachers in the Southwest section for inflicting corporal punishment upon boarding-school children, Collier wrote, "It is, or should be, self-evident that so long as physical force and acts of humiliation directed against the children, are used, no healthy or happy morale will be possible. . . ." Collier to all Field Supervisors of Education and Superintendents, August 23, 1934, 1934-801-General Service (hereafter cited as GS), NA.

22. Flandreau pupil to Miss Carrie Alberta Lyford, November 19, 1930, Office File of Carrie A. Lyford, 1929–32, NA.

23. R. (illegible), Acting Commissioner, to J. R. Wise, Superintendent, Indian School, Chilocco, Oklahoma, January 9, 1909, 74805-821-GS, NA.

24. Henry J. Scattergood to Miss Florence Bayard Kane, May 1, 1930, 1930-821-GS, NA.

25. Ibid.

26. Oliver La Farge, "Revolution with Reservations," *New Republic* 84 (October 9, 1935):233.

27. Kenneth Dale, "Navajo Indian Educational Administration," Ed.D. diss., University of North Dakota, 1949, pp. 132–33.

28. *The Problem of Indian Administration,* p. 33.

29. Ibid., p. 32.

30. Ibid., p. 35.

31. *New York Times,* April 16, 1929. Ironically, the *Times* entitled its editorial "A New Deal for the Indians," a nomenclature that Collier preferred to reserve for his administration.

32. Francis Fisher Kane, "East and West: The Atlantic City Conference on the American Indian," *Survey Graphic* 61 (January 15, 1929):474.

33. Harold L. Ickes, Letter to the editor, *Illinois Law Review* (n.d.), June 25, 1929 (letter date), p. 575.

34. *American Indian Life,* bull. 16 (July 1930):20. This initiated an exchange of letters between Dr. Haven Emerson, president of the American Indian Defense Association board of directors, and Secretary Wilbur. Hereafter, Wilbur became the sworn enemy of the association and, in particular, of its executive secretary, Collier, whom he engaged in acrimonious debate in the following years.

35. This mammoth project continued from 1928 to 1943 and was published in forty-three parts *(Survey of Conditions of the Indians).* In 1933 Senator King submitted to Congress the report of the committee that exposed the infamous fact that the Indian land base had dwindled by nearly 90 million acres since 1887. This report spurred the introduction of the Wheeler-Howard Bill in 1934, which was enacted in revised form as the Indian Reorganization Act (hereafter cited as the IRA).

36. *Congressional Record* (hereafter cited as *CR*), vol. 75, part 1, 72d Cong., 1st sess., March 4, 1932, p. 5,547.

37. Ibid., March 9, 1932, p. 5,770.

38. E. E. Dale, *Indians of the Southwest*, 1955.

39. Ruby A. Black, "A New Deal for the Red Man," *The Nation* 130 (April 2, 1930):390.

40. See, for example, Kelly, *The Navajo Indians and Federal Indian Policy*, who concludes that Rhoads "placed the major recommendations of the Meriam Report into action, but beyond that he was unwilling or unable to go" (p. 153). Randolph Downes agrees that Collier "accelerated reform to a degree to which Rhoads was incapable." He adds, "the Collier administration was an acceleration, and not a break." "A Crusade for Indian Reform," *MVHR*, p. 350.

41. In the early 1970s, members of Congress asked the same question with no greater degree of success in learning the answer.

42. Circular on Student Control, March 20, 1930, Rhoads to John T. Bramhall, June 20, 1930, 22991-1930-821-GS, NA.

43. Rhoads to Miss Amelia E. White, April 23, 1930, ibid.

44. This issue did not flair up again until 1934 when Collier himself was forced to deal with the issue of corporal punishment. Despite the efforts of Rhoads, Collier, and Ryan to discourage unjust punishment, the Old Guard retained their bastions of control.

45. *Annual Report of the Secretary of the Interior*, 1931, p. 83. For further discussion, see *Federal Relations to Education*, pp. 53, 280. This is the report of the National Advisory Commission on Education, appointed by President Hoover in 1929.

46. *American Indian Life* bull. 16 (July 1930):39.

47. Ibid., bull. 17 (January 1931):6.

48. Ibid.

49. In 1933, Collier reiterated this by observing that the reduction of the boarding schools and increase of the day schools was not an "innovation" but an "established policy," whose success was "fully demonstrated." *Annual Report of the Secretary of the Interior*, 1933, p. 72.

50. Ryan, "Federal-State Cooperation in Education," *School and Society* 34 (September 26, 1931):422.

51. *Annual Report of the Secretary of the Interior*, 1930, p. 27.

52. From 1928 to 1933 the number of day schools increased by a scant three, from 129 to 132. Ibid., 1928, p. 278; 1933, p. 52.

53. W. Carson Ryan to Samuel Thompson, March 22, 1935, Office File of W. Carson Ryan, Director of Education, 1931–35, NA.

54. *CR*, vol. 78, part I, 73rd Cong., 2d sess., January 18, 1934, p. 903.

55. Carson Ryan and Rose K. Brandt, "Indian Education Today," *Progressive Education* 9 (February 1932):85.

56. Ann Nolan Clark, teacher at Santa Fe boarding school at this time and later author of several of the bilingual stories used in Bureau schools in the early 1940s, was one exception.

57. Bacone was a junior college established for Indians in Bacone, Oklahoma, by two home mission societies of the Northern Baptist Convention.

58. Lewis Meriam, "Indian Education Moves Ahead," *Survey* 66 (June 1, 1931):257.

59. George F. Miller to W. Carson Ryan, July 25, 1932, Office File of Ryan, "Pierre, S.D.," NA.

60. Ibid., January 11, 1933, "Phoenix Indian School."

61. See Chapters 8 and 14 for chronological description of the change in federal-state relations.

62. *Federal Relations to Education*, p. 52.

63. Homer H. Howard, *In Step with the States*, introduction by Willard Beatty, p. 7.

64. *The Problem of Indian Administration*, p. 15.

65. Collier, "Mexico: A Challenge," *Progressive Education* 9 (February 1932):94, 97.

66. *Survey of Conditions of the Indians*, part 14 (November 1930), pp. 6, 589.

67. Ibid., part 17 (April 1931), p. 8,063.

68. Samuel Thompson to John Collier, April 17, 1934, Office File of Ryan, NA.

CHAPTER 4
John Collier and Willard Walcott Beatty:
New Deal Achitects of Education

1. John Collier, "The Indian Bureau's Record," *The Nation* 135 (November 5, 1932):304.

2. Mary Austin to Wilbur, October 3, 1932, 47863-1932-806-GS, NA.

3. Wilbur to Mary Austin, October 24, 1932, ibid.

4. U.S. Senate, *Conditions of Indians in the United States*, document no. 214, 72d Cong., 2d sess., February 8, 1933.

5. *New York Times*, April 16, 1933.

6. All Pueblo Council Resolution, January 12, 1933, *American Indian Life*, bull. 21 (January 1933):32.

7. For more detail on the hassle over Collier's appointment, see Collier, *From Every Zenith*, pp. 169–72, Harold L. Ickes, *The First Thousand Days*, p. 20, and *American Indian Life*, bulls. 21, 22.

8. Oliver La Farge's *Laughing Boy* was considered a classic—fictionalized and antiwhite—and in the 1930s it caught the mood of the reformers and of Collier's Indian New Deal. Later, in the 1950s, as president of the Association of American Indian Affairs, La Farge became one of the sharpest critics of the termination trend of the Dillon S. Myer, Glenn L. Emmons administrations. When Indian self-determination began to grow in the 1960s, however, La Farge himself became the object of ridicule by Indian writers such as Rupert Costo and Vine Deloria, Jr. Both men attacked La Farge for assuming the role of "protector" of the Indian.

9. Oliver La Farge, "Revolution Within Reservations," *New Republic* 84 (October 9, 1935):234.

10. *The Nation* 136 (April 26, 1933):459.

11. *New York Times*, April 16, 1933.

12. These figures included Senators King and Wheeler and Congressman Howard.

13. Collier, *From Every Zenith*, p. 164.

14. Ibid., p. 173.

15. *Annual Report of the Secretary of the Interior*, 1938, p. 263.

16. Donald L. Parman, "The Indian and the CCC," *Pacific Historical Review* 40 (February 1971):54.

17. John Collier, "The People's Institute," *The Independent* 72 (May 1912):1144.

18. Frederick C. Howe, *Confessions of a Reformer*, p. 250.

19. In 1926, James Archibald Frear (Republican, Wisconsin), who exemplified this type of congressman, made his first trip to the Southwest to tour Indian reservations. His companion and guide on the trip was Collier. See *CR*, vol. 68, part 1, 69th Cong., 2d sess., December 13, 1926, January 4, 1927, pp. 385, 393, 1067.

20. Speech delivered by Collier to the American Federation of Arts, Washington, D.C., May 14, 1934, reprinted in *Indians at Work* 1 (June 1, 1934):9.

21. "The Indian as Viewed by the Indian Educational Service in 1898," *Indians at Work* 3 (June 1936):28. This publication began as an "Emergency Conservation News Sheet" in June 1934, but was soon broadened into a general news bulletin for the Indian Service. Until 1945, when the stringency of the war budget forced it to cease publication (shortly after Collier left his position), Collier used this small bulletin as a podium to expound his opinions and to praise both Indians and the Indian Service. Its success in this direction, however, led congressmen to attack it in the late thirties.

22. Ryan remained as Education Director until the summer of 1935. At this time he asked for leave to become a consultant with the Commonwealth Fund of New York City. Between 1940 and 1956, while serving as professor and chairman of the Department of Education, University of North Carolina, he continued his consultant and editorial services. On Ryan's death in 1968, a memorial in his name was entered in the permanent minutes of the university's faculty council. It praised his contributions, saying that "few men in the 20th century made the impact upon professional education that Carson Ryan made."

23. For a discussion of the background and development of the Winnetka experiment, see *The National Society for the Study of Education, Twenty Fourth Year Book* (1925), part 2; also, Carleton Washburn, "Winnetka," *School and Society* 29 (1929):37–50; Carleton Washburn and Edward Yeomans, "The Inception of the Winnetka Technique," *Journal of the AAUW* 20 (1930):129–36.

24. *Bronxville Press* as quoted in *Indians at Work* 3 (March 1, 1936):8.

25. *Time* 27 (February 10, 1936):36.

26. Hildegard Thompson to writer, November 26, 1971.

27. One person who had been an employee of the Bureau since the late 1940s suggested that what the Bureau was lacking in the 1960s was effective leadership. "All of the great thinkers," he commented, "all of the fine minds are gone. . . . There is no longer anyone like Carson Ryan or Beatty or John Collier. . . . Most of the ideas of today are a rehash of those begun by Collier." Interview with Bureau employee of the Education Division, Bureau of Indian Affairs, Washington, D.C., July 1970, in writer's personal collection.

28. H. Thompson to writer, November 26, 1971.

29. Samuel H. Thompson to Beatty, March 17, 1937, 42811-1936-800-GS, NA.

30. Beatty, *Education for Action*, p. 260.

31. Beatty to Edward Huberman, March 22, 1937, 16696-1937-800-GS, NA.

32. Collier, *From Every Zenith*, p. 196.

CHAPTER 5
New Deal Innovations: Progressive Education and Anthropology

1. Lawrence Cremin, *The Transformation of the School: Progressivism in American Education, 1876–1950*, p. 325.

2. John Dewey, *Experience and Education*, p. vii.

3. Beatty to Winona Winfred (n.d.), 1938-810-Haskell, NA.

4. Cremin, *Transformation of the School*, p. x.

5. Dewey, *School and Society*, pp. 27–28.

6. Dewey asserted that traditional 3 Rs education is worth very little if the child "loses his appreciation of things worthwhile, of the values to which these things are relative; if he loses desire to apply what he has learned and, above all, loses the ability to extract meaning from his future experiences as they occur." Dewey, *Experience and Education*, pp. 48, 50.

7. I. L. Kandel, *The Cult of Uncertainty*, p. 128.

8. Dewey, *Experience and Education*, pp. 75–76.

9. Three years later Ryan described the PEA (Progressive Education Association) as "an association sufficiently interested in Indian work to have made one of its most important issues, that of February, 1932, a wholly Indian issue. . . ." Ryan to A. C. Monahan, January 4, 1935, 1286-1935-800-GS, NA.

10. Ryan and Brandt, "Indian Education Today," *Progressive Education*, p. 83. Rose Brandt was an experienced educator who had been state supervisor of elementary education for the Indian Service. She was a good example of the professional educator whom Ryan began to employ.

11. In February 1935, the Education Division planned a special program for the annual meeting of the Progressive Education Association. Ryan to Monahan, January 4, 1935.

12. Byron J. Brophy, Superintendent of Flandreau Indian School, S.D., to John Collier, January 31, 1935, 1286-1935-800-GS, NA.

13. Beatty, *Education for Action*, p. 14.

14. *Indians at Work* 1 (July 1, 1934):11.

15. Frederick Webb Hodge, ed., *Bureau of American Ethnology* bull. 30, 2 vols. (1907, 1910).

16. Although the university terminated the contract in 1944, the project was continued through a second contract secured with the Society for Applied Anthropology. This organization was founded in 1941 and was the publisher of *Applied Anthropology*, a quarterly that later became *Human Organization*. The final report was submitted to the society on September 23, 1947, and the project was officially terminated by the Secretary of the Interior on December 31, 1947.

17. These included Laura Thompson and Alice Joseph, M.D., *The Hopi Way* (Chicago, 1944); Gordon MacGregor, *Warriors without Weapons* (Chicago, 1946); Clyde Kluckhohn and Dorothea Leighton, *The Navaho* (Cambridge, Mass., 1946) and *Children of the People* (Cambridge, Mass., 1947); Alice Joseph, M.D., Rosamond B. Spicer, and Jane Chesky, *The Desert People* (Chicago, 1949); and Dorothea C. Leighton, M.D., and John Adair, *People of the Middle Place* (New Haven, Conn., 1966).

18. See Collier's introduction to Laura Thompson, *Personality and Government, Findings and Recommendations of the Indian Administration Research* and Collier, *From Every Zenith*, p. 222.

19. "Comment on Ethnological Training for Indian Service People," *Indians at Work* 2 (October 15, 1934):30.

20. Carson Ryan, "Anthropologists and the Indian Program," *Indians at Work* 2 (January 15, 1935):35.

21. Ibid., pp. 35–36.

22. H. G. Barnett, *Anthropology in Administration*, p. 82.

23. Mekeel, "An Appraisal of the I.R.A.," *American Anthropologist* 46 (April-June 1944):213.

24. Collier, "Collier Replies to Mekeel," ibid., p. 424.

CHAPTER 6
Theory Confronts Reality: Cross-Cultural Education

1. *Annual Report of the Secretary of the Interior*, 1934, p. 84. This was the most spectacular year. The number of schools dropped to fifty-five and the number of boarding school pupils fell from 17,500 in 1933 to 13,000 in 1934. Ibid. From 1932 to 1934 the drop was even sharper, from 22,000 to 13,000, for a total of 9,000.

2. The push for public-school enrollment had also led to a rapid increase in this area and by 1940 there were 45,000 children attending public schools. Ibid., 1940, p. 389.

3. As late as 1938 the Bureau noted that there were 10,390 children not in school and 8,457 who were "unknown." Ibid., 1938, p. 245.

4. For a discussion of the reaction of intellectuals to this period, see R. Jackson Wilson, *In Quest of Community: Social Philosophy in the United States, 1860–1920*.

5. However, scattered attempts to achieve community, such as the utopian experiments in the Jacksonian period and the more successful Mormon colonization of Utah, indicated that Americans may have felt a need for this missing portion of their heritage.

6. Resolution by the Council of New Mexico Pueblos (later known as the All Indian Pueblo Council), November 23, 1930, 61916-1930-806-GS, NA.

7. Chief Charlie Washoe et al. to John Collier, June 15, 1934, 18862-1934-803-GS, NA.

8. Beatty pointed out that this policy was "inaugurated" by Carson Ryan. Beatty, "Planning

Indian Education in Terms of Pupil and Community Needs," *Indians at Work* (September 1, 1936):5.

9. Two-thirds of the 1933 PWA funding that initiated this project was to be used in Arizona and New Mexico. "Day School Building under Public Works," *Indians at Work* 1 (November 15, 1933):32.

10. This was also an acute problem on the Sioux reservations where, by 1936, there were about forty day schools. Joe Jennings, "The Government Indian Day School as a Community Center," *Indians at Work* 3 (August 1936):37. On the Cheyenne River Reservation eight out of nine day schools hauled their "potable" water from ten to fifty miles. Allan Hulsizer to Joe Jennings, December 14, 1936, 800-Cheyenne River, NA. One observer commented, "At almost all of these places the water situation doesn't exist because there isn't any water." Samuel Thompson to John Collier, September 18, 1936, ibid.

11. See L. Madison Coombs's study of the special postwar Navajo education program, *Doorway toward the Light*, p. 4.

12. Interviews with Leola Kessler, October 20, 26, 1971, Albuquerque, Indian History Project. Also see Donald L. Parman, *The Navajos and the New Deal* (New Haven, 1976).

13. S. M. Johnson to J. C. McCaskill, April 19, 1935, 26976-1935-810-Albuquerque, NA.

14. Interview with Pablita Velarde, February 9, 1972.

15. L. E. Correll, superintendent of Chilocco from 1926 to 1956, exemplified this approach.

16. General Statement of Policy Relating to Secondary Schools, 1935, accompanying letter: A. C. Monahan to James T. Ryan, Superintendent, Salem Boarding School, May 25, 1935, Office File of Mary Stewart, Assistant Director of Education, 1929–36, "Approved Programs and Letters," NA.

17. In the 1940–41 school year Chemawa offered a "Reservation Survey Course" for all students from seventh to twelfth grade. 73193-1940-810-Chemawa, NA.

18. J. Henry Scattergood to supervisors and superintendents of schools, September 4, 1931, Lyford Office File, NA.

19. Beatty, "Planning Indian Education in Terms of Pupil and Community Needs," p. 7.

20. Ibid., p. 6.

21. There is little point in teaching the girls home economics suited to "living or working in a well-to-do home in a city," Alida C. Bowler, Superintendent at Carson Indian School reasoned. Rather, we should prepare them for their "probable future homes," which are likely to have a "limited economic basis." Five Year Report, Carson Indian School, February, 1940, 37969-1940-800-Carson, NA.

22. Edward Sapir, "Culture, Genuine and Spurious," in David Mandelbaum, ed., *Selected Writings of Edward Sapir*, pp. 314–15.

23. Ryan and Brandt, "Indian Education Today," *Progressive Education*, p. 84.

24. Mrs. Lucy Suazo (Acoma) explained that her family had no car and so she could not go home (to Acomita) except in the summer. Interview, December 10, 1970, Albuquerque, Indian History Project.

25. However, they could choose between the Catholic or the Protestant church.

26. Elaine G. Eastman, "Does Uncle Sam Foster Paganism?" *Christian Century* 51 (August 8, 1934):1016–18; John Collier, reply, ibid., pp. 1018–20.

27. A. C. Monahan to Vivian C. Hayman, December 12, 1935, 1956-851-Chilocco, NA (no accession number).

28. The course was planned for the 1936–37 school year. In 1944 it was described as seeking to "develop an interest in the early background of the Indian people and a pride in racial heritage through a study of the culture and language groups, individual research in tribal histories, and a study of the present-day trends and policies in Indian sociology." 26871-1944-819.1-GS-Chilocco, WNRC.

29. Interview with Pablita Velarde, February 9, 1972.

30. Articles on the New York exposition as well as on Indian art itself began to appear in

national publications at this time. See, for example, *The Nation* 133 (December 30, 1931):725; Hartley Alexander, "The Art of the American Indian," ibid. 132 (May 6, 1931), 501–3; *New York Times* editorial, December 1, 1931. Forty years later, however, when the Whitney Museum of New York City opened an exposition entitled "Two Hundred Years of North American Indian Art," the press commented, "North American Indian art finally is coming into its own." *Albuquerque Tribune*, November 25, 1971.

31. *Annual Report of the Secretary of the Interior*, 1936, p. 165.

32. J. J. Brody, *Indian Painters and White Patrons*, p. 72.

33. Art instruction was also begun at Albuquerque Indian School, but the program was less extensive.

34. For a brief description of the flavor of this period, see Mary Austin's autobiography, *Earth Horizon*, pp. 360–68. A more detailed account is in Alice Marriott's biography of Maria Martinez, *Maria: The Potter of San Ildefonso* (Norman, Okla., 1948). Also see Dorothy Dunn, *American Indian Painting of the Southwest and Plains Areas*, a firsthand account of the establishment of the Santa Fe school of painting; and Brody, *Indian Painters and White Patrons*, a more critical account. Brody concludes that during the first half of the twentieth century Indian artists produced solely for the pleasure of white patrons, who chose to confine them to an "Indian school" of art. This school, he adds, conformed to the romantic stereotype of how the traditional Indian should express himself artistically.

35. The New Mexico Association on Indian Affairs sought to encourage Indian artists by judging and awarding prizes for their work during Indian pueblo fiestas. The Indian Arts Fund encouraged Indian artists through another means. It was organized by a group of Santa Feans who began collecting specimens of Southwest Indian art, which would be available for students but primarily for Indian artists in order that they might have "free access to the best of their own arts of past generations." The fund was the brainchild of Kenneth Chapman, curator of the collection, which was housed in the Laboratory of Anthropology, Santa Fe, a building donated by John D. Rockefeller, Jr., and completed in 1931. For a detailed account of these events, see Kenneth Chapman, "America's Most Ancient Art," *School Arts Magazine* 30 (March 1931):387–402. This entire issue is devoted to Southwest Indian art.

36. *Indians at Work* 1 (June 1, 1934):9.

37. Dunn, *American Indian Painting*, p. 250.

38. Ryan and Brandt, "Indian Education Today," p. 84.

39. *Report of the Commissioner*, 1887, p. 186.

40. Interview with Robert Young, January 14, 1972, Albuquerque, Indian History Project.

41. Ibid.

42. Beatty to Leo C. Favrot (Field Agent, General Education Board), February 22, 1936, 45839-1936-808-GS, NA.

43. Underhill, *Hawk Over Whirlpools*, p. 60.

44. Ann Clark, "Reading Readiness," in Beatty, *Education for Cultural Change*, p. 207.

45. Collier, *From Every Zenith*, p. 196.

46. Beatty to Winona Winfred.

47. In spite of Beatty's good intentions, reaction to the program was not entirely favorable. At least one teacher involved in the apprentice training was very critical of the program. He said it was discriminatory to require that Indian graduates from colleges of education receive more training (and, incidentally, less pay) than non-Indians with the same degree, and pointed out that the implementation of the program was not always as exemplary as Beatty might have wished.

48. Interview with Robert Young, January 14, 1972.

49. Hildegard Thompson to writer, November 26, 1971.

50. Beatty, *Education for Cultural Change*, p. 400.

51. Beatty, "Indian Service Schools: Their Aims and Some Results," *Indians at Work* 6 (October, 1938):4.

52. Collier editorial, *Indians at Work* 3 (February 1, 1936):4.

53. J. C. McCaskill, Supervisor of Boys Activities, Haskell Institute. This first appeared in *The Indian Leader*, Lawrence, Kansas, and was reprinted in *Indians at Work* 3 (February 1, 1936):12.

54. Clyde Kluckhohn and Dorothea Leighton, *The Navaho*, p. 321.

55. Sapir, "Culture, Genuine and Spurious," p. 315. The culture Sapir chose as an example of one that had not achieved this goal was that of white America.

56. H. Scudder Mekeel, "An Anthropologist's Observation on Indian Education," *Progressive Education* 14 (March 1936):155.

57. Translated by Herbert Joseph Spinden, *Songs of the Tewa: With an Essay on American Indian Poetry* (New York, 1933); quoted by A. Grove Day, *The Sky Clears* (Lincoln: University of Nebraska Press, 1970), p. 76.

58. Frank Waters (who is part Indian himself) has analyzed some Hopi concepts in *Pumpkin Seed Point*, p. 105.

59. A. Irving Hallowell, *Culture and Experience*, p. 234.

60. Ibid., p. 231.

61. Waters, *Pumpkin Seed Point*, pp. 103–4.

62. Lynn White, Jr., "Christian Myth and Christian History," in his book, *Machina Ex Deo*, pp. 37–38.

63. Sapir, "Culture, Genuine and Spurious," p. 318.

CHAPTER 7
Training Teachers for Cross-Cultural Education

1. Dr. Reichard was a professor at Barnard College and the author of a number of books on the Navajo, including *Spider Woman* (New York, 1934).

2. At this time Dr. Underhill was an assistant in anthropology at Barnard College; later, she became a well-known author of a number of books on Southwest Indians, including *The Navajos* (Norman, Okla., 1956).

3. A. C. Monahan, editorial notes, *Indians at Work* 2 (May 13, 1935):45.

4. Monahan to Miss Irene A. Smith and Miss Ida L. Peterson, May 9, 1935, 11940-1935-806-GS, NA.

5. "Extracts from Reports on Special Summer Schools," *Indians at Work* 2 (July 15, 1935):35.

6. Hildegarde Thompson to writer, November 26, 1971.

7. Allan Hulsizer, "Summer School at Pine Ridge, S.D.," *Indians at Work* 4 (September 1, 1936):39.

8. The report for the 1937 sessions suggested that Alaska employees often made "plans about coming out" as much as two years in advance and consequently they had not had adequate notice. It added that the choice of a location in Alaska would be "more desirable." "Indian Service Summer Schools, Sherman, Chemawa," 61877-1937-808-GS, NA.

9. Homer Howard to various superintendents, May 26, 1937, 11562-1937-808-GS, NA.

10. H. Thompson to writer, November 26, 1971.

11. The same comment has been applied to experienced Indian Service teachers of the 1960s, according to an Albuquerque Indian School teacher. Interview, November 12, 1970, in writer's personal collection.

12. Memo to Indian Service by Professor Fay-Cooper Cole, January 30, 1935, 6097-1935-810-GS, NA.

13. Ruth Underhill to Beatty, April 7, 1936, 12450-1936-810-GS, NA.

14. Summary of Indian Service Summer Schools, 1938, Sherman, Chemawa, NA, ibid.

15. Douglas to Homer Howard, November 6, 1937, 61877-1937-808-GS, NA.

16. John Collier to the Secretary of the Interior, January 13, 1938, NA, ibid.

17. Ryan's plans for a bulletin apparently failed to materialize. Edna Groves, supervisor, Home Economics, wrote in 1931, "I have had in mind the matter of a news letter for a number of years but there never seems to be time to take care of it. . . . Dr. Ryan has in mind a house letter for the entire Service. . . . Just how soon we will get to this I cannot tell you." Groves to Carrie Lyford, September 19, 1931, Lyford Office File, NA.

18. Edward Huberman to Beatty, March 19, 1936, 16996-1937-800-GS, NA.

19. On more than one occasion they were adopted in the decade of the sixties.

20. Huberman to Beatty, March 18, 1937.

CHAPTER 8
The Johnson-O'Malley Act: Indian Children and Public Schools, 1928–45

1. *Annual Report of the Secretary of the Interior*, 1900, p. 27; *Fiscal Year 1970 Statistics Concerning Indian Education*, p. 6.

2. *Fiscal Year 1970 Statistics*, p. 21.

3. *The Problem of Indian Administration*, p. 36.

4. Ryan to N. D. Showalter, State Superintendent of Public Instruction, Washington State, September 15, 1931, 55897-800-GS, NA.

5. Ryan, "Federal-State Cooperation in Indian Education," *School and Society* 34 (September 26, 1931):419.

6. Ryan to Showalter, September 15, 1931.

7. Sherman Institute, California, a federal boarding school, was the only exception, but its status was not affected by the state contracts.

8. Ryan had looked for the passage of the Swing-Johnson bill as early as 1931–32.

9. In 1936 the act was amended (U.S. *Stat.*, vol. 49, p. 1458) to include state schools and state or private corporations, agencies, or institutions.

10. Representative Roy E. Ayers (D., Montana), CR, vol. 78, part 7, 73d Cong., 2d sess., May 6, 1935, p. 7018. See also part 3, February 28, pp. 2774–76, and part 9, May 21, p. 9194.

11. Samuel Thompson to William Zimmerman, Jr., February 9, 1936, 42133-1934-803-GS, NA.

12. *Annual Report of the Secretary of the Interior*, 1936, p. 169.

13. "It is, therefore, quite obvious," wrote the Oregon Indian Superintendent at Large, "that any problems arising from the attendance of Indian children in the public schools immediately become questions for the local authorities . . . and the influence of the position of local administration must be clearly recognized, and the sentiment of the particular community must be carefully considered." Superintendent of Indian Schools at Large (no name), Financial Report of Public Schools (n.d.), 4575-1935-800-GS, NA.

14. Washington state relied on state income for 60 percent of the cost of public-school education. William Zimmerman, Jr., to Senator Elmer Thomas, Chairman, Committee on Indian Affairs, November 4, 1936, 42133-1934-803-GS, part 1, NA.

15. This was facilitated by an enabling act, which the California state legislature had passed in 1928 in anticipation of the eventuality of state contracting.

16. In 1928 Congress passed legislation (U.S. *Stat.*, vol. 45, p. 602) that entitled the "Indians of California" to sue the United States in the U.S. Court of Claims for lands taken from them without their consent. A net award of about $5 million was made in 1944. In 1946, however, when the Indian Claims Commission was established, further claims were filed by the "Indians of California" and by individual tribes. In 1964 the Court of Claims settled all of the claims of these groups for $29.1 million. Harrison Loesch, Assistant Secretary of the Interior, to Spiro T.

Agnew, President of the Senate, November 17, 1971; *American Indian Law Newsletter* 4 (December 1, 1971):269–72 (hereafter cited as *AILN*).

17. Tomas Arviso, spokesman, Rincon Reservation and Member of Valley Center School Board to Walter Dexter, Superintendent of Public Instruction, July 27, 1940, 18862-1934-803-GS, NA.

18. Beatty to Mary Stewart, May 4, 1937, 18862-1934-803-GS, part 3, NA.

19. Beatty to Mary Stewart (n.d. except 1941), *Indians at Work* 10 (Spring 1943):35.

20. Beatty to Mary Stewart, May 4, 1937.

21. Beatty to Byron J. Brophy, Superintendent of Indian Education (Washington state), March 6, 1941, 42133-1934-803-GS, part 5, NA.

22. Samuel Thompson to Beatty, May 4, 1936, 61017-1935-803-GS, part 1, NA.

23. Ibid. Sande was so well thought of by the Education Division that he became a Bureau administrator shortly thereafter.

24. Collier to Benjamin Drake, Sr., January 10, 1941, 61017-1935-803-GS, part 4, NA. In spite of the overwhelming praise given to the Minnesota system, criticism was not entirely lacking. At least one Bureau field representative in the state wrote that there was "still a very real, even serious gap between the ideals of Brothers Rockwell and Sande and the Indian education actualities." Louis Balsam, Consolidated Chippewa Agency, Cass Lake, Minnesota, to Beatty, February 12, 1938, ibid.

25. According to 1937 statistics, the California contract was for $173,000 and the Washington and Minnesota contracts were for $100,000 each. The Arizona contract for the first year was approximately $33,000.

26. Beatty to H. E. Hendrix, Superintendent of Public Instruction, Arizona, April 9, 1938, 37544-1937-803-GS, NA.

27. H. E. Hendrix to Carl Hickerson, County School Superintendent, Prescott, Arizona, March 25, 1938, 37544-1937-803-GS, NA.

28. Beatty to Hendrix, April 9, 1938, ibid.

29. *The Problem of Indian Administration*, p. 36.

30. *Annual Report of the Secretary of the Interior*, 1934, p. 89.

31. Byron J. Brophy, Superintendent of Indian Education, Washington State, to Paul Fickinger, Associate Director of Education, June 14, 1941, 42133-1934-803-GS, NA.

32. Ibid.

33. Irene M. Berven points out that the only tribe that expressed an "indifferent attitude" toward public school attendance was the Kootenai, the "least acculturated of the three tribes on the reservation." Berven, "History of Indian Education on the Flathead Reservation," M.A. thesis, Montana State University, 1959, p. 76.

34. Beatty, "Twenty Years of Indian Education," in Baerreis, *The Indian in Modern America*, pp. 45, 46.

35. The superintendent was quoted in a letter from Samuel H. Thompson, supervisor of Public School Relations, to Beatty, January 19, 1938, 37544-1937-803-GS, NA. Thompson was in charge of public-school relations throughout this experimental period of J-O'M programs in the mid and late 1930s. He traveled extensively, keeping the Bureau's eye on as many areas as possible that fell within the J-O'M contract states, and instead of using the telephone he wrote voluminous letters describing literally hundreds of schools, their staffs, the children, the lunch menus, the physical condition of the schools, etc. In view of the numerous times when he encountered deplorable conditions, he was perhaps overly optimistic about the potential for Indian education through J-O'M funding. These letters provide a detailed source for the status of rural American schools in the later years of the Depression.

36. Collier to Henry Roe Cloud, Superintendent, Haskell Institute, October 6, 1933, 27990-1933-803-GS, NA.

37. Parents of the white children who lived near this small public school transported their children into Redwood Falls. This type of discrimination persisted despite the Bureau's hopes

for assimilation through the J-O'M program. Janet Russel, "Indian Children Attend Public School," *Minnesota Journal of Education* 30 (September 1949):24.

38. George C. Wells to Ryan, March 16, 1934, 18897-1934-800-GS, NA.

39. *Annual Report of the Secretary of the Interior*, 1934, p. 89.

40. This does not mean that all Indian children were in school. In 1934, out of a total of 3,400 Indian children of school age, the Bureau had records for only 1,700 for whom the federal government was paying tuition to the public schools. There were also 1,337 illiterate children between the ages of 10 and 21, as well as 1,323 adults who were illiterate. Homer L. Morrison, Superintendent, Indian Education, to Charles O. Roos, Special Representative, Hoaquiam, Washington, January 3, 1934, 2547-1935-800-GS, NA. Three years later the records showed a completely different picture, which was due, according to Samuel Thompson, to the prodigious efforts of Morrison. In 1937, out of 3,496 Indian children, 3,080 were enrolled in public school. Thompson to Collier, April 6, 1937, 42133-1934-803-GS, NA.

CHAPTER 9
World War II and the Postwar Years

1. John Adair develops this thesis with regard to the Navajos, concluding that "it would be difficult to find four years when the cultures of these people have been subjected to such an impact as during these war years." Adair, "The Navajo and Pueblo Veteran," *The American Indian* 4, no. 1 (1947):6. The fact that the Navajos were among the least acculturated Indians suggests that in some cases the war may have had a more unsettling influence on less acculturated tribes than on those that had been forced to adopt a life style more similar to the whites'.

2. The Nebraska (Santee) Reservation of the Santee Sioux suffered a 65 percent population loss between 1940 and 1960. Apparently many of those who left for war work never returned. One of the reasons for this, as Roy W. Meyer points out, was that Santee is the only Santee Indian community that is not close to a "fair sized town within reasonable commuting distance." Meyer, *History of the Santee Sioux*, pp. 312–13. The Navajos left their reservation in such numbers that they depleted the population by perhaps a fourth. According to Adair, about 15,000 Navajos moved away during the war. Adair, "The Navajo and Pueblo Veteran," p. 5.

3. Bureau educational funding for building was severely cut during the war. The building allocation declined from $462,200 in 1940 to $320,215 in 1945. *Digest of Appropriations*, 1940, p. 383; 1945, p. 348. Since this budget included construction, maintenance, and repair, the cut meant that the program for expansion of community schools was destroyed. In addition both community schools and boarding schools found it increasingly difficult to remain open.

4. Dale, "Navajo Indian Education Administration," p. 149.

5. One employee on the Navajo Reservation recalled that the children slept so close together they had to be put head to foot, side to side, to prevent the spread of disease. Interview with Leola Kessler, October 20, 1971, Indian History Project. Dr. George A. Boyce, a noted authority on Navajo education and the director of education on this reservation during the war, recently related his experiences in his book, *When Navajos Had Too Many Sheep: the 1940's* (San Francisco: Indian Historian Press, 1974).

6. U.S. House of Representatives, Report 2091, *Report of the Select Committee to Investigate Indian Affairs and Conditions in the United States*, 78th Cong., 2d sess., 1944, p. 9.

7. Brightman, "Mental Genocide (Some Notes on Federal Boarding Schools for Indians)," *Inequality in Education* 7 (February 1971):17.

8. *Annual Report of the Secretary of the Interior*, 1945, p. 245.

9. Spaulding to Beatty, May 25, 1941, 33535-1941-820-Haskell, WNRC.

10. Foster to Paul Fickinger, February 26, 1942, 18090-1941-810-Carson, WNRC.

11. The budget of the Education Division declined by over a million dollars during the war years. Between 1940 and 1942 funding for Bureau education was cut by 10 percent. The 1940 budget was $10,683,548. By 1942 it had dropped to the wartime low of $9,388,335. *Digest of Appropriations*, 1940, pp. 382–86; 1942, pp. 346–49.

12. U.S. House of Representatives, Interior Department Appropriation Hearings for 1944, part 2, Bureau of Indian Affairs, 78th Cong., 1st sess., 1943, p. 258.

13. M. L. Burns, Acting Superintendent, Cheyenne River Reservation, to John Collier, August 23, 1944, 42811-1936-Cheyenne River, NA.

14. U.S. House of Representatives, Interior Department Appropriation Hearings for 1946, 79th Cong., 1st sess., 1945, pp. 34–35.

15. However, during these years the Indian Service added a new program. The experience and well-earned reputation of the Education Division's summer training sessions led to a request for the Indian Service to teach special courses to American citizens of Japanese ancestry who were held at the Colorado River War Relocation Center in Poston, Arizona. (The Indian Service itself administered this camp, which was located on reservation lands.) These programs were coordinated with California's college system in order that credits would transfer and eventually earn for the candidates teacher certification by the California Department of Education.

16. Collier pointed out that the decrease in funding actually began in the late thirties. Emergency funding, such as the Indian CCC, began to dwindle as early as 1935; funding for IRA programs began to decline at about the same time. Collier, editorial, *Indians at Work* 12 (November-December 1944):5–6.

17. William Zimmerman, "Role of the Bureau of Indian Affairs Since 1933," *Annals of the American Academy of Political and Social Science* (May 1957):34.

18. Collier, *Indians at Work* 12 (November-December 1944):6.

19. Collier, editorial, *Indians at Work* 11 (July-August 1943):4.

20. O. K. Armstrong was on the *Reader's Digest* editorial staff. Armstrong, "Set the American Indians Free," *Reader's Digest* 47 (August 1945):47–52.

21. Ibid., p. 52.

22. One of the measures approved by Congress during this period was the formation of the Hoover Commission. This commission, headed by former President Hoover, was appointed by President Harry S Truman in 1947. In the next two years it completed a comprehensive study of the executive branch of the government, making a number of recommendations for consolidation of federal departments and agencies in order to achieve a greater economy in government. In revised form, most of the recommendations were approved by Congress in 1949. The Report of the Task Force on Indian Affairs, one of eighteen task force reports made for the commission, criticized the Collier approach to Indian affairs and supported the argument for assimilation. While it was not as hard on the New Deal Indian education programs, it stressed the need for improved enrollment, even though this might require more boarding schools; it also encouraged state control of J-O'M contracts, and, eventually, state and local control of all Indian Service schools. John Leiper Freeman, Jr., "A Program for Indian Affairs," *American Indian* 7 (Spring 1954):48–62.

23. These included the Menominee, Klamath, and western Oregon tribes, the Paiute Bands of southern Utah, the mixed-blood population of the Uintah and Ouray reservations, and the Alabama-Coushattas. In August 1953, Congress had declared its intention to terminate Indians as rapidly as possible in House Concurrent Resolution 108. A second measure that gave the states increased authority over reservations was P.L. 83-280 (August 15, 1953). Most tribes were hostile to this act because of their fear of state control. Consequently, they fought P.L. 280 until Congress passed an amendment (P.L. 90-284) that required tribal consent before a state could assume jurisdiction over a reservation. A large number of termination bills were also introduced.

24. This group inherited the reform mantle from the 1937 merger of the Indian Defense Association and the Eastern Association on Indian Affairs.

25. Unable to leave the field entirely, a number of reformers continued to defend the Indian through writing, and some of the most penetrating arguments against termination were developed by people like Oliver La Farge, president of the American Association on Indian Affairs during the termination fight. See *The Annals of the American Academy of Political and Social Science* 311 (May 1957), which is devoted to Indian problems. The foregoing discussion is based partially on interviews with John Rainer (Taos), March 21 and April 25, 1972, and John Belindo (Kiowa-Navajo), December 8, 1971, and February 11, 1972, Albuquerque, Indian History Project.

26. At least one tribe reserved funds paid as a claim settlement by the federal government. When the traditional fishing site of the Yakima Indians was destroyed by the Dalles Dam, the Yakimas established the settlement as a trust fund for tribal young people to attend college. By the late 1950s, twenty-four tribes had established scholarships for college. Doris K. Holmes and Elizabeth C. Rosenthal, "Of Students and Scholarships," *The American Indian* 8 (Winter 1958–59):46. This was the journal of the American Association on Indian Affairs.

27. Alice Henderson Rossin, "Cabinet Room," *The American Indian* 3 (Summer 1946):18.

28. That this was four years before the Navajo-Hopi Rehabilitation Act (April 19, 1950) only serves to emphasize that Beatty was well ahead of Congress in his awareness of the needs of these people and his willingness to respond. The rehabilitation legislation provided financial assistance to these tribes for a ten-year period, including a sum of $24 million for health and school facilities. Although bills to furnish aid to other tribes were introduced, none of them was passed.

29. Coombs, *Doorway toward the Light*, p. 29. This is the standard Bureau study of the program. As the Bureau's leading expert in the testing of Indian children, Coombs was responsible for much of the testing policy. His best known work is *The Indian Child Goes to School*. On Navajo education see also Hildegard Thompson, *The Navajos' Long Walk for Education* (Tsaile, Navajo Nation, Arizona, 1975), a warm reminiscence encompassing twenty-four years (1941–65) of experience with the Navajo.

30. In the second year of the program new units were opened at Chilocco, Phoenix, and Stewart. A year later, Albuquerque, Chemawa, and Cheyenne-Arapaho schools, all of which had seen a decline in enrollment during the war, were included.

31. For the girls, these included day-school housekeeping, practical home nursing, and general service—hotel and motel work and hospital ward attendant. For the boys, training included auto mechanics, furniture upholstery and repair, masonry, printing, and dairying. Coombs, *Doorway Toward the Light*, p. 79.

32. *Report to Schools on Progress of the Special Program of Eight Off-Reservation Indian Schools, 1953–1954* (n.p., n.d.), p. 25. If this approach had been adopted in the regular boarding schools, they might have achieved similar success.

33. By 1959 all but 65 of 580 graduates of the Special Navajo Program had found jobs through the aid of their schools. Coombs, *Doorway toward the Light*, p. 116.

34. See N. Scott Momaday, *House Made of Dawn* (New York: Harper and Row, 1969).

35. In the mid thirties, Bureau educators had discussed the possibility of setting aside one school for children whose behavior separated them from most of the other pupils.

36. Beatty, "The Indian in the Postwar Period," *The American Indian* 3 (Winter 1946):2.

37. Ibid., p. 5.

38. Beatty, *Education for Cultural Change*, p. 11.

39. Ibid., p. 44.

40. However, the Navajo situation did not lend itself to such a simple analysis. In one respect, Beatty was not responsible for this failure. He was fully aware of the Navajo desire for local education, and promoted a plan for new reservation schools to meet the need, but he was directed by the Bureau of the Budget to fill off-reservation boarding schools, which had

declined in enrollment during the war. Until these schools were filled, the Bureau of the Budget refused to allocate extensive funds for reservation schools. Interview with Boyce, May 18, 1972, Santa Fe, Indian History Project.

41. Bureau of Indian Affairs Inspection of Haskell Institute, 1958, 8875-1956-813-Haskell, WNRC.

42. In 1970, these included Aberdeen, Albuquerque, Anadarko, Billings, Juneau, Minneapolis, Muskogee, Navajo, Phoenix, Portland, and Sacramento.

43. Beatty remained very active in educational work after he left the Bureau. He served as Director of Education for UNESCO until 1953. From this position, he moved to become educational consultant for Perkins and Will, School Architects. In 1958 he became Associate Program Director for Save the Children Federation and the Community Development Foundation. Two years later he moved to the vice presidency of this foundation. In 1961, he accepted the chairmanship of the Indian Arts and Crafts Board. His death came, however, on the day of his acceptance.

CHAPTER 10
Hildegard Thompson: Education for a Technological Society

1. Hildegard Thompson to writer, November 26, 1971.

2. Interview with Bureau administrator, July 1970, Washington, D.C. In writer's personal collection.

3. Thompson speech, Cheyenne River School graduation, May 28, 1959, Indian Bureau.

4. *Annual Report of the Secretary of the Interior, 1959*, p. 235. These facilities were located in seven towns bordering the Navajo Reservation, including Aztec, Flagstaff, Holbrook, Manuelito-Hall (Gallup), Richfield, Snowflake, and Winslow. Another dormitory was at Albuquerque Indian School. In the 1960s their enrollment declined and by 1970 there were only 2,146 students in the program.

5. In 1940 slightly more than 6,000 Navajo children were in school and the average daily attendance in day schools was 1,760. Beatty, *Education for Cultural Change*, p. 38. In 1968, out of a total of 23,591 Navajo children enrolled in schools operated by the Indian Bureau, only 1,022 attended day school. Although over 20,000 were in reservation boarding schools, this often meant that they were still a long distance from home. In addition, over 2,000 children still attended off-reservation boarding schools. Finally, there were 18,372 enrolled in public school. *Statistics Concerning Indian Education, 1968*, pp. 10, 15, 25, 36.

6. These included Mt. Edgecumb, Wrangell Institute, William E. Beltz, and Chemawa, Oregon.

7. "Notes on Alaskan Student Enrollment at Chilocco" (n.d.), 5397-1966-803-GS-Chilocco, Indian Bureau.

8. In the fall of 1966 Chilocco reported the achievement levels for the newly arrived ninth grade Alaskan students. They were: reading, grade 5.1–5.5; mathematics, grade 6.1–6.5; language, grade 5.6–6.0. Scores for ninth-grade Navajos were identical. Ninth-grade students at the school, other than Alaskan or Navajo, were about two or three grades above these averages. Ibid.

9. Owen Morten (?) to Leon Wall, Superintendent, Chilocco Indian School, October 28, 1966. Ibid. In the first year of the Alaska program, students were given no choice as to school preference; later some effort was made to consider student desires. In the 1968–69 school year, however, only 9 percent of the eligible Alaskan boarding-school students selected Chilocco. Ibid.

10. Hildegard Thompson, "Education Among American Indians: Institutional Aspects," p. 101.

11. George Boyce, "Some Possibilities in Summertime Programs for Indian Children," October 1959, 16216-1959-808-GS, WNRC.

12. Robert A. Roessel, Jr., *Indian Communities in Action,* section 2, p. 123.

13. Reservation Principal, San Carlos Agency, to Area Director of Schools, September 28, 1962, 16216-1959-808-GS, WNRC.

14. Richard M. Balsiger, Assistant Area Director, Community Services, Portland Area Office, to Assistant Commissioner, Education, October 10, 1967, Portland Area Office, 600 GS, Indian Bureau. Records of Area Offices that reported the progress of these students from the 1965–66 summer sessions revealed that: out of a total of sixty-five students, twenty-five had withdrawn from colleges; eight averaged an F or failing grade; ten averaged a D; eighteen, a C; two, a B or above average; and three were unknown. Letters from Area Offices at Anadarko, Minneapolis, Billings, Muskogee, Portland, and Juneau to Acting Assistant Commissioner, Education, September-October 1967, 600-GS, Indian Bureau.

15. In the fall of 1961 a questionnaire was sent out to all Indian Service teachers. "Workshop: Quest for Quality Teaching," *Indian Education* (October 1962):4, 13095-1961-830-GS, WNRC.

16. Hildegard Thompson to Almira D. Franchville, Assistant Chief, Branch of Education, June 19, 1962, 7232-1962-800-GS, WNRC.

17. A phenomenon of these decades, educational specialists often had long careers in Indian Service education, ranging from actual teaching to supervisory positions, including that of boarding-school superintendent. At this time, usually late in their careers, they were transformed into educational specialists, and it was not unusual for the Director of Education to rely heavily on their experience in making major decisions.

18. Recommendations of National Congress of American Indians Convention, St. Paul, Minnesota, July 21–24, 1951, NCAI Convention Files, 1944–54, Records of the National Congress of American Indians, Washington, D.C.

19. Hildegard Thompson, "Challenges to Education in the 1960s," address delivered at the guidance Workshop, Intermountain School, June 12–26, 1961, 10358-1961-800-GS, WNRC.

20. Ibid.

21. Hildegard Thompson to Selene Gifford, August 20, 1962, 4487-1963-813-GS-Haskell, WNRC.

22. In a critical analysis of the stress on technological careers, home economics instructors at a 1963 workshop session recommended that "special attention continue to be devoted to training students in home living. With the emphasis on space age," they concluded, "administration seems to have lost sight of the great importance of preparing Indian boys and girls to have a satisfactory home and family life." "1963 Workshop Recommends," Home Economics Discussion Group, 11172-1962-800-GS, WNRC.

23. W. Wade Head, Area Director, Gallup Area Office, "The Future of Indian Education," address delivered at School Administrators Workshop, Intermountain Indian School, Brigham City, Utah, June, 1957, 9692-1957-808-GS, WNRC.

24. The long-range goal established by Commissioner Nash was 90 percent graduation from high school and 50 percent of the graduates attending college. Nash address, 1965, *Indian Education* 428 (February 1966):5.

25. *Annual Report of the Secretary of the Interior,* 1961, p. 291. In 1968 there were 181 graduates.

26. A group known as the Society of University Indians of America asserted in 1937 that there were several hundred Indians who held "degrees of higher learning." *Indians at Work* 4 (February 1, 1937):43.

27. Ruth Bronson, "Advanced Education Survey," 1932, 10972-1933-800-GS, NA.

28. A survey of higher education among Southwest Indians, conducted between September 1958 and January 1962, revealed that out of 416 students, a total of 237 dropouts were identified. This was better than 50 percent. Thirty-five percent of the Indians in school had less than a C (2.00) average; and only 26 out of 402 Indians in school (for whom grade point

averages were available) had an average of 2.75 or higher. G. D. McGrath, Robert Roessel, et al., *Higher Education of Southwestern Indians with Reference to Success and Failure*, pp. 264, 266.

29. Madison Coombs pointed out in a comparative study of Indian and white pupils in eleven states that non-Indian pupils invariably tested higher than Indian pupils. However, Indian pupils in public schools tested higher than those who attended federal and mission schools. Coombs, et al., *The Indian Child Goes to School*, p. 4.

30. Tribal funds had also increased in the 1960s. By 1967 the number of tribes that set aside higher education funds had jumped from twenty-four to forty, in less than ten years. In 1968 total tribal funding amounted to over $1.3 million. *A Progress Report from the Commissioner of Indian Affairs* (USGPO, 1968), p. 8 (hereafter cited as *Progress Report*). Nonetheless, the combined funds of all scholarship aid were still insufficient. In 1968 the Director of Education admitted that the scholarship fund was already inadequate, which meant that the Bureau had been forced to refuse students for lack of funds. Charles N. Zellers to Area Directors, September 26, 1968, 853-GS, Indian Bureau. In 1970 a new source of funding was made available with the founding of the American Indian Scholarships Program.

31. The most popular programs at Chilocco were dry cleaning, auto mechanics, welding, and printing, all of which were fairly successful in terms of job placement for graduates. "Chilocco Indian School, Program Review," January 22, 1969, 2346-1968-806-GC-Chilocco, Indian Bureau.

32. In 1963 the 150 students of the Institute represented seventy-four tribes and came from twenty states. *Annual Report of the Secretary of the Interior, 1962*, p. 17. In 1971 the first phase of construction was completed on the Bureau's newest addition to the post–high school vocational schools. This was the controversial Southwestern Indian Polytechnic Institute in Albuquerque. The subject of extensive debate by public-school officials, local residents, congressmen, and the Bureau for a period of at least five years, the institute was initially just one of several choices for federal school expansion. The fact that it was chosen indicates the strength of the trend toward post–high school vocational training. Although the school opened in the fall of 1971, final construction was scheduled to be completed in 1973, with a total cost estimated at $18.5 million. Enrollment was to be a maximum of 1,000 students, many of them married and living off campus. By the end of 1973, however, the second phase of construction had not been started, the student enrollment was under 500, and members of the all-Indian Board of Regents were questioning the "validity" of their contribution. "We should be a policy making board," commented Joe Herrera, board member (Cochiti), "but our roles as members of the board have never been defined." *Albuquerque Tribune*, June 8, 1973. Although the school had placed over 150 graduates by the end of 1973, its direction and success were seriously questioned by Indian leaders. "SIPI is being run by 'bureaucrats,'" observed Ernest Lovato, secretary of the All Indian Pueblo Council, but this school and all other Indian schools with Indian advisory boards should be under the "actual direction" of Indians. Interview, January 25, 1974, in writer's personal collection.

33. In 1964 more than 600 Indians participated in training programs of the Area Redevelopment Administration (Department of Commerce) and the Manpower Development Training Act of 1962 (76 *Stat.*, 23–33). *Progress Report*, 1964. After 1963 the Report of the Commissioner of Indian Affairs was published separately.

34. *Progress Report*, 1964, p. 10; 1966, p. 11.

35. Although a number of articles on relocation have been published since the 1950s (see, for example, Joan Ablon, "Relocated American Indians in the San Francisco Bay Area: Social Interaction and Human Identity," *Human Organization* 23 [Spring-Winter 1964]:296–304), very little research has been done on the education of the children whose families moved to urban areas. *The National Study of Indian Education: Education of Indian Children and Youth*, sponsored by the United States Office of Education (1970), dealt with this topic as one of several varieties of Indian schooling. What is needed, however, is a monograph that deals exclusively with urban

schooling and that would contribute to an understanding of the problems and pressures of these second-generation relocated Indians.

36. When the Bureau developed the Branch of Relocation Services in 1954, it depended partially on the success of job placement in the Navajo Special Education Program. However, both the relocation program and the traditional boarding schools were less successful than this carefully planned experiment.

37. The National Congress of American Indians asserted that the Bureau was moving untrained Indians to urban areas where they became a "pool of cheap, unskilled labor," and were "always the first to be laid off." Thus, they became victims of the "worst side of the white man's life." Quoted in the Episcopal Church-News, April 15, 1956. In 1955, the National Congress sent to Congress a Point Nine Program "to alleviate the present poverty, lack of education and training, and the present ill health of the country's 450,000 Indians." This plan suggested that development of reservation resources would solve the problems of the Indian people. As Dorothy Van de Mark points out, it was "lost" in the morass of congressional legislation. Van de Mark, "The Raid on the Reservations," *Harper's Magazine,* 212 (March 1956):52–53.

38. For a critical analysis of relocation, see Ruth Mulvey Harmer, "Uprooting the Indians," *Atlantic Monthly* 197 (March 1956):54–57. A second, more general analysis of relocation is Edith R. Mirrielees, "The Cloud of Mistrust," *Atlantic Monthly* 199 (February 1957):55–59. Another critical essay on Emmons's administration is Van de Mark, "The Raid on the Reservations," pp. 48–53. During this decade the Indian Bureau was deluged with criticism.

39. Thompson, "Report on procedures used in implementing Public Law 762, 83d Congress, for termination of the Paiute Bands of Southern Utah," March 25, 1957, 12217-1954-819-GS, WNRC.

40. Ibid.

41. Commissioner Emmons's attitude toward Indian participation in decision making was well known. On one occasion he pointed out to a group of Indian delegates that "consent by the Indian people would consistent [*sic*] participation on their part, which would be much too costly for the U.S. government and the tribes." Zimmerman, "The Role of the Bureau of Indian Affairs Since 1935," *Annals of the American Academy of Political and Social Science* (May 1957):32, 33.

42. "Indian Education and Training Program, Narrative Summary, Coastal Program," March 10, 1955–August 13, 1956, 12217-1954-819-GS, WNRC.

43. John O. Crow, Superintendent, to "Friend," June 26, 1956, Office of Indian Affairs, Field Service, Uintah and Ouray Agency, ibid.

44. James Ring, Acting Area Director, Phoenix, to Commissioner, July 27, 1955, ibid.

45. In the Klamath situation, out of 146 students who enrolled in school, at the end of the training period 9 had finished technical or business school and 34 were still enrolled; none had completed college and 18 were still enrolled. "Summary, Klamath Indian Education and Training Program," December 31, 1956, ibid., 1-A-1, WNRC. Among the Menominnee, approximately 700 out of the 3,200 tribal members took part in the special termination program.

46. Interview with retired Bureau education administrator, May 18, 1972, in writer's personal collection.

CHAPTER 11
New Directions in Federal Control

1. One analysis of Udall's move suggests that he was embarrassed by the lack of noticeable progress, particularly economic improvement, within the Indian community. Anxious to

achieve some obvious change, he became impatient with Philleo Nash. Despite the fact that Nash achieved a level of confidence with many Indian people (as an anthropologist, the commissioner attempted to work in some areas within the perspective of Indian needs), Secretary Udall believed that Nash simply was not moving fast enough. Needless to say, changes could not be made overnight, but often authoritative figures in the administration believed this possible. A similar response was evidenced by the ill-planned termination legislation of the 1950s. See D'Arcy McNickle, "Indian Tests the Mainstream," *The Nation* 203 (September 26, 1966):275–79. Opinions from Bureau leaders during this period tend to support this position. When Nash resigned the *New York Times* described him as "the most popular Indian Commissioner in years," and quoted a letter from President Johnson, who wrote to Nash that the Indian people had "renewed their confidence in government" during his incumbency. *New York Times*, March 13, 1966; also see March 23, 1966.

2. Coombs, "Changing Times," *Indian Education* 435 (May 15, 1966):1.

3. Hearings before a Special Subcommittee on Indian Education, of the Committee on Labor and Public Welfare, U.S. Senate, 91st Cong., 1st sess., February 24, 1969, pp. 316–17. Carl L. Marburger testimony. This information was also clarified through correspondence with former Bureau administrators (June 1972, February 1977).

4. Roessel to Marburger, June 16, 1967, 3089-66-Navajo Area Office-411 GS, Indian Bureau.

5. Early in his eight-month tenure, Franklin proposed a reorganization of the Bureau's central office. During the July 1973 Senate hearings on this proposal, however, it was revealed that Franklin's nomination had not been submitted to the Senate for approval, and, subsequently, he was removed from his position. *Realinement of the Bureau of Indian Affairs Central Office*, Hearings before the Subcommittee on Indian Affairs of the Committee on Interior and Insular Affairs, U.S. Senate, 93d Cong., 1st sess., June 25, July 10, 1973.

Franklin's reorganization plan remained in limbo until the approval of Commissioner Thompson. During the interim, some Bureau positions were temporarily shifted; Hawkins was transferred from Director of Education Programs to Acting Special Assistant, at first to Franklin and then to Thompson.

6. In the 1960s criticism of the public school led to experiments in "open education." As a current author notes, it is ironic "that the failures cited by recent critics were in many cases the same conditions the earlier reformers [of the 1930s] thought they were correcting." Irving J. Hendrik, "Federal Policy Affecting the Education of Indians in California, 1849–1934," *History of Education Quarterly* 16 (Summer 1976):26. Indian Service educators gradually introduced these concepts into traditionally structured Bureau schools. Both Concho (Oklahoma) and Pierre instituted upgraded programs of instruction, while Intermountain adjusted to the irregularities of "flexible scheduling." In order to brief education personnel on the current educational scene, the National Indian Training Center (entitled the Instructional Services Center from 1968 to 1972) at Brigham City, Utah, offered three-day courses on "Innovations and New Trends in Education."

7. The important differences between the late sixties and the early seventies indicated that the year 1970 served essentially as a dividing line between introductory changes and the beginnings of a dynamic shift recognized and acted upon by the Indian people. In these years the Navajos began to organize, plan, and direct their own summer training sessions for new Indian Bureau education personnel in the Navajo Area. In Michigan, the Inter-tribal Council began to direct educational scholarships through a contract with the Bureau, which had always handled the program. In the Southwest, the newly formed Navajo Division of Education also took over this responsibility from the Bureau.

8. Chief among these was the report prepared by the Commission on the Rights, Liberties and Responsibilities of the American Indian, established in 1957 by the Fund for the Republic. William A. Brophy and Sophie Aberle, *The Indian: America's Unfinished Business*, 1966. Three years later a far more critical study appeared. This was the result of research by the Citizen's

Advocate Center, directed by Edgar S. Cahn, *Our Brother's Keeper: The Indian in White America*, 1969.

9. Among educators see, for example, Horatio Ulibarri, "Teacher Awareness of Socio-Cultural Differences in Multi-Cultural Classrooms," Ed.D., University of New Mexico, 1959; Miles V. Zintz, *Education Across Cultures* (Dubuque, Iowa: William C. Brown, 1963). Anthropologists include, among others, Edward P. Dozier (Santa Clara), author of a number of articles and books, including *The Hopi Tewa of Arizona* (Berkeley: University of California Press, 1954); and Rosalie Wax, who, with her husband, Murray Wax (a sociologist), has written a number of articles including "Education for What?" *Midcontinent American Studies Journal* 6 (Fall 1965):164–70, and "Cultural Deprivation as an Educational Ideology," *Journal of American Indian Education* 3 (January 1964):15–18, as well as their recent study, *Indian Education in Eastern Oklahoma* (Lawrence: University of Kansas Press, 1969). Psychologists include Dr. John F. Bryde, "A Rationale for Indian Education," *Journal of American Indian Education* 8 (January 1969):11-14.

10. Dozier, paper read at Bureau conference on early childhood, 1968, as quoted by Anne Smith, *Indian Education in New Mexico*, p. 28.

11. Kluckhohn and Leighton, *The Navajo*, p. 321.

12. Mekeel, "An Anthropologist's Observation on Indian Education," p. 152.

13. Murray Wax and Rosalie Wax, "The Ogalala Sioux Educational Project" (Atlanta, 1963), quoted by Edward Parmee, *Apache Indian Community*, p. 28.

14. Bryde, "A Rationale for Indian Education," p. 12.

15. W. W. Keeler, Chairman, et al., *Report to the Secretary of the Interior by the Task Force on Indian Affairs* (n.p., July 10, 1961), pp. 25–26.

16. Brophy, Aberle, *The Indian: America's Unfinished Business*, p. 146.

17. Alvin M. Josephy, Jr., *The American Indian and the Bureau of Indian Affairs, A Study, with Recommendations*, February 11, 1969, quoted in Josephy, *Red Power*, pp. 117, 118, 123.

18. Estelle Fuchs and Robert J. Havighurst, *To Live on This Earth*, p. 21.

19. After Jackson's bitter fight against the Senate vote that awarded Blue Lake to Taos Pueblo (December 2, 1970), he succumbed to the threat of similar pressure in the Alaskan Native claims settlement and sought to compromise on this issue by vastly increasing the amount of land to be awarded to the Alaskan Natives. As a politician, Jackson "was not inclined to suffer another Taos Blue Lake catastrophe on the floor of the Senate," wrote Adrian Parmeter in "A Personal View of the Indian Affairs Reform Movement—The Alaska Native Land Claims," Indian Legal Information Development Service, *Legislative Review* 1 (April 1972):41.

20. Josephy suggests that the Presidential Task Force recommendation of 1966 to move the Bureau of Indian Affairs from the Department of the Interior to Health, Education and Welfare was effectively squelched by the House Interior and Insular Affairs Committee. According to Josephy, this was due to the fact that the move also implied the "transfer of Indian affairs to other Committees in Congress and to other sections of the Bureau of the Budget." Josephy, *Red Power*, pp. 109–10.

21. National Indian Education Consultation, February 7-10, 1972, American Indian Press Association press release, February 18, 1972, as quoted in *AILN* 5 (February 15, 1972):13.

22. Mondale, Address to the First National Indian Education Conference, November, 1969, Minneapolis, 115 CR 198, S 15342-S 15344, as quoted in *AILN* 2 (December 23, 1969):327.

23. Senator Fannin has written articles on Indian education, including "Indian Education—A Test Case for Democracy," *Arizona Law Review* 10 (Winter 1968):661–73.

24. According to Adrian Parmeter, Staff-Director for the Senate Special Subcommittee on Indian Education, Senator Fannin had first tried to establish the subcommittee under the Interior Committee, of which he was a member. Parmeter, "A Personal View of the Indian Affairs Reform Movement," p. 38.

25. *Indian Education: A National Tragedy—A National Challenge,* 1969 Report of the Committee on Labor and Public Welfare, Special Sub-committee on Indian Education, U.S. Sen. Res. 80, 91st Cong., 1st sess. (Washington, D.C., 1969), p. 1.

26. Ibid., p. 21.

27. See Brewton Berry, *The Education of American Indians, A Survey of the Literature.*

28. These included: preschool programs and kindergarten, summer school, adult education, easily accessible community colleges, financial aid to college students in terms of "need" rather than "location" (this referred to Bureau policy of refusing to aid Indian students who had moved away from their reservations), vocational and technical training related to employment opportunities, and treatment for alcoholism and narcotics addiction. The report also recommended full funding for the Bilingual Education Act (Title VII of the Elementary and Secondary Education Act), and that the Act be extended to include schools operated for Indians by nonprofit institutions. *Indian Education: A National Tragedy—A National Challenge,* pp. 111–30. This recommendation was enacted in May 1970.

29. Ibid., p. 113.

30. Coombs also suggested that the original intent of the subcommittee was the "dissolution" of the Indian Bureau, or at least the transfer of Indian education to the Department of Health, Education and Welfare. However, due to the consistently negative reaction to this suggestion by Indian leaders, the subcommittee had to delete this recommendation. Thus, he added that "people who do a great deal of talking about Indian self-determination had better start listening to them." "The Indian Student Is *Not* Low Man on the Totem Pole" (Lawrence, Kansas: Haskell Press, 1970), pp. 1, 2, 7, 8. Coombs's article originally appeared in the *Journal of American Indian Education* 9 (May 1970):1–9.

31. Coombs, "Changing Times," p. 2.

32. *Progress Report,* 1968, p. 7. In the early 1970s Head Start programs operating under the Indian and Migrant Program Division and the Office of Child Development under Health, Education and Welfare continued to make an impact on early education for Indian youngsters. Designed for flexibility, the programs were developed to meet the needs of individual communities. They often reflected a dual purpose: learning English and the "white man's ways" in order to adjust to public school; and preserving the tribe's own language and culture. In 1973 there were Head Start programs in all nineteen New Mexico pueblos, and even here emphasis varied widely, according to the traditions and environment of each community. A Pueblo teacher at the Paraje Head Start school suggested some results: "I ask my five children," she said, "Are you proud of what you are? I'm an Indian. I cannot be anything else. I'm proud of what I am. We were so timid before. . . ." *Albuquerque Journal,* December 16, 1973.

33. 117 *CR,* November 23, 1971, 181, S 19442, quoted in *AILN* 4 (December 15, 1971):294.

34. The 1971 Bureau budget for education-related programs was $114.1 million. Ibid.

35. *Progress Report,* 1968, p. 6.

36. In the early 1970s the Bureau continued to expand the number of schools using bilingual programs funded by Title VII (ESEA). Separate projects were also developed to provide materials for this new approach. At the University of New Mexico the Navajo Reading Study, directed by Robert Young, developed books to be used in Bureau schools on the Navajo Reservation. Young had been one of the key linguists in Beatty's bilingual program of the late thirties and early forties, and the renewed need for his talents in the late sixties and early seventies reiterates the continuing relevance of Beatty's prewar bilingual program. In the early seventies, however, the lack of Indian teachers that Young encountered in the thirties was no longer a staggering problem, and Young was able to employ Navajos in the university's College of Education to write the books. Young and William Morgan, who had been his assistant in 1940, also were revising their Navajo-English dictionary, first published in 1943.

37. *Education Dialogue,* November 1968, n.p. More recent experiments in course development include the University of Arizona and University of New Mexico contracts with Health,

Education and Welfare to design social studies curriculum improvements for Navajo schools. The College of Education at the University of New Mexico initiated its project in 1967 and began distributing curriculum unit kits to all Bureau schools on the Navajo Reservation in the early 1970s. Since the purpose of the contract was to encourage Navajo culture, the project staff developed unique materials. These included, among others: a second-grade unit on "My Community," a fifth-grade unit on "My Indian Heritage," and high school units on "Assets and Problems of Navajo Youth" and "Folklore, Mirror of Culture."

CHAPTER 12
Indian Organization and Leadership

1. Josephy, *Red Power*, pp. 5, 6.
2. *New York Times*, April 14, 1966.
3. Ibid., April 15, 1966.
4. Ibid., December 15, 1967.
5. Ibid.
6. Interview with John Rainer, April 25, 1972, Albuquerque, Indian History Project.
7. D'Arcy McNickle, a member of the Confederated Salish and Kootenai tribes of Montana, exemplifies this generation. An anthropologist, McNickle coauthored with Harold E. Fey *Indians and Other Americans* (New York: Harper & Brothers, 1959). This is a brief history of Indian-white relations, with primary emphasis on the twentieth century. It contains a cursory summary of Indian education before World War II (pp. 125–41). McNickle has also published a number of other works.
8. Momaday, an English professor at Berkeley, is best known for his Pulitzer Prize winning *House Made of Dawn*. He has also published *The Way to Rainy Mountain* (Albuquerque: University of New Mexico Press, 1969). Deloria published in rapid sequence *Custer Died for Your Sins* and *We Talk, You Listen*. Both authors have also appeared in national magazines. Deloria's article, "The War Between the Redskins and the Feds," appeared in the *New York Times Magazine* section, December 7, 1969. Momaday has written a number of book reviews for the *New York Times* and the *New York Review of Books*. See, for example, "Bringing on the Indians," *New York Review of Books*, April 8, 1971.
9. In the spring of 1972 it appeared as though a number of social science textbooks would not be printed because of a suit filed by a multiracial task force of the state of California. The suit contended that the books could generate inferiority feelings among minority group students "and tend to make them ashamed of all their natural and ancestral backgrounds." *Albuquerque Journal*, May 7, 1972. The issues at stake in California were also raised in other states. In the previous year Navajo parents conducted a sit-in at the administration building of Shiprock (New Mexico) Consolidated Schools to protest use of a textbook that referred to Indians as "savage barbarians." As a result, the superintendent "told teachers not to use the book anymore." *Albuquerque Journal*, May 14, 15, 1971.
10. Another concrete example was the Yakima tribal experiment with the use of film production to depict the growth of their education programs.
11. Although he did not specify the particular conference, Costo probably referred to the

National Indian Workshop on School Affairs held in Ogden, Utah, March 24–28, 1969, which received extensive coverage in the *Ogden Standard Examiner.* Costo, *Textbooks and the American Indian,* p. 249.

12. In addition to the eight Indian members, led by John Rainer, the National Council was composed of eight cabinet-level positions. Established by executive order, it was ratified by Congress in 1970. A copy of the statement of the Indian members (January 26, 1970) can be found in *AILN* 2 (April 1, 1970):50–62. The statement was an inclusive summary of their opinions on current Indian problems. The concurrence of this statement with that of the Kennedy Report led Madison Coombs to link the two reports in his critique, "The Indian Is *Not* Low Man on the Totem Pole."

13. "Control–Change–Choose: Indian Education," brochure for the Third National Indian Education Conference, November 4–6, 1971, Albuquerque, New Mexico.

14. Demmert was director of the American Indian Program in the Harvard University Graduate School of Education.

15. Part of the reason for this was the complexity of the legislation. Often, only experts such as Demmert himself could comprehend it clearly enough to make an intelligent decision. One section of a questionnaire offered this choice: "There should be a special department of Indian education; there should not be a special department of Indian education; there should be two departments of Indian education—one for Indians NOT under the Bureau of Indian Affairs, and one for Indians presently under the B.I.A.; the department of Indian education in the Office of Education and the Bureau of Indian Affairs should remain as they are; a department of Indian education should be placed in the Executive Office of the President; a department of Indian education should be in the Department of Interior on an equal level with the B.I.A." Demmert to Fellow Native American, February 17, 1972.

16. Within a short period of time the National Tribal Chairman's Association (NTCA) became the voice for one political extreme in the polarization of Indian people in the early 1970s. At the other extreme were the activists or Red Power advocates, who generally represented urban-based Indians. Opponents of NTCA labeled it an administration group. In return, NTCA accused activists of destroying most of the recent gains for the Indian people through the use of violence. In the aftermath of the 1972 Bureau seizure, NTCA censured those responsible for the destruction. These years, therefore, witnessed an Indian power struggle of urban versus reservation, activist versus conservative, which was by no means resolved at the end of 1973.

17. Project Outreach, prepared for the National Council on Indian Opportunity, Office of the Vice President, Washington, D.C., April 28, 1970, John Belindo, Project Coordinator. Another organization established at this time was the American Indian Scholarships Program, funded in 1971. Although the Bureau had increased its scholarship funding, this program gave larger individual grants and, in addition, was under Indian direction. The first director was John Rainer.

18. The coalition was particularly concerned with resistance at the area office level, and for this reason it opposed Marvin Franklin's reorganization proposal of 1973, which would have given the area directors "all the decision-making powers." "The Executive Director Speaks Out," interview with Gerald M. Clifford, Executive Director of CICSB, *Education Journal* (of the Institute for the Development of Indian Law) 1 (April 1973):6.

19. "CICSB Urges More Control at Local Level," ibid., p. 7.

20. *Project Outreach,* p. 12.

21. This organization was founded on April 1, 1970, by a group of young Indian leaders, including John Belindo, former Executive Director of the National Congress of American Indians, who became the first director (April 1970–April 1972). Myron Jones, the second director, was responsible for the initiation of the J-O'M project. The organization was funded by the Ford Foundation and was initially concerned with economic problems on reservations. On July 1, 1973, NILT became an independent corporation with the title Indian Education

Training, Inc. No longer involved with economic problems, it planned to expand its area of educational training. Having already added Arizona to its New Mexico base, it also began to work with parents in Nevada and Oklahoma. Indian Education Training, Inc., also cooperated closely with The Coalition of Indian Controlled School Boards (CICSB), particularly on the national level.

22. Jones's point of view represents one side of a dichotomy that developed among Indian educators. At the other extreme was the trend of the late sixties toward increasing professionalization. The annual meeting of the National Indian Education Association came to be dominated by individuals who had earned not only a college degree but an advanced degree as well. Opponents of professionalization included some of the more radical youth, who asserted that they had more respect for the wisdom of tribal members who did not even speak English than they did for an Indian with a label after his name. Jones felt that professionalization should not be encouraged at the expense of parental control, even though parents often had very little schooling themselves. Interview, February 2, 1972, Albuquerque, Indian History Project. Joe Cochineau, a representative of the Indian Association of Alberta, who spoke at the National Indian Education Association meeting in Albuquerque (1972), pointed out that the newly established Alberta Indian Education Center was seriously concerned about preservation of heritage and planned to tape interviews with tribal elders and to use them in course instruction. A similar acknowledgment of tribal elders was part of the curriculum of Navajo Community College. See also, The Zuni People, *The Zunis: Self-Portrayals* (Albuquerque: University of New Mexico Press, 1972).

23. Interview with Smartlowit, August 12, 1970, Yakima Indian Reservation.

24. In 1968 the average level of education completed by the Yakimas was fifth grade.

25. Speech by Wayne Newell (Passamaquoddy), National Indian Education Conference, 1971, Albuquerque, Indian History Project.

26. *Seattle Post Intelligencer,* December 6, 1969.

27. Walter Hickel, Secretary of the Interior, to Vernon Ashley, Chairman, Governors Interstate Indian Council, April 8, 1969, 2346-806-Chilocco, Indian Bureau.

28. Pyramid Lake Paiute Tribal Council to Congressman Walter W. Baring, March 1, 1968, 11306-1962-411-GS-Nevada-Stewart School, Indian Bureau.

29. See, for example, Joseph N. Bell, "America's Oldest Debt: Justice for the Indians," *Good Housekeeping* (January 1971):78–80, 146–50; William Hedgepeth, "America's Indians, Reawakening of a Conquered People," *Look* 34 (June 2, 1970):23–45; *Life* special issue on "Our Indian Heritage," 71 (July 2, 1971). *Saturday Review* carried several articles on Indian education, including those by Estelle Fuchs, professor of education, Hunter College: "American Indian Education: Time to Redeem an Old Promise" (January 24, 1970):54–57, 74–75; and "The Navajos Build a College" (March 4, 1972):58–62. In 1972 Dr. Fuchs coauthored with Robert J. Havighurst *To Live on This Earth: American Indian Education* (Garden City, New York: Doubleday & Co.), based on the *National Study of Indian Education,* 1970.

30. Indian studies programs took a variety of names. In some schools, Native American Studies was adopted, to include Alaskan Natives; others chose Indian Studies; and others preferred Ethnic Studies, to include Chicano and Black groups.

31. In 1937 the University of Oklahoma established an Institute of Indian Education (later changed to the American Indian Institute), which coordinated programs concerned with Indians. It sought to encourage Indians to understand white society as well as to further knowledge about the Indian people.

32. These included the University of Michigan, the University of Minnesota, and the University of California, Berkeley.

33. A similar program to develop administrators for Indian schools and Indian education programs was established at the University of Minnesota in 1970. By 1973 Minnesota had awarded fifteen master's degrees and two doctorates. Four additional doctoral candidates were in the program, all of whom were Indian.

34. Fort Lewis College had been established with the stipulation that it would permit Indian students to enroll tuition free. The school encountered no difficulty in supporting these students until the fall of 1970 when, for the first time, the number of applicants (247) exceeded the usual pattern, which was 10 percent of the student body. In order to help the college out of its predicament, in April 1971 the state legislature passed a law that continued free tuition for Colorado Indians only.

35. Interview with Roessel, October 5, 1970, Indian History Project.

36. The Yakima Tribe persuaded the local television station to defray the cost of making at least two films on their educational programs. As Smartlowit pointed out, since the Federal Communications Commission required a minimum of public service projects of this type for broadcasting stations, there was no reason why this station should not donate its obligation to an Indian tribe.

CHAPTER 13
Indian-Controlled Schools

1. Roessel, *Indian Communities in Action,* p. 43.

2. In 1969 the Kennedy Report asserted that the Bureau had never "requested" or "required" a study of this reservation that "would show the effect of road construction on proposed school construction and operations." *Indian Education: A National Tragedy—A National Challenge,* p. 70. Beatty encountered this problem during the war years and after the war was over, he concluded that the expense was too great for the result that might be obtained.

3. Ibid., p. 86. Roessel left the Bureau and became director of the Indian Community Action Center at Arizona State University. Within a short period, however, he reentered the field of Navajo community education as a temporary troubleshooter and by 1966 he had returned to the reservation.

4. "The Small School Also Serves," "Values of the Small School, Can We Preserve Them?" Hildegard Thompson, *Education for Cross-Cultural Enrichment,* pp. 56, 58.

5. Yazzie was a well-known leader whose encouragement of self-determination in Indian education was one of the most instrumental factors in bringing about Rough Rock. In 1965, the year before Rough Rock was begun, the first demonstration school was established at Lukachukai, under an OEO grant. This school proved to be unsatisfactory because its administration was under the control of the Indian Bureau rather than the local community. When the Rough Rock plant became available the experiment was moved to the new location.

6. DINE stands for Demonstration in Navajo Education, but *Diné* also is the Navajo word for themselves, meaning "The People."

7. In Rough Rock's first two years, more than 10,000 people made the trek to this remote, beautiful spot at the foot of Black Mesa.

8. The Bureau provided almost half of the joint funds.

9. Donald A. Erickson and Henrietta Schwartz, *Community School at Rough Rock.* The critique was: Robert Bergman, Joseph Muskrat, Sol Tax, Oswald Werner, and Gary Witherspoon, "Problems of Cross-Cultural Educational Research and Evaluation" (mimeo, 1969), as quoted in *School Review* 79 (November 1970):58. Most of this issue, entitled "Skirmish at Rough Rock," is devoted to the debate over Erickson's report. See also the viewpoint of a disenchanted former Rough Rock teacher: Guy Blackburn, "A View from Within," *The Arizona Teacher* (January 1972):5, 6, 19, 22, 23.

10. Ironically, one of the critics of the school was Rupert Costo, who submitted that Rough Rock still committed the error of relying on boarding schools. "To alleviate homesickness" at the school, he wrote, Indian adults are invited to tell them stories and to speak to them. "This," he added, "is small comfort to the youngster who longs to go home." Costo, *Textbooks*

and the American Indian, p. 247. In defense of the boarding-school system, Anita Pfeiffer, Navajo staff member, pointed out that they were willing to take the children home anytime, roads permitting. Interview with Pfeiffer, October 6, 1970, Rough Rock, Indian History Project.

11. Dillon Platero and Gary Witherspoon, "Rough Rock Demonstration School Proposal for 1968–69," Indian Bureau.

12. Early titles included: Roessel and Platero, eds., *Coyote Stories of the Navaho People* (Chinle, Arizona: Rough Rock Demonstration School, 1968); Vada Carlson and Witherspoon, *Black Mountain Boy* (1968); Sydney M. Callaway, et al., *Grandfather Stories of the Navahos* (1968). Another project that sought to remedy the lack of written material was the Navajo Reading Program, established at the University of New Mexico through a contract between the school, the Bureau, and the Ford Foundation. As of 1972, however, in spite of the seeming duplication of these two projects, there was no coordination between them. Interview with Robert Young, Director of the Program (1971–72), June 26, 1972, Albuquerque, Indian History Project.

13. In 1970, Dillon Platero was very defensive on this point. He explained that the experimental nature of the school necessitated the larger budget. Interview with Platero, September 6, 1970, Rough Rock, Indian History Project. Nonetheless, the gap between the Rough Rock budget and the average boarding-school budget remained too wide to justify either extreme. In 1969, the average amount budgeted for a boarding school child was $1,650, or about half of the amount allocated for a child attending a private school. Bennett address to Dartmouth College, May 17, 1969. The Rough Rock budget, which was planned for an enrollment of 240, was roughly the equivalent of $3,000 per pupil. As Bennett pointed out, "we cannot do justice to Indian youth on such a penny-pinching scale."

14. Roessel to Robert Bennett, Commissioner of Indian Affairs, July 20, 1966, 3089-66-411-GS, Navajo Area Office, Indian Bureau.

15. In the preface to the report, the Rough Rock Board of Education made it quite clear what it thought of analysis by professional educators. Observing that the evaluators "all spoke fluent Navajo," and were "all Navajos," and thus could draw conclusions that would "be accepted with confidence by other Navajos," the board added, "We didn't want some high sounding mishmash of research terms that do nothing but add further confusion. We wanted, and received, a clear, down to earth exposition of just what these Navajo leaders think of this school. . . ." John Y. Begaye, et al., *Navajo Evaluators Look at Rough Rock Demonstration School* (Chinle, Arizona: Rough Rock Demonstration School 1969), pp. 28, 29, 32, 34.

16. In 1973 Rough Rock was a participant in one of the Health, Education and Welfare contract programs negotiated between certain Southwest tribes and the University of New Mexico and University of Arizona. Specifically designed to enable Indians to obtain college degrees (either bachelor or associate of arts, depending on the plan), these projects were geared to bring education to the teacher. In each case, university professors traveled to the community to offer instruction.

The Navajo Teacher Education Development Program (NTEDP), which was implemented though contracts negotiated between the Navajo Tribe and the two universities, sought to correct the imbalance between Indian and non-Indian teachers in Navajo Reservation schools. In 1973, of the 2,800 Navajo Reservation teachers, fewer than 200 were Navajo. Negotiated by Dillon Platero, who had moved from director of Rough Rock to director of the Navajo Division of Education, this program was based on a five-year goal. In this period, Platero hoped to increase the number of Navajo teachers by 400 percent, which meant that by 1978, 1,000 Navajos would be serving in reservation schools. (Late in 1973 the Navajo Tribe was preparing proposed federal legislation that would make it possible for Indian tribes to take over supervision of all reservation schools.)

Another contract was negotiated between the University of New Mexico and the All Indian Pueblo Council, and provided for associate of arts degrees for Pueblo Indian teachers. In 1973, 150 Pueblo teacher aides in seven different pueblos were taking courses from the university. This degree represented two years of course work plus two summers on the university campus. (The associate of arts programs were coordinated by Anita Pfeiffer, formerly on the staff at Rough Rock and currently a doctoral candidate at Harvard University and a member of the College of Education faculty, University of New Mexico.)

The potential of these programs was far greater than any past efforts made by the Indian Bureau. They demonstrated the enthusiasm that often accompanied projects developed under Indian direction, and they also revealed the impact of federal funding made available through contract negotiations.

17. Several members of the community sought to keep the school open through court action. There was also an effort to force the school district to improve transportation, but neither action was successful. *Albuquerque Journal,* September 6, 1970.

18. Although this was only one year after Commissioner Bennett had observed that cost per pupil for boarding schools was $1,650, the amount provided for Ramah was figured at $2,204 per pupil. Thus, for the 167 pupils estimated, the total grant was $368,068. This was a significant increase over the previous year. Ibid.

19. *Washington Post,* April 9, 1970.

20. When Rough Rock was initiated Coombs was Deputy Director of Education. Even in the early stages of its development, however, he was critical of its method. He recalled later, "There was never room for a spirit of open and free inquiry as to how theories were working." Rather, its "purpose" was one of demonstrating "theories which their proponents had long before assured themselves were sound and right." Coombs, "Rough Rock Revisited: The Indian Voice in Education, How Can It Best Be Heard?" *The Arizona Teacher* (March-April 1972):11, 24.

21. The Navajo evaluators of Rough Rock recommended a followup evaluation of every student leaving the school. Only through this means could the school gauge its long-range effectiveness. *Navajo Evaluators Look at Rough Rock Demonstration School,* p. 34.

22. The school received funds from Health, Education and Welfare and from the Indian Bureau. However, its funding from Johnson-O'Malley programs was grossly inadequate due to the fact that when the county superintendent of schools split the J-O'M budget he allocated 90 percent to the Havre District and 10 percent to the Rocky Boy District. NAACP Legal Defense and Education Fund, Inc., with the cooperation of the Center for Law and Education, Harvard University, *An Even Chance,* p. 55.

23. Interview with Roessel, Navajo Community College, October 5, 1970, Indian History Project.

24. The Navajo Tribe also donated 2,000 acres of land at Tsaile Lake, where the new campus would be built; and an additional 500 acres at Many Farms for an agricultural program.

25. Interview with Roessel, October 5, 1970.

26. Ibid.

27. Interview with Hatathli, October 5, 1970, Navajo Community College, Indian History Project. Roessel became chancellor after his term of office and then was aptly chosen for the challenging task of securing funds for the school.

28. Ibid.

29. Even in the very early stages NCC's directors were aware of the need for accreditation and sought to meet the necessary standards. Thus, when the first team of evaluators visited the school, late in 1971, its preliminary report was favorable. *Albuquerque Tribune,* February 17, 1972.

30. Although the influence of NCC has spread beyond the Navajo Reservation (among Indian institutions begun in the early 1970s were Standing Rock Community College, North Dakota, and Sinte Gleska College on the Rosebud Reservation, South Dakota; DQU, a two-year university in northern California, was designed to serve Indians and Chicanos), no other Indian reservation college has received the broad financial backing and congressional support which have made NCC a unique institution.

31. Interview with Roessel, October 5, 1970.

32. *Albuquerque Tribune,* April 22, 1971.

CHAPTER 14
Indian Children and Public Schools, 1945–73

1. In 1970 Congress amended this law again in order to give Indian schools "equal priority" with other requests (P.L. 91-230, Sec. 206). But, as the NAACP points out, the United States Office of Education still would not be able to fund all the "back requests" under Sec. 14. Fiscal year 1971 appropriations of $15 million for P.L. 815 would support only $6 million of Sec. 14 requests. NAACP, *An Even Chance,* p. 6

2. Ibid.

3. These two were Oregon and Florida. Oklahoma was the only state of the eighteen that participated in J-O'M and also received funds under P.L. 874. This was due to the fact that Oklahoma was the only state that had a "predominantly special services program under J-O'M funding rather than an Enrichment aid program." Enrichment provided for maintenance and operation, while special services included lunches, supplies, fees, books, transportation, etc.

4. This was Wisconsin, which preferred J-O'M programming only.

5. In school districts eligible for funding under P.L. 874 (as amended), "supplemental aid" under the J-O'M program "will be limited to meeting educational problems under extraordinary or exceptional circumstances." *Code of Federal Regulations* (hereafter cited CFR), *Title 25—Indians* (Revised as of January 1, 1968), 33.4(c). In terms of financial output for the Bureau of Indian Affairs, the new legislation meant an immediate reduction in the J-O'M budget. In 1959 the total J-O'M budget was $5,201,000. Without P.L. 874 assistance, it would have been $8,500,000. *Annual Report of the Secretary of the Interior,* 1959, p. 234.

6. " 'Educationally deprived children' . . . includes children who are handicapped or whose needs for such special educational assistance result from poverty, neglect, delinquency or cultural or linguistic isolation from the community at large." 45 *CFR,* 116.17(g).

7. The average income of an Indian family is $1,500, which is 75 percent below the national average. *Indian Education: A National Tragedy—A National Challenge.* p. x.

8. Ibid., p. 92.

9. More than two-thirds of all public-school districts participate in Title I programs. *An Even Chance,* p. 27.

10. Not until the end of the 1960s was there any foreseeable change in this misuse of funds. In the fall of 1969 the city of Albuquerque began a new system of accounting for its J-O'M funds, and instituted special programs for the Indian students that made use of the funds allocated for these students. Even in the short time that this change had been in effect, the coordinator of the programs observed that the results in terms of parental involvement and student interest were much more positive than the school system had expected. Interview with Johnny Caton, Coordinator of special Indian programs for the Albuquerque Public Schools, March 2, 1972, Albuquerque, Indian History Project.

11. In the 1965 nationwide median test scores, twelfth-grade Indian students were below the national average in every criterion, ranging from 8.4 percent in verbal skills to 4.9 percent in nonverbal skills. In response to questions in the individual motivation survey of the same year, only a third (36 percent) of the twelfth-grade students said they would "do anything to stay in school"; less than a third (31 percent) said they believed they were "brighter than average"; and over a third (44 percent) said "I just can't learn." James S. Coleman, et al., *Equality of Educational Opportunity,* p. 24. *Indian Education: A National Tragedy—A National Challenge* also points out that the achievement levels of Indian children are two to three years below those of white students (p. ix).

EPILOGUE

1. News Release from the Office of the White House Press Secretary, July 8, 1970.

2. Before the final draft of the bill was completed, the Indian Education Subcommittee made specific changes as requested by Indians. One of these was the deletion of a provision to establish a National Board of Indian Education. The original bill provided for the transfer of administration of Indian education programs from the Indian Bureau to this National Board. This proposal to "fragment" the Bureau was unequivocally opposed by some tribes.

3. Senate debate and vote on S. 2482 (Indian Education Act). *CR* 117, Part 27, 92d Cong., 1st sess., October 8, 1971, pp. 35, 642.

4. Herschel Sahmaunt, "An Indian Education Leader Speaks Out," *Education Journal* 1 (March 1973):7.

5. Ibid., p. 9.

6. The budget for the Indian Education Act was approximately $202 million.

7. Two separate suits were filed, each on behalf of several clients. The first action was taken by the Native American Rights Fund of Boulder, Colorado. The second was initiated by four Indian attorneys—John Ghostbear (Sioux), Ralph Keen (Cherokee), Kirke Kickingbird (Kiowa), Executive Director, Institute for the Development of Indian Law, and Vine DeLoria, Jr., currently President of the Board of the Institute for the Development of Indian Law—on behalf of a number of clients, including the Coalition of Indian Controlled School Boards.

8. Part A grants were awarded to 436 local educational agencies for development of elementary and secondary school programs to meet the special needs of Indian children. Part B grants went to fifty special programs and projects. Part C grants went to ten adult education programs. Over thirty states were represented in the allocation funding. While the heaviest concentration of grants was in those states with large Indian populations, for the first time the East Coast, from Maine to Florida, was also represented. "Title IV Distribution Map," *Education Journal* 1 (June–July 1973):10–11.

9. "Proposed Johnson-O'Malley Regulations," Jointly Submitted by Alaska Federation of Natives, All Indian Pueblo Council of New Mexico, American Association of Junior and Community Colleges, American Indian Law Center, et al. Mimeo, February 28, 1974. (Courtesy of Indian Education Training, Inc.)

10. *Education Dialogue* (March 1975):3.

BIBLIOGRAPHY

MANUSCRIPTS

The National Archives of the United States
  Records of the Bureau of Indian Affairs. Record Group 75
  Central Classified Files—General Services File
    General and Statistical
    Finance and Accounts
    Health and Social Relations
    Education
    Industries and Employment
Washington National Records Center, Suitland, Maryland
  Records of the Bureau of Indian Affairs. Record Group 75
Bureau of Indian Affairs, Washington, D.C.
  Records of the Bureau of Indian Affairs. Record Group 75
    Boarding and Day Schools: Navajo Area, Cheyenne River, Haskell,
      Chilocco, Albuquerque Area, and Nevada
    General Services File
    Education
National Congress of American Indians, Washington, D.C.
  Records of Conventions
  Correspondence of Staff

Interviews
  Unless otherwise noted, these interviews are located in the American Indian History
  Research Project files, Zimmerman Library, University of New Mexico.
  Mort Abromowitz, Navajo Community College, October 5, 1970.
  Willard Bass, Southwest Cooperative Education Laboratory, Albuquerque, September 23,
    1971. In writer's collection.
  John Belindo, Kiowa-Navajo, National Indian Leadership Training Program, Albuquerque,
    December 8, 1971, February 11, 1972.
  Dr. George Boyce, Santa Fe, May 18, 1972.

233

Johnny Caton, Special Indian Programs, Albuquerque Public Schools, Albuquerque, February 2, 1972.

Madison Coombs, Arlington, Virginia, July 14, 1970. In writer's collection.

Donald J. Fosdick, Bureau of Indian Affairs, Washington D.C., July 13, 1970. In writer's collection.

Grace Funk, teacher, and several pupils, Albuquerque Indian School, November 12, 1970; April 3, 1971. (Second interview in writer's collection.)

Helen Hardin, Santa Clara, Albuquerque, April 11, 1972.

Ned Hatathli, Navajo, Navajo Community College, October 5, 1970.

Myron Jones, Tuscarora, National Indian Leadership Training Program, Albuquerque, February 22, 1972.

Leola Kessler, Albuquerque, October 20, 26, 1971.

Keith Lamb, Superintendent, Albuquerque Indian School, April 8, 1971. In writer's collection.

Roby Leighton, Rough Rock Demonstration School, October 6, 1970. In writer's collection.

Ernest Lovato, Secretary, All Indian Pueblo Council, Albuquerque, January 25, 1974. In writer's collection.

Heinz Meyer, Bureau of Indian Affairs, Washington, D.C., July 13, 1970. In writer's collection.

Anita Bradley Pfeiffer, Navajo, Rough Rock Demonstration School, October 6, 1970. In writer's collection.

Dillon Platero, Navajo, Rough Rock Demonstration School, October 6, 1970.

John Rainer, Taos, American Indian Graduate Scholarship Program, Albuquerque, March 21, April 25, 1972.

Bernard E. Richardson, Library, Navajo Community College, October 5, 1970. In writer's collection.

Robert A. Roessel, Jr., Navajo Community College, October 5, 1970.

Pauline Sam, Yakima, Albuquerque, November 5, 1970.

Joe Sando, Jemez, Southwest Cooperative Education Laboratory, Albuquerque, September 30, 1971.

Stanley Smartlowit, Yakima, Yakima Tribal Headquarters, Toppenish, Washington, August 12, 18, 1970. In writer's collection.

Jerry Suazo, Taos, Albuquerque, April 27, 1972.

Mrs. Lucy Suazo, Acoma, Albuquerque, December 10, 1970. In writer's collection.

Pablita Velarde, Santa Clara, Albuquerque, February 9, 1972.

Henry A. Wall, Albuquerque Area Office, May 26, 1970. In writer's collection.

Robert Young, University of New Mexico, January 14, February 1, 1972.

THESES AND DISSERTATIONS

Adair, Mildred L. *The Establishment, Growth, Development and Functioning of the Federal Day School on the Navaho Reservation Since 1935.* M.A. thesis, Florida State University, 1938.

Berven, Irene M. *History of Indian Education on the Flathead Reservation.* M.A. thesis, Montana State University, 1959.

Crook, Clifton. *A Study of Indian Education in Washington.* M.A. thesis, University of Washington, 1941.

Dale, Kenneth I. *Navajo Indian Educational Administration.* Ed.D. diss., University of North Dakota, 1949.

Fischbacher, Theodore. *A Study of the Role of the Federal Government in the Education of the American Indian.* Ed.D. diss., Arizona State University, 1967.

Hemsing, William M. *The History and Trends of Indian Education in New Mexico under the Administration of Federal and State Governments.* M.A. thesis, University of New Mexico, 1953.

Hopkins, David A. *A Brief History of Indian Education on the Tongue River Reservation.* M.A. thesis, Montana State University, 1951.

Johnson, Milo C. *The History of Education on the Fort Peck Reservation, 1885–1935.* M.A. thesis, University of Minnesota, 1937.

McClellan, Kenneth R. *The Ute Indians and Their Educational Programs.* M.A. thesis, University of Utah, 1953.

Poole, Charles P. *Two Centuries of Education in Alaska.* Ph.D. diss., University of Washington, 1948.

Ulibarri, Horacio. *Teacher Awareness of Socio-Cultural Differences in Multi-Cultural Classrooms.* Ed.D. diss., University of New Mexico, 1959.

Vrettos, Louis. *The Education of Indians with Special Reference to the Shoshone Indian Reservation in Wyoming.* M.A. thesis, University of Wyoming, 1949.

Wall, Claude Leon. *History of Indian Education in Nevada, 1861–1951.* M.A. thesis, University of Nevada, 1952.

DOCUMENTS

FEDERAL

U.S., Bureau of Indian Affairs. *Adult Education Series, 1956.* Lawrence, Kansas: Haskell Press, 1956.

————. *Annual Reports of the Commissioner of Indian Affairs, 1880–1970.* Between 1897 and 1963 this report appeared in the U.S. Department of the Interior, *Annual Report of the Secretary of the Interior.* Between 1964 and 1970 it was published separately, as *Indian Affairs, A Progress Report from the Commissioner of Indian Affairs.*

————. *Basic Goals for Elementary Children.* 2 vols. Lawrence, Kansas: Haskell Press, 1964.

————. *Doorway toward the Light,* by L. Madison Coombs. Lawrence, Kansas: Haskell Press, 1962.

————. *Education for Action,* ed. Willard W. Beatty. Chilocco, Oklahoma: Chilocco Agricultural School, 1944.

————. *Education for Better Living,* by George A. Dale. Lawrence, Kansas: Haskell Press, 1955.

————. *Education for Cross-Cultural Enrichment,* ed. Hildegard Thompson. Lawrence, Kansas: Haskell Press, 1964.

————. *Education for Cultural Change,* ed. Willard W. Beatty. Chilocco, Oklahoma: Chilocco Agricultural School, 1953.

————. *The Educational Achievement of Indian Children,* by Kenneth E. Anderson, E. Gordon Collister, and Carl L. Ladd. Lawrence, Kansas: Haskell Institute Print Shop, 1953.

————. *How Well Are Indian Children Educated?* by Shailer Peterson. Lawrence, Kansas: Haskell Institute Print Shop, 1948.

————. *In Step with the States,* by Homer H. Howard. Lawrence, Kansas: Haskell Institute Print Shop, 1949.

————. *The Indian Child Goes to School,* by L. Madison Coombs, et al. Lawrence, Kansas: Haskell Institute, 1958.

————. *Indian Education.* 12 vols. Chilocco, Oklahoma: Chilocco Agricultural School, 1936–1948.

————. *Indian Service Trachoma Control.* Lawrence, Kansas: Haskell Institute, 1941.

————. *Indians in non-Indian Communities.* Mimeographed. Window Rock, Arizona: U.S. Indian Service, 1953.

————. *Instructional Material for Use in Indian Schools: Money Series.* Washington, D.C.: Bureau of Indian Affairs, 1953.

————. *Minimum Essential Goals.* Lawrence, Kansas: Haskell Institute Press, 1952.

————. *Program for the Termination of Indian Bureau Activities in the State of California.* Sacramento, California: U.S. Indian Service, 1949.

————. *Reforms of the Indian Office and Withdrawal of the Federal Supervision over Indian Affairs,* by Ruth F. Kirk. Mimeographed. n.p.: 1945 (?).

————. *Report to Schools on Progress of the Special Five-Year Program at Eight Off-Reservation Indian Schools.* Multilithed. Brigham City, Utah: Intermountain Indian School, 1952.

————. *Report to Schools on Progress of the Special Program at Eight Off-Reservation Indian Schools.* n.p.: Bureau of Indian Affairs, 1953–54.

————. *Scholarships for American Indian Youth,* by Amanda H. Finley. Washington, D.C.: USGPO, 1963.

————. *Statistics Concerning Indian Education.* Lawrence, Kansas: Haskell Press, 1968–1971.

————. *Suggested Books for Indian Schools.* Lawrence, Kansas: Haskell Press, 1959.

————. *Summary Report: First and Second Sessions, Workshop—June 6–July 1, 1955.* 2 vols. Washington, D.C.: Bureau of Indian Affairs, 1955.

————. *Summary Report, School Administrators Workshop, Brigham City, June 3–14, 1957.* Lawrence, Kansas: Haskell Institute Press, 1957.

————. *Vocational Training Programs for American Indians,* by Virginia S. Hart. n.p., n.d. (reprinted from *Training Facts,* no. 15, December 1964, Office of Planning and Standards for Manpower Development, U.S. Department of Labor).

————. *We Teach in Alaska,* by Eunice and Dorothy Johnson. Juneau, Alaska: Bureau of Indian Affairs Area Office, 1957.

————. *The Withdrawal of Federal Supervision of the American Indian,* by John H. Provinse. Paper presented at National Conference of Social Work, San Francisco, California, April 15, 1947. Mimeographed. n.p.: 1947 (?).

U.S., *Code of Federal Regulations,* Title 25. Washington, D.C.: USGPO, January 1, 1968.

U.S., *Congressional Record.*

U.S., **Department of Commerce. Doc. PB 184571.** *Community School at Rough Rock,* **by Donald A. Erickson and Henrietta Schwartz. Springfield, Virginia, 1969.**

U.S., Department of the Interior. *Federal Relations to Education.* Washington, D.C.: National Capital Press, 1931.

————. *Indian Administration in the United States.* Address by Philleo Nash, University of Toronto, Toronto, Ontario, December 6, 1962. News Release, December 7, 1962.

————. *Report of the Acting Secretary of the Interior on H.R. 7260 (S. 2597), August 9, 1937, Making Provision for Inservice Training for Indian Service.* Washington, D.C.: 1937.

————. *Report to the Secretary of the Interior by the Task Force on Indian Affairs.* Mimeographed. n.p.: 1961.

U.S., Department of the Treasury. *Digest of Appropriations.* Washington, D.C.: USGPO, 1930–1945.

U.S., House of Representatives. *Hearings on S. 2103, An Act to Exempt Certain Indians and Indian Tribes from the Provisions of the Act of June 18, 1934 (48 Stat., 984) As Amended.* 76th Cong., 3d sess., 1940.

————. *Survey Report on the Bureau of Indian Affairs.* 83d Cong., 2d sess., 1954.

————. Report No. 2091, *Report of the Select Committee to Investigate Indian Affairs and Conditions in the United States.* 78th Cong., 2d sess., 1944.

————. Report No. 2680, *Report with Respect to the House Resolution Authorizing the Committee to Conduct an Investigation of the Bureau of Indian Affairs.* 83d Cong., 2d sess., 1954.

————. *Interior Department Appropriations Hearings,* for 1944, 1946.

————. *Present Relations of the Federal Government to the American Indian.* 85th Cong., 2d sess., 1959.

————. *Operation Bootstrap for the American Indian.* 86th Cong., 2d sess., May 31, June 1, 1960.

U.S., Office of Education. *Equality of Educational Opportunity,* by James S. Coleman, et al. Washington, D.C.: USGPO, 1966.

————. *National Study of Indian Education.* Education of Indian Children and Youth. Summary Report and Recommendations. n.p., 1970.

————. *The Educational Disadvantage of the Indian American Student,* by L. Madison Coombs. Las Cruces, New Mexico: New Mexico State University (ERIC Clearinghouse on Rural Education and Small Schools), 1970.

U.S., Office of the Vice President. *Project Outreach,* by John Belindo, Project Coordinator. Prepared for the National Council on Indian Opportunity. Washington, D.C.: 1970.

U.S., Senate. *Survey of Conditions of the Indians in the United States,* parts 1–43. Washington, D.C.: USGPO, 1928–1943.

————. Document 214. 72d Cong., 2d sess., 1933.

————. *Realinement of the Bureau of Indian Affairs Central Office.* Hearings before the Subcommittee of the Committee on Interior and Insular Affairs. 93d Cong., 1st sess., June 25, July 10, 1973.

————. *The Education of American Indians: Field Investigation and Research Reports.* 91st Cong., 1st sess., 1969.

————. *The Education of American Indians: The Organization Question.* 91st Cong., 1st sess., 1969.

————. *The Education of American Indians: A Compendium of Boarding School Evaluations.* 91st Cong., 1st sess., 1969.

————. *The Education of American Indians: A Compilation of Statutes.* 91st Cong., 1st sess., 1969.

————. *The Education of American Indians: A Survey of the Literature.* 91st Cong., 1st sess., 1969.

————. *Indian Education: A National Tragedy—A National Challenge.* 91st Cong., 1st sess., 1969.

STATE

Progress Report to the Governor and the Legislature by the Advisory Commission on Indian Affairs on Indians in Rural and Reservation Areas. Sacramento, California: California Office of State Printing, February 1966.

NEWSPAPERS

Albuquerque Journal
Albuquerque Tribune
Minneapolis Tribune
New York Times
Seattle Post Intelligencer
Spokesman Review, Spokane, Washington
Washington (D.C.) *Post*
Yakima (Washington) *Herald*
Yakima (Washington) *Republic*

BOOKS

Adams, Evelyn C. *American Indian Education.* Morningside Heights, N.Y.: King Crown's Press, 1946.

Austin, Mary. *Earth Horizon.* Boston and New York: Houghton Mifflin Co., 1932.

Baerreis, David A., ed. *The Indian in Modern America.* Madison, Wis.: State Historical Society of Wisconsin, 1956.

Barnett, H. G. *Anthropology in Administration.* Evanston, Ill.: Row, Peterson and Company, 1956.

Begaye, John Y., et al. *Navajo Evaluators Look at Rough Rock Demonstration School.* Chinle, Arizona: Rough Rock Demonstration School, 1969.

Biographical Directory of the American Congress. Washington, D.C.: USGPO, 1961.

Brody, J. J. *Indian Painters and White Patrons.* Albuquerque: University of New Mexico Press, 1971.

Bronson, Ruth M. *Indians Are People, Too.* New York: Friendship Press, 1944.

Brophy, William A. and Sophie Aberle. *The Indian: America's Unfinished Business. Report of the Commission of the Rights, Liberties, and Responsibilities of the American Indian.* Norman: University of Oklahoma Press, 1966.

Cahn, Edgar S. *Our Brother's Keeper: The Indian in White America.* Cleveland, Ohio: World Publishing Co., 1969.

Chapman, William M. *Remember the Wind.* Philadelphia and New York: J. B. Lippincott Co., 1965.

Clapp, Elsie Ripley. *The Uses of Resources in Education.* New York: Harper and Brothers, 1952.

Collier, John. *From Every Zenith.* Denver: Sage Books, 1963.

———. *Indians of the Americas.* New York: New American Library, 1947.

Costo, Rupert, ed. *Textbooks and the American Indian.* San Francisco: The Indian Historian Press, Inc., 1970.

Cremin, Lawrence A. *The Transformation of the School.* New York: Columbia University Press, 1961.

Dale, E. E. *Indians of the Southwest.* Norman: University of Oklahoma Press, 1949.

Deloria, Vine, Jr. *Custer Died for Your Sins.* London: Collier, MacMillan, Ltd., 1969.

———. *God Is Red.* New York: Grosset and Dunlap, 1973.

———. *We Talk, You Listen.* New York: The Macmillan Co., 1970.

———, ed. *Of Utmost Good Faith.* New York: Bantam Books, 1972.

Dewey, John. *Experience and Education.* New York: The MacMillan Co., 1938.

———. *School and Society.* Chicago: University of Chicago Press, 1915.

Dockstadter, Frederick J. *The American Indian in Graduate Studies.* New York: Heye Foundation, 1957.

Dunn, Dorothy. *American Indian Painting of the Southwest and Plains Areas.* Albuquerque: University of New Mexico Press, 1968.

Eels, Kenneth, Allison Davis, Robert J. Havighurst, et al. *Intelligence and Culture Differences.* Chicago: University of Chicago Press, 1951.

Erickson, Erik H. *Childhood and Society.* New York: W. W. Norton and Company, 1963.

Fey, Harold E., and D'Arcy McNickle. *Indians and Other Americans.* New York and Evanston, Ill.: Harper and Row, 1970.

Fiedler, Leslie A. *The Return of the Vanishing American.* New York: Stein and Day, 1968.

Fritz, Henry E. *The Movement for Indian Assimilation, 1860–1890.* Philadelphia: University of Pennsylvania Press, 1963.

Fuchs, Estelle, and Robert J. Havighurst. *To Live on This Earth.* Garden City, New York: Doubleday and Company, 1972.

Gessner, Robert. *Massacre.* New York: Jonathon Cape and Harrison Smith, 1931.

Gittler, J. B., ed. *Understanding Minority Groups.* New York: John Wiley and Sons, 1956.

Hallowell, A. Irving. *Culture and Experience.* Philadelphia: University of Pennsylvania Press, 1955.

Havighurst, Robert J., and Bernice L. Neugarten, *American Indian and White Children.* Chicago: University of Chicago Press, 1954.

Hodge, Frederick Webb, ed. *Handbook of American Indians North of Mexico.* Bureau of American Ethnology Bulletin 30. 2 vols. Washington, D.C.: Smithsonian Institution, 1907–10.

Hodge, William H. *The Albuquerque Navajos.* Tucson: University of Arizona Anthropology Paper, no. 11, 1969.

Hook, Sidney. *Education for Modern Man.* New York: Alfred A. Knopf, 1963.

Howe, Frederick C. *Confessions of a Reformer.* New York: Charles Scribner's Sons, 1926

Ickes, Harold L. *The First Thousand Days: The Secret Diary of Harold L. Ickes.* New York: Simon and Schuster, 1953.

Josephy, Alvin M., Jr. *Red Power.* New York: McGraw-Hill, 1971.

Kandel, I. L. *The Cult of Uncertainty.* New York: The Macmillan Co., 1943.

Kelly, Lawrence C. *The Navajo Indians and Federal Indian Policy.* Tucson: University of Arizona Press, 1968.

Kilpatrick, William H., ed. *The Educational Frontier.* New York: The Century Co., 1933.

Kinney, J. P. *A Continent Lost—A Civilization Won: Indian Land Tenure in America.* Baltimore: Johns Hopkins Press, 1937.

Kluckhohn, Clyde, and Dorothea Leighton. *The Navaho.* Garden City, N.Y.: Doubleday and Co., Inc., 1962.

La Farge, Oliver, ed. *The Changing Indian.* Norman: University of Oklahoma Press, 1942.

McGrath, G. D., Robert Roessel, et al. *Higher Education of Southwestern Indians with Reference to Success and Failure.* Tempe: Arizona State University, 1962.

Mandelbaum, David, ed. *Selected Writings of Edward Sapir.* Berkeley: University of California Press, 1949.

Marinsek, Edward A. *The Effect of Cultural Difference in the Education of Pueblo Indians.* University of New Mexico Research Study, The Adjustment of Indian and Non-Indian Children in the Public Schools of New Mexico. Albuquerque: University of New Mexico, 1958.

May, Henry F. *The End of American Innocence.* New York: Alfred A. Knopf, 1959.

Meyer, Roy W. *History of the Santee Sioux.* Lincoln: University of Nebraska Press, 1967.

Meriam, Lewis, et al. *The Problem of Indian Administration.* Baltimore: Johns Hopkins, 1928.

NAACP Legal Defense and Educational Fund, Inc., with the Cooperation of the Center for Law and Education, Harvard University. *An Even Chance.* Annandale, Virginia: Graphics 4, 1971.

National Society for the Study of Education, Twenty Fourth Year Book. Part 20, 1925.

National Study of Indian Education: The Education of Indian Children and Youth. n.p., USOE, 1970. Also, Educational Resources Information Center (ERIC) Clearing House on Rural Education and Small Schools (CRESS) ED045275. April 1971.

O'Neil, William L. *Coming Apart.* Chicago: Quadrangle Books, 1971.

Parmee, Edward A. *A Modern Apache Indian Community and Government Education Programs.* Tucson: University of Arizona Press, 1968.

———. *Formal Education and Cultural Change.* Tucson: University of Arizona Press, 1968.

Pearce, Roy Harvey. *Savagism and Civilization.* Baltimore: Johns Hopkins Paperbacks, 1967.

Roessel, Robert A., Jr. *Amerindian Handbook of Indian Education.* Los Angeles: Amerindian Publishing Company, 1962.

———. *Indian Communities in Action.* Tempe: Arizona State University, 1962.

Smith, Anne Marie. *Indian Education in New Mexico.* Albuquerque: University of New Mexico Press, 1968.

———. *New Mexico Indians.* Santa Fe: Museum of New Mexico, 1966.

Schmeckebier, Lawrence F. *The Office of Indian Affairs.* Baltimore: Johns Hopkins University Press, 1927.

Spicer, Edward H. *Cycles of Conquest.* Tucson: University of Arizona Press, 1962.

———, ed. *Perspectives in American Indian Culture Change.* Chicago: University of Chicago Press, 1961.

Thompson, Laura. *Culture in Crisis.* New York: Harper and Brothers, 1950.

———. *Personality and Government: Findings and Recommendations of the Indian Administration Research.* Panuco, 63 Mexico, D.F.: Ediciones del Instituto Indigenista Inter-Americano, 1951.

Tiedt, Sidney W. *The Role of the Federal Government in Education.* New York: Oxford University Press, 1966.

Underhill, Ruth M. *Hawk Over Whirlpools.* New York: J. J. Augustin, 1940.

Utley, Robert M. *The Last Days of the Sioux Nation.* New Haven and London: Yale University Press, 1963.

Waters, Frank. *Pumpkin Seed Point.* Chicago: Sage Books, 1969.

Wheeler, Burton K. *Yankee from the West.* New York: Doubleday and Co., 1962.
White, Lynn, Jr. *Machina ex Deo.* Cambridge: Massachusetts Institute of Technology Press, 1968.
Who's Who in American Education. Vol. 2, 1929–30. New York: Robert C. Cook Co., 1930.
Wilson, Edmund. *Apologies to the Iroquois.* New York: Vintage Books, 1960.
Wilson, R. Jackson. *In Quest of Community.* New York: John Wiley and Sons, Inc., 1968.

ARTICLES

Ablon, Joan. "Relocated American Indians in the San Francisco Bay Area: Social Interaction and Human Identity." *Human Organization* 23 (Spring-Winter 1964):296–304.
———. "Acculturation: An Explanatory Formulation." *American Anthropologist* 56 (December 1954): 973–1002.
Adair, John. "The Navajo and Pueblo Veteran." *The American Indian* 4 (1947):5–11.
———, and Evon Z. Vogt. "Navaho and Zuni Veterans: A Study of Contrasting Modes of Culture Change." *American Anthropologist* 51 (October-December 1949):597–61.
Alexander, Hartley. "The Art of the American Indian." *The Nation* 132 (May 6, 1931):501–3.
Armsby, E. Raymond, and John G. Rockwell. "New Directions Among Northern California Indians." *The American Indian* 4, no. 3 (1948):12–23.
Armstrong, O. K., "Set the American Indians Free." *Reader's Digest* 47 (August 1945):47–52.
"Arizona State University Indian Education Center, An Overview of Activities." *Journal of American Indian Education* 6 (May 1967):18–20.
"Beatty to Indians." *Time* 27 (February 10, 1936):36.
Beatty, Willard Walcott. "Forty Thousand First Americans Who Can't Speak English." *Today's Education* 36 (April 1947):300–301.
———. "Planning Indian Education in Terms of Pupil and Community Needs." *Indians at Work* 4 (September 1, 1936):5–7.
———. "Twenty Years of Indian Education." In David A. Baerreis, ed., *The Indian in Modern America.*
———. "Uncle Sam Develops a New Kind of Rural School." *Elementary School Journal* 41 (November 1940):185–94.
———. "What Makes an American?" *Today's Education* 21 (February 1943):55–56.
Beltran, Enrique. "The Place of the Biological Sciences in Educational Programs." *Progressive Education* 13 (1936):92–97.
Benham, William J. "A Foundation for Indian, Cross-Cultured Education." *Journal of American Indian Education* 8 (January 1969):26–31.
Bennett, Robert L. "Indian-State Relations in their Historical Perspective." *New Mexico Business* 20 (July 1967):17–20.
Blackburn, Guy. "A View from Within." *The Arizona Teacher* (January 1972):5, 6, 19, 22, 23.
Brightman, Lehman. "Mental Genocide (Some Notes on Federal Boarding Schools for Indians)." *Inequality in Education* 7 (February 1971):15–19.
Bruce, Louis R. "Remarks on Education to a Conference on Modern American Indians." Claremont Men's College, February 27, 1970. *American Indian Law Newsletter* 3 (March 27, 1970):36–39.
Bryde, John F. "A Rationale for Indian Education." *Journal of American Indian Education* 8 (January 1969):11–14.
"CICSB Urges More Control at Local Level." *Education Journal* 1 (April 1973):7–12.
"Civilizing the Indian." *The Nation* 138 (January 10, 1934):33–34.
Clifford, Francis. "The Practice Cottage Plan." *Indians at Work* 6 (October 1938):50–51.

Collier, John. "Collier's Reply to Eastman." *Christian Century* 51 (August 8, 1934):1018.
——. "Collier Replies to Mekeel." *American Anthropologist* 46 (July-September 1944):422–26.
——. "The Indian Bureau's Record." *The Nation* 135 (October 5, 1932):303–5.
——. "Indian Takeaway, Betrayal of a Trust." *The Nation* 179 (October 2, 1954):290.
——. "The Keystone of the Arch." *The Survey* 27 (November 18, 1911):1,200.
——. "The Last of the Referendums." *Indians at Work* 2 (July 15, 1935)):1–5.
——. "Mexico: A Challenge." *Progressive Education* 9 (February 1932):95–98.
——. "The People's Institute." *The Independent* 72 (May 1912):1144–48.
——. "Self-Determination in Community Enterprise." *The Survey* 42 (September 1919): 870–72.
——, and Theodore H. Haas. "The United States Indian." In J. B. Gittler, ed., *Understanding Minority Groups.*
"Commissioner Nash on Indian Needs." *Christian Century* 80 (April 10, 1963):463–64.
Coombs, L. Madison. "Rough Rock Revisited: The Indian Voice in Education, How Can it Best Be Heard?" *The Arizona Teacher* (March-April 1972):11, 22–24.
Downes, Ralph C. "A Crusade for Indian Reform." *Mississippi Valley Historical Review* 32 (December 1945):331–54.
Dozier, Edward P. "An Anthropologist Looks at Early Childhood." Paper read at Bureau of Indian Affairs conference on Early Childhood Education, Albuquerque, March 5, 1968. Quoted in Anne Marie Smith, *Indian Education in New Mexico.*
——, George E. Simpson, and J. Milton Yinger. "The Integration of Americans of Indian Descent." *Annals of the American Academy of Political and Social Science.* 311 (May 1957):158–65.
Eastman, Elaine Goodale. "Does Uncle Sam Foster Paganism?" *Christian Century* 51 (August 8, 1934):16–20.
——. "Uncle Sam and Paganism: Rejoinder to John Collier." Letter to editor. *Christian Century* 51 (August 22, 1934):1,073.
"Educational Leadership Training Program at Arizona State University." *American Indian Law Newsletter* 3 (June 3, 1970):116–17.
"The Executive Director Speaks Out." *Education Journal* 1 (April 1973):4–6.
Evvard, Evelyn, and George C. Mitchell. "Sally, Dick and Jane at Lukachukai." *Journal of American Indian Education* 5 (May 1966):2–6.
Fannin, Paul J. "Indian Education—A Test Case for Democracy." *Arizona Law Review* 10 (Winter 1968):661–73.
"Federal Appropriations to Schools for Indian Children." *School and Society* 31 (May 24, 1930):702–3.
"The Fight on the New Indian Policy." *The Nation* 140 (April 24, 1935):479–80.
Forbes, Jack D. "An American Indian University: A Proposal for Survival." *Journal of American Indian Education* 2 (January 1966):1–7.
Freeman, John Leiper, Jr. "A Program for Indian Affairs, Summary of the Report of the Hoover Commission Task Force on Indian Affairs." *The American Indian* 7 (Spring 1954):48–62.
Fuchs, Estelle. "American Indian Education: Time to Redeem an Old Promise." *Saturday Review* (January 24, 1970):54–57, 74–75.
——. "Learning to be Navaho-Americans: Innovations at Rough Rock." *Saturday Review* (September 16, 1967):82–84, 98–99.
——. "The Navajos Build a College." *Saturday Review* (March 4, 1972):58–62.
Haas, Theodore H., and John E. Jay. "Toward Effective Indian Government." *The American Indian* 6 (Summer 1951):17–25.
Hallowell, A. Irving. "The Impact of the American Indian on American Culture." *American Anthropologist* 59 (April 1957):201–17.
Harmer, Ruth Mulvey. "Uprooting the Indians." *Atlantic Monthly* 197 (March 1956):54–57.
Harper, Allen G. "Navajo Education." *The American Indian* 5 (Fall 1950):3–10.

Hawley, Florence. "An Examination of Problems Basic to Acculturation in the Rio Grande Pueblos." *American Anthropologist* 50 (October-December 1948):613–24.

Hoebel, E. Adamson, "To End Their Status." In David A. Baerreis, ed., *The Indian in Modern America*.

"Indian Children and the Public Schools." *School and Society* 33 (May 2, 1931):582.

"Indian Education in the United States." *School and Society* 55 (June 29, 1940):775–76.

"Indianizing the Red Man." *Newsweek* 17 (April 14, 1941):77.

"In-Service Training for Indian Reservations." *School and Society* 44 (December 5, 1936):727.

"J-O'M Rip-off in Oklahoma." *Education Journal* 2 (August 1973):1–24.

Kennedy, Robert F. "America's Forgotten Children." *Parent's Magazine* 43 (June 1968):30.

Kobrick, Jeffrey W. "The Compelling Case for Bilingual Education." *Saturday Review* (April 29, 1972):54–58.

Kramer, Max. "An Experiment in Indian Education." *Progressive Education* 12 (January 1935):155–59.

La Farge, Oliver. "Revolution with Reservations." *New Republic* 84 (October 9, 1935):232–34.

————. "Termination of Federal Supervision: Disintegration and the American Indians." *Annals of the American Academy of Political and Social Science* 311 (May 1957):41–46.

Lewis, Rod. "Indian Education Legislation." *Inequality in Education*, no. 10 (December 1971):19–21. (Center for Law and Education, Harvard University).

McNickle, D'Arcy. "Indian Tests the Mainstream." *The Nation* 203 (September 26, 1966): 275–79.

Mather, P. B. "Tama Indians Fight for Their Own Schools." *Christian Century* 85 (October 2, 1968):1251–52.

Mekeel, Scudder. "The American Indian as a Minority Group Problem." *The American Indian* 2 (1944):3–11.

————. "An Appraisal of the I.R.A." *American Anthropologist* 46 (April-June 1944):209–17.

————. "An Anthropologist's Observation on Indian Education." *Progressive Education* 14 (March 1936):151–59.

McKittrick, Margaret. "Lost: A Tradition." *School Arts Magazine* 30 (March 1931):449–53.

Meriam, Lewis. "Indian Education Moves Ahead." *The Survey* 66 (June 1, 1931):253–57.

Mirrielees, Edith. "Cloud of Mistrust." *Atlantic Monthly* 199 (February 1957):55–59.

Momaday, N. Scott. "Bring on the Indians." *New York Review of Books* (April 8, 1971).

"More Trouble for the Indians." *New Republic* 90 (March 31, 1937):226.

Nash, Philleo. "The Education Mission of the Bureau of Indian Affairs." *Journal of American Indian Education* 3 (January 1964):1–4.

————. "Education—the Chance to Choose." *Indian Education*, issue 428 (February 1, 1966).

Overby, H. D. "Tell it Like it Is." *Today's Education* 58 (November 1969):55–56.

Parman, Donald L. "The Indian and the Civilian Conservation Corps." *Pacific Historical Review* 40 (February 1971):39–56.

Parmeter, Adrian. "A Personal View of the Indian Affairs Reform Movement—The Alaska Native Land Claims." *Legislative Review* (Indian Legal Information Development Service) I (April 1972):36–41.

Provinse, John, et al. "The American Indian in Transition." *American Anthropologist* 56 (June 1954):388–92.

Prucha, Francis Paul. "New Approaches to the Study of the Administration of Indian Policy." *Prologue* 3 (Spring 1971):15–19.

Roessel, Robert, Jr. "An Overview of the Rough Rock Demonstration School." *Journal of American Indian Education* 7 (May 1968):2–41.

————. "The Right to be Wrong and the Right to Be Right." *Journal of American Indian Education* 7 (January 1968):1–6.

Russel, Janet. "Indian Children Attend Public School." *Minnesota Journal of Education* 30 (September 1949):19, 24.

Ryan, W. Carson, Jr., "Federal-State Cooperation in Indian Education." *School and Society* 34 (September 26, 1931):418–23.

———, and Rose K. Brandt. "Indian Education Today." *Progressive Education* 9 (February 1932):81–86.

Sahmaunt, Herschel. "An Indian Education Leader Speaks Out." *Education Journal* 1 (March 1973):4–10.

Sapir, Edward. "Culture, Genuine and Spurious." In David Mandelbaum, ed., *Selected Writings of Edward Sapir.*

Shepard, Ward. "Land Problems of an Expanding Indian Population." In Oliver La Farge, ed., *The Changing Indian.*

Steiner, Stan. "The American Indian, Ghettos in the Desert." *The Nation* 198 (June 22, 1964):624–27.

Thompson, Hildegard. "Education Among American Indians: Institutional Aspects." *Annals of the American Academy of Political and Social Science* 311 (May 1957):95–104.

"Title IV Distribution Map." *Education Journal* (June-July 1973):10–11.

Van de Mark, Dorothy. "The Raid on the Reservations." *Harper's Magazine* 212 (March 1956):48–53.

Vogt, Evon Z. "The Acculturation of American Indians." *Annals of the American Academy of Political and Social Science* 311 (May 1957):137–46.

Wallace, A. F. C. "Dreams and the Wishes of the Soul: A Type of Psycho-Analytic Theory Among the Seventeenth Century Iroquois." *American Anthropologist* 60 (April 1958):234–48.

Washburne, Carleton, and Edward Yeomans. "The Inception of the Winnetka Technique." *Journal of the AAUW* 23 (1930):129–36.

———. "Winnetka." *School and Society* 29 (January 12, 1929):37–50.

Watkins, Arthur V. "Termination of Federal Supervision: The Removal of Restrictions over Indian Property and Person." *Annals of the American Academy of Political and Social Science* 311 (May 1957):47–55.

Wax, Murray, and Rosalie Wax. "Cultural Deprivation as an Educational Ideology." *Journal of American Indian Education* 3 (January 1964):15–18.

———. "Education for What?" *Midcontinent American Studies Journal* 6 (Fall 1965):164–70. (Fall 1965):164–70.

Wax, Rosalie, and Robert H. Thomas. "American Indians and White People." *Phylon* 22 (Winter 1961):305–17.

Wigmore, John H. "The Federal Senate as a Fifth Wheel." *Illinois Law Review* (May 1929):89–96.

Woehlke, Walter W. "Starving the Nation's Wards." *Sunset* 61 (November 1928):11–14, 69–70.

Wright, Frank. "BIA: The Red Man's Burden." *Minneapolis Tribune.* Series of articles reprinted in the *Congressional Record* and then in *American Indian Law Newsletter* 3 (June 29, 1970):122–35.

Young, Biloine W. "The American Indian: Citizen in Captivity." *Saturday Review* 48 (December 11, 1965):25–26.

Zimmerman, William, Jr. "The Role of the Bureau of Indian Affairs Since 1933." *Annals of the American Academy of Political and Social Science* (May 1957):31–40.

Zintz, Miles V. "Indian Children Are Different." *New Mexico School Review* 40 (October 1960):26–27.

INDEX